Phonological Development in Children   18 TO 72 MONTHS

Edited by John V. Irwin and Seok P. Wong / With a Foreword by Daniel S. Beasley

Southern Illinois University Press   Carbondale and Edwardsville

Library of Congress Cataloging in Publication Data
Main entry under title:

Phonological development in children 18 to 72 months.

   Bibliography: p.
   Includes index.
   Contents: Review of literature / Leslie Paschall and John V. Irwin — Methodology /
Seok P. Wong and John V. Irwin — Development at 18 months / Leslie Paschall — [etc.]
   1. Language acquisition—Addresses, essays, lectures. 2. Grammar, Comparative and
general—Phonology—Addresses, essays, lectures. I. Irwin, John V. II. Wong, Seok P.,
1939–   . III. Title: Phonological development in children eighteen to seventy-two
months.
P118.P48 1983   401'.9   82–5893
ISBN 0–8093–1057–0   AACR2

Edited by Stephen W. Smith
Designed by David Ford
Production supervised by John DeBacher

Contents

Tables vii

Figures xi

Foreword xiii

Notes on Contributors xvii

1 Review of Literature 1
Leslie Paschall and John V. Irwin

2 Methodology 9
Seok P. Wong and John V. Irwin

3 Development at 18 Months 27
Leslie Paschall

4 Development at 2 Years 55
Gayle Hare

5 Development at 3 Years 87
Patricia Larkins

6 Development at 4 Years 107
Cynthia Bassi

7 Development at 6 Years 133
Electa Harmon and Stephen Harmon

8   Summary   153
          John V. Irwin and Seok P. Wong

          References   181

          Index   185

Contents

Tables

2.1 English Vowels, Phonemic Diphthongs, and Syllabics by Irwin-Wong Features as Stored for Computer Processing   12

2.2 English Consonants by Irwin-Wong Features as Stored for Computer Processing   13

2.3 English Vowels, Phonemic Diphthongs, and Syllabics by Chomsky-Halle Features as Extended and Stored for Computer Processing   18

2.4 English Consonants by Chomsky-Halle Features as Extended and Stored for Computer Processing   19

2.5 Sample Utterance Output   22

2.6 Traditional Classification of 24 Consonants by Manner, Voicing, and Place of Constriction   25

3.1 Percentage of Occurrence of Individual Vowellike and Consonant Sounds Based on Total Phoneme Sample (N = 12,775)   31

3.2 Percentage of Correct Production of Individual Vowellike Sounds Based on Total Occurrence of Each Phoneme   32

3.3 Percentage of Correct Production of Individual Consonants Based on Total Occurrence of Each Phoneme   33

3.4 Error Type Distribution (Percent Omissions and Percent Substitutions) for Each Vowellike Sound   34

3.5 Error Type Distribution (Percent Omissions and Percent Substitutions) for Each Consonant   35

3.6 Correct Usage of Irwin-Wong Feature Sets and Feature Specifications by Percent and Number Based on Total Sample   36

3.7 Comparison of Individual Subjects with Group Means by Percentage of Correct Usage of Irwin-Wong Feature Sets   38

3.8 Correct Usage of Modified Chomsky-Halle Feature Sets and Feature Specifications by Percent and Number Based on Total Sample   40

3.9 Comparison of Individual Subjects with Group Means by Percentage of Correct Usage of Modified Chomsky-Halle Feature Sets   42

3.10 Error Productions by Replacement, Frequency of Replacement, and Feature/ Degree Differences of Replacement as Specified in Irwin-Wong System   44

3.11 Mean Feature/Degree Difference Values by Phoneme as Specified in Irwin-Wong System   47

3.12 Error Productions by Replacement, Frequency of Replacement, and Feature Differences of Replacement as Specified in Modified Chomsky-Halle System   48

3.13 Mean Feature Difference Values as Specified in Modified Chomsky-Halle System   50

4.1 Percentage of Occurrence of Individual Vowellike and Consonant Sounds Based on Total Phoneme Sample (N = 14,711)   60

4.2 Percentage of Correct Production of Individual Vowellike Sounds Based on Total Occurrence of Each Phoneme   60

4.3 Percentage of Correct Production of Individual Consonants Based on Total Occurrence of Each Phoneme   61

4.4 Error Type Distribution (Percent Omissions and Percent Substitutions) for Each Vowellike Sound   62

4.5 Error Type Distribution (Percent Omissions and Percent Substitutions) for Each Consonant   63

4.6 Correct Usage of Irwin-Wong Feature Sets and Feature Specifications by Percent and Number Based on Total Sample   64

4.7 Comparison of Individual Subjects with Group Means by Percentage of Correct Usage of Irwin-Wong Feature Sets   66

4.8 Correct Usage of Modified Chomsky-Halle Feature Sets and Feature Specifications by Percent and Number Based on Total Sample   68

4.9 Comparison of Individual Subjects with Group Means by Percentage of Correct Usage of Modified Chomsky-Halle Feature Sets   70

4.10 Error Productions by Replacement, Frequency of Replacement, and Feature/Degree Differences of Replacement as Specified in Irwin-Wong System   72

4.11 Mean Feature/Degree Difference Values as Specified in Irwin-Wong System   75

4.12 Error Productions by Replacement, Frequency of Replacement, and Feature Differences of Replacement as Specified in Modified Chomsky-Halle System   76

4.13 Mean Feature Difference Values as Specified in Modified Chomsky-Halle System   79

5.1 Percentage of Occurrence of Individual Vowellike and Consonant Sounds Based on Total Phoneme Sample (N = 37,989)   89

5.2 Percentage of Correct Production of Individual Vowellike Sounds Based on Total Occurrence of Each Phoneme   90

5.3 Percentage of Correct Production of Individual Consonants Based on Total Occurrence of Each Phoneme   91

5.4 Error Type Distribution (Percent Omissions and Percent Substitutions) for Each Vowellike Sound   92

5.5 Error Type Distribution (Percent Omissions and Percent Substitutions) for Each Consonant   93

5.6 Correct Usage of Irwin-Wong Feature Sets and Feature Specifications by Percent and Number Based on Total Sample   94

5.7 Comparison of Individual Subjects with Group Means by Percentage of Correct Usage of Irwin-Wong Feature Sets   96

5.8 Correct Usage of Modified Chomsky-Halle Feature Sets and Feature Specifications by Percent and Number Based on Total Sample   98

5.9 Comparison of Individual Subjects with Group Means by Percentage of Correct Usage of Modified Chomsky-Halle Feature Sets   100

5.10 Error Productions by Replacement, Frequency of Replacement, and Feature/Degree Differences of Replacement as Specified in Irwin-Wong System   102

5.11 Mean Feature/Degree Difference Values by Phoneme as Specified in Irwin-Wong System   103

5.12 Error Productions by Replacement, Frequency of Replacement, and Feature Differences of Replacement as Specified in Modified Chomsky-Halle System   104

5.13 Mean Feature Difference Values as Specified in Modified Chomsky-Halle System   105

6.1 Percentage of Occurrence of Individual Vowellike and Consonant Phonemes Based on Total Phoneme Sample (N = 16,199)   111

6.2 Percentage of Correct Production of Individual Vowellike Sounds Based on Total Occurrence of Each Phoneme   112

6.3	Percentage of Correct Production of Individual Consonants Based on Total Occurrence of Each Phoneme	113
6.4	Error Type Distribution (Percent Omissions and Percent Substitutions) for Each Vowellike Sound	114
6.5	Error Type Distribution (Percent Omissions and Percent Substitutions) for Each Consonant	115
6.6	Correct Usage of Irwin-Wong Feature Sets and Feature Specifications by Percent and Number Based on Total Sample	116
6.7	Comparison of Individual Subjects with Group Means by Percentage of Correct Usage of Irwin-Wong Feature Sets	118
6.8	Correct Usage of Modified Chomsky-Halle Feature Sets and Feature Specifications by Percent and Number Based on Total Sample	120
6.9	Comparison of Individual Subjects with Group Means by Percentage of Correct Usage of Modified Chomsky-Halle Feature Sets	122
6.10	Error Productions by Replacement, Frequency of Replacement, and Feature/Degree Differences of Replacement as Specified in Irwin-Wong System	124
6.11	Mean Feature/Degree Difference Values by Phoneme as Specified in Irwin-Wong System	126
6.12	Error Productions by Replacement, Frequency of Replacement, and Feature Differences of Replacement as Specified in Modified Chomsky-Halle System	130
6.13	Mean Feature Difference Values as Specified in Modified Chomsky-Halle System	132
7.1	Percentage of Occurrence of Individual Vowellike and Consonant Sounds Based on Total Phoneme Sample (N = 4,906)	134
7.2	Percentage of Correct Production of Individual Vowellike Sounds Based on Total Occurrence of Each Phoneme	135
7.3	Percentage of Correct Production of Individual Consonants Based on Total Occurrence of Each Phoneme	136
7.4	Error Type Distribution (Percent Omissions and Percent Substitutions) for Each Vowellike Sound	137
7.5	Error Type Distribution (Percent Omissions and Percent Substitutions) for Each Consonant	138
7.6	Correct Usage of Irwin-Wong Feature Sets and Feature Specifications by Percent and Number Based on Total Sample	140
7.7	Comparison of Individual Subjects with Group Means by Percentage of Correct Usage of Irwin-Wong Feature Sets	142
7.8	Correct Usage of Modified Chomsky-Halle Feature Sets and Feature Specifications by Percent and Number Based on Total Sample	144
7.9	Comparison of Individual Subjects with Group Means by Percentage of Correct Usage of Modified Chomsky-Halle Feature Sets	146
7.10	Error Productions by Replacement, Frequency of Replacement, and Feature/Degree Differences of Replacement as Specified in Irwin-Wong System	148
7.11	Mean Feature/Degree Difference Values by Phoneme as Specified in Irwin-Wong System	149
7.12	Error Productions by Replacement, Frequency of Replacement, and Feature Differences of Replacement as Specified in Modified Chomsky-Halle System	150
7.13	Mean Feature Difference Values as Specified in Modified Chomsky-Halle System	151
8.1	Phoneme Frequency by Basic Phonetic Classification and Age Group	153
8.2	Percent of Vowellike and Consonant Sounds from Children in Project and from Two Adult Studies	154
8.3	Frequency Distribution of Vowellike Sounds by Age Groups	155
8.4	Frequency Distribution of Consonants by Age Group	156
8.5	Three Most Frequent Vowellike Sounds by Age and Percentage of Distribution	157
8.6	Three Most Frequent Consonants by Age and Percentage of Distribution	157
8.7	Phonemes Not Entered in Adult Form	157
8.8	Phonemes Appearing as Additions	157

Tables

8.9	Percentage of Correct Usage of Vowellike Sounds by Age	158
8.10	Percentage of Correct Usage of Consonants by Age	159
8.11	Phonemes 100 Percent Correct by Age	159
8.12	Phonemes Most Frequently in Error by Age and Percent	160
8.13	/θ/ Replacements by Phoneme and Frequency of Replacement	161
8.14	/ð/ Replacements by Phoneme and Frequency of Replacement	161
8.15	Correlation Matrix for Two Feature Systems by Differences Between All Possible Pairs (1,081) of 47 Phonemes	162
8.16	Place-3 (Linguadental) Percent Correct and Replacement Percent by Age	163
8.17	Mean Percent Correct for /s/ and /z/ by Age and Inflection	163
8.18	Percent of Correct Production by Phoneme Type, Age, and Sex	165
8.19	t Tests of Difference in Percent Correct Production of Vowels and Consonants by Age	166
8.20	Traditional Classification of 18 Selected Consonants by Manner, Voicing, and Place of Constriction	167
8.21	Means and Standard Deviations by Age Group and Phoneme	167
8.22	Profile Analysis for Six Pairs of Cognates	168
8.23	Multivariate Analyses of Variance for Five Age Groups on Six Pairs of Cognates	168
8.24	Univariate Analyses of Variance for Five Age Groups on Six Pairs of Cognates	168
8.25	Bonferroni Multiple Comparison of Five Age Groups	169
8.26	Comparisons of Six Cognate Pairs by Age Group	169
8.27	Mean Percentages Correct and Standard Deviations by Age and Two Phoneme Groups	170
8.28	Profile Analyses for Five Age Groups on Voiced and Unvoiced Plosives and Fricatives	171
8.29	Multivariate Analyses of Variance for Five Age Groups on Voiced and Unvoiced Plosives and Fricatives	171
8.30	Univariate Analyses of Variance for Five Age Groups on Voiced and Unvoiced Plosives and Fricatives	171
8.31	Bonferroni Multiple Comparisons for Five Age Groups	172
8.32	Bonferroni Multiple Comparisons of Unvoiced Plosives vs. Voiced Plosives and Unvoiced Fricatives vs. Voiced Fricatives	173
8.33	Means and Standard Deviations by Age Group and Four Groups of Phonemes Classified by Manner	173
8.34	Profile Analysis for Five Age Groups on Four Phonetic Classifications by Manner	173
8.35	Multivariate Analysis of Variance for Five Age Groups Using Plosives, Fricatives, Nasals, and Liquids and Glides as Criterion Variables	173
8.36	Univariate Analyses of Variance for Five Age Groups on Four Groups of Phonemes Classified by Manner	174
8.37	Bonferroni Multiple Comparison of Five Age Groups	174
8.38	Bonferroni Multiple Comparison of Four Manner Groups by Age Group	175
8.39	Means and Standard Deviations by Age Group and Phonetic Classification by Place	176
8.40	Profile Analyses for Five Age Groups on Five Phonetic Classifications by Place	176
8.41	Multivariate Analysis of Variance for Five Age Groups Using Five Places as Criterion Variables	176
8.42	Univariate Analyses of Variance for Five Age Groups on Five Groups of Phonemes Classified by Place	176
8.43	Bonferroni Multiple Comparisons of Five Age Groups	177
8.44	Bonferroni Multiple Comparisons of Five Place Groups by Age Groups	177

Tables

Figures

2.1	Data entry system	10
8.1	Distribution of vowels and consonants by percentage of occurrence for five age groups and two adult studies	154
8.2	Number of Irwin-Wong features occurring with less than 50 percent or less than 90 percent correctness by subject age in years	164
8.3	Number of Chomsky-Halle features occurring with less than 50 percent or less than 90 percent correctness by subject age in years	164

Foreword

There has been an extraordinary expansion of literature in the professional areas of speech-language pathology, audiology, and speech and hearing science in recent years. No place is this activity better exemplified than in the study of children's speech and language development. The results of this myriad of research activities have had significant positive impact upon our knowledge-base, but an associated difficulty has evolved out of our attempt to remain professionally current in view of the variety of directions that the many theories and investigations have taken. Thus, a treatise occasionally is necessary to bring order out of apparent chaos, and so it is with the present volume edited by John V. Irwin and Seok P. Wong. In this work, the editors have attempted to bring their thoughts relative to distinctive feature theory to bear upon speech development as it relates to phonological systems. In doing so, they have provided the professional reader with insights into the value of such knowledge as well as how distinctive feature systems relate to classical research findings pertaining to phoneme acquisition. Equally important, John V. Irwin, whose understanding of and contributions to the communication sciences are legend, and Seok P. Wong, a mathematician and computer scientist, have described how a feature system can be developed for applied purposes. Further, they have shown by example the value of the computer scientist as an ally to the clinical investigator and they have provided the empirical documentation to support their notions.

The theory of distinctive features as the foundation for the explanation to articulatory production and perception dates back at least to the late 1920s and early thirties and the early classification systems of Trubetzkoy (1939, translated by Baltaxe, 1969) and the subsequent evolution of the distinctive feature system presented by Jakobson and his colleagues to American science with the 1952 publication of *Preliminaries to Speech Analysis*. Distinctive feature theory received early acceptance by speech and hearing scientists, linguists, and mathematicians who recognized its intuitive appeal and inherent value. As with any theory, the idea of phonemes being the result of a combination and interaction of articulatory and acoustic features has gone through a variety of modifications since its initial appearance, but the basic tenets of the theory have remained intact (Baltaxe, 1978; Soli, 1980).

Significant changes in distinctive feature theory over the past 20 or so years have included the development of a broader viewpoint of the universal nature of features for the phonetic as well as the phonemic bases of language (Chomsky and Halle, 1968). Simultaneously, additional feature systems have evolved which are in fact language-specific, such as the system developed by Irwin and Wong, and these newer distinctive feature systems have permitted research investigators to develop strategies for application of the theory. As a result, speech scientists have derived a broad array of applications for the distinctive feature concept, from enhancement of understanding the short-term memory process (Wickelgren 1965, 1966), to improvement in the diagnosis and remediation of speech and language problems (Singh, 1976). Using the system developed by Chomsky and Halle (1968), for example, McReynolds and Huston (1971) presented the results of pioneer research which clearly showed the significant role played by phonemic features in the misarticulations of young children. McReynolds and Huston elicited their samples by using a standardized articulation testing procedure. Gooze (1974), on the other hand, used spontaneous speech samples obtained from young misarticulating children in order to study the consistency of misarticulations relative to distinctive feature analysis. In addition, she suggested a training program based upon the distinctive feature idea for the remediation of these misarticulations. Fairchild and Beasley (1974) presented data based upon three children from one family, each of whom exhibited significant speech articulation disorders, and they found consistencies within and among the three subjects in their articulatory feature errors. These examples and the historical developments described by Irwin and Wong in this volume illustrate a phenomenon that pervades (and often frustrates) science: namely, that here exists an idea with a relatively lengthy history and which is recognized and accepted as valid (in some form), but which only relatively recently has received concerted interest as to its potential as an applied clinical activity.

Irwin and Wong, in conjunction with their students, have provided the structure and methodology to enhance the application of distinctive feature theory to speech development and disorders. In doing so, they make a convincing case for the need to discover the role played by distinctive features in normal language acquisition. There can be little argument with the fact that knowledge about normal speech and language development can provide useful reference levels for diagnosis and remediation of speech and language disorders. Such a systematic investigation relative to distinctive feature theory, to date, has not been presented. Irwin and Wong have gone beyond this first step, however, and have attempted to show the relationships between the functional development of distinctive features and the previously established data pertaining to phoneme acquisition. They duly recognize the value of classical feature systems such as that of Chomsky and Halle, but put forth the notion that their modified version may have greater applicability to speech and language pathologists. In the process, they have developed the bases for computerization of speech samples in the analyses of the distinctive features as reflected in the language of children and have suggested a rationale and the means for modifying current feature systems in order to accommodate timely evaluation of diagnostic data.

Investigations of the type presented in this volume invariably suffer from experimental problems and can be readily criticized for such lapses. For example, in each of the several investigations presented the population sizes are limited, thereby potentially limiting the generalizability of the results. Further, each investigator uses different populations from which to obtain his or her subjects, and it might be argued that such variability could very well contaminate the general conclusions pertaining to the developmental nature of distinctive features. Another argument could be leveled against the use of conversational speech samples as the corpus from which to extract the distinctive feature data. The nature of coarticulation in phoneme acquisition largely has been ignored, and yet are we not acutely aware of the effects that coarticulation has upon speech and language production (Daniloff, Schuckers, and Feth, 1980)? And what effects do the development of distinctive features have upon the phonetic nature of the speech signal? And, of course, how might other feature systems fare in an investigation similar to the Irwin and Wong series?

The list of potential questions is lengthy. Indeed, Irwin and Wong are quite aware of what has *not* been done in the series of investigations as reported in their volume. The internal consistency and logically developmental progression in the reported findings by Irwin and Wong and their colleagues and the agreement with earlier investigations, nevertheless, should generate a sense of optimism for those investigators and clinicians who support the notions of the distinctive feature theorist. More importantly, perhaps, is the fact that Irwin and Wong have fulfilled a valued purpose inherent in any research activity, namely, to provide the theoretical, methodological, and empirical foundation for the derivation of increasingly definitive questions which, in turn, lead to a clearer understanding of the problem area. In this case, the answers to these questions will allow interested professionals to better deal with the intricacies of normal speech and language development and, consequently, the variant behaviors experienced by children who suffer communication disorders.

Daniel S. Beasley

Memphis State University
Memphis, Tennessee
January 1983

Notes on Contributors

Cynthia Bassi was a graduate student at Memphis State University at the time she collected the data on the 4-year-old children. A former speech therapist at the Madonna Day School in Memphis, she currently is in private practice in Paducah, Kentucky.

Daniel Beasley is Chairman of the Department of Audiology and Speech Pathology at Memphis State University and Director of the Memphis Speech and Hearing Center. With strong interests in the sciences underlying normal and disordered communication, Beasley is a frequent contributor to both professional and scientific societies.

Gayle Hare is a Memphis State graduate who has participated in national meetings. She is currently serving as speech and language pathologist in the Anoka-Hennepin Independent School District No. 11, Minnesota.

Stephen Harmon was on the professional staff of the Memphis Speech and Hearing Center and his wife, Electa Harmon, was a candidate for the Master's degree and a therapist in the West Memphis, Arkansas, schools at the time of this study. One thesis and one baby later, Mr. Harmon is still on the professional staff at the Center but Ms. Harmon is in private practice.

John Irwin, Pope M. Farrington Professor Emeritus at Memphis State University, is presently Distinguished Consultant and Lecturer at Eastern Kentucky University. Irwin's recent research interests have emphasized computer applications to the analysis of developmental and clinical behaviors.

Patricia Larkins, who completed her doctoral work at Memphis State, is an assistant professor in the Department of Communication Arts and Sciences at Howard University and a consultant for the Clinical Center at the National Institutes of Health, Bethesda, Maryland. A frequent contributor at professional meetings, she recently presented a paper at the World Congress on Black Communication at the University of Nairobi, Nairobi, Kenya.

Leslie Paschall, who completed his Master's degree at Memphis State, is presently working as a therapist and consultant for the profoundly retarded at Pennhurst Center, Spring City, Pennsylvania.

Seok Wong earned his Ph.D. degree in mathematical statistics at the University of Illinois. Currently a professor in the Department of Mathematical Sciences at Memphis State University, he has contributed both to concepts of theoretical statistics and to computer applications of statistics in educational and clinical fields.

Phonological Development in Children

1 Review of Literature

Leslie Paschall and John V. Irwin

In historical perspective, child language acquisition studies can be seen as having followed two directions of inquiry. One has been to record surface events, that is, to describe the actual language output. The second has been to discover any principles that may have governed this output. Normative research in sound acquisition has typically chosen either a phonemic or a distinctive feature approach to developmental process. Such research has contributed significantly to our understanding of developmental phonology despite many acknowledged theoretical and methodological difficulties. One purpose of this review is to examine the relevant developmental literature and to indicate how previous studies have helped shape the material to be presented. For in a broad sense, the five studies offered in this work are an extension of previous investigations using either phonemic or distinctive feature analysis. It is hoped that these findings will represent a refined extension.

David Ingram (1976) divided research on phonological development into three historical periods. The first period extended from the latter part of the nineteenth century to the 1930s. The studies predominant in this period have been called the "diary studies" by Winitz (1969), Olmstead (1971), Ingram (1976), Hare (1977), and Bassi (1979). These investigations typically involved only one or two children. The second period began with the widely cited pioneer studies of Wellman, Case, Mengert, and Bradbury (1931) and Poole (1934), and lasted until the early part of the 1950s. These studies will be discussed in greater detail later. Since the 1950s, a fairly significant shift has occurred in child language research. Developments within the field of linguistics have strongly influenced this change. As pointed out by Olmstead (1971) and Ingram (1976), language scientists became interested in discovering or determining the rules behind phonological acquisition. A new analytical model was offered with the distinctive feature theory of Jakobson, Fant, and Halle (1952); a new approach to child language research followed.

Distinctive feature analysis has been applied to two major areas of language development research: the first has focused upon normal phonological development, and the second has examined deviant phonology. The studies of Menyuk (1968), Prather, Hedrick, and Kern (1975), Singh (1976), Hare (1977), and Bassi (1979) are representative of normative research, while McReynolds and Huston (1971), McReynolds and Bennett (1972), Pollack and Rees (1972), McReynolds and Engman (1975), Costello (1975), Costello and Onstine (1976), and Blache (1978) have sought both to describe deviant phonological development and to design remedial strategies using distinctive feature analysis.

Obviously, not all major contributions to understanding sound acquisition fall neatly into Ingram's chronological divisions. Specifically, Templin (1957), Olmstead (1971), Sander (1972), and Prather et al. (1975) represent more recent attempts to understand normal phoneme acquisition. In addition, distinctive feature theory has roots which date as early as 1912, yet gained wide recognition only after English translations and publications of the theory became available (Olmstead, 1971; Baltaxe, 1978; Blache, 1978).

A complete critical exposition of phoneme and distinctive feature research is beyond the scope of this review. Yet, as mentioned earlier, the five studies included in this monograph have profited from the strengths and weaknesses of previous research. Consequently, this review will deal primarily with the body of literature which has in some way influenced the choice of methods of either data collection or data analysis used in this research.

PHONEME ACQUISITION RESEARCH

As has been noted, early language acquisition research began with rather detailed diaries tracing the language growth of a small number of children. The authors of these early diaries often used their own children as subjects (Ingram, 1976). The records kept were probably extremely representative of the language behavior of the individual children. Yet the methods of data collection lacked uniformity across diaries, and the small number of subjects makes it difficult to generalize to the whole population. It is ironic that some of the early linguists, as pointed out by Olmstead (1971), used these early diary studies as a basis for developing certain aspects of their theories of *universal* feature acquisition. Finally, of the early diaries cited in the literature (Olmstead, 1971; Ingram, 1976), few were in English. Unfortunately for those who are interested in English phonological research, the early English diaries did not report all the data collected (Ingram, 1976), and since these early diaries, relatively few have appeared in English. The works of Leopold (1947) and Smith (1973) are excellent examples of this type of single-subject, longitudinal research.

The works of Wellman et al. (1931), Poole (1934), and Templin (1957) represent some of the first group studies whose goals included the establishment of the developmental age sequence for phoneme acquisition. Wellman et al. (1931) sampled 204 children between ages 2 and 6.5 years. Through systematic sound elicitation, production data for 23 consonants were obtained for three word positions: initial, medial, and final. Criterion was considered achieved when 75 percent of the children within each age group produced the sound correctly. Poole (1934) conducted a similar study applying a more stringent standard for sound mastery; namely, that 100 percent of the children could produce the sound correctly. A third study performed by Templin (1957) investigated consonants and vowellike sounds in single-word responses.

The strengths of the studies are noteworthy. First, they represent a significant attempt to analyze the phonemic repertoire and development of large groups of children within specific age ranges. Second, while the individual studies vary slightly in methods of sound elicitation, all employ a systematic approach in obtaining the data. For example, Wellman et al. (1931) used picture stimuli to obtain the production of a sound in each of three positions in a word, and the same pictures and target words were used with all the children. Finally, taken collectively, the three studies pose the possibility of phonemic developmental patterns. That is, a comparison of the three studies reveals some agreement as to the ages at which certain sounds are mastered.

Certainly, these studies are phonological landmarks; any criticisms should acknowledge that they represent first attempts at understanding a complicated process. It is, however, important to review certain criticisms that have been made. Prather et al. (1975), Olmstead (1971), and Ingram (1976) have each indicated that the method of elicitation used in the three aforementioned studies has some unfortunate consequences. Wellman et al., Poole, and Templin all used examiner-determined words which they elicited through pictorial or object stimuli. While this method allows quick sampling of a large number of children, the resultant data can be misleading.

As Olmstead (1971) pointed out, the child is given one chance to produce a given sound within a word. This "all or nothing" trial does not allow for the possibility of correct production within another word. Moreover, it obscures the fact that the child may be producing the target phoneme with some accuracy, but not at the time of elicitation. Ingram (1976) noted that examiner-determined words within these studies did not take into consideration the unequal frequency of phoneme occurrence within a given language. Finally, Prather et al. found that it is often very difficult to elicit examiner-determined words from small children since, due to short attention spans, they have difficulty in attending to the stimuli presented. An alternative sampling method, spontaneous speech sampling, will be discussed below.

Another criticism of these studies has been made by Sander (1972), a researcher interested in determining alternative methods of organizing the previous data. Specifically, Sander noted that subtle developmental patterns may be obscured by imposing arbitrary percentages as criteria for the mastery of a sound. Rather than imposing the stringent percentages used by Wellman, Poole, and Templin, Sander used the criterion of correct production more often than incorrect; that is, criterion was achieved when more than 50 percent of the children produced the sound correctly. He found that children varied considerably in their correct production of certain sounds and that this variation could be better represented by a broader interpretation of the developmental data. Ironically, Sander's 51 percent criterion also obscures developmental data, a fact which may suggest that developmental data are most representative when the actual percentages of correct production are reported.

It seems, then, that "normality" may encompass a wider age range for acquisition of speech sounds than the pioneer studies indicate. The point is especially significant when these traditional data are used as diagnostic and remedial tools. That is, while the studies do indicate that some sounds are learned before others and that phonemic mastery is complete around 8 years of age (Templin, 1957), certain inconsistencies in the ages at which specific phonemes are learned emerge when the studies are compared collectively. As summarized by Winitz (1969), the three studies concur on the age of acquisition for five sounds, yet differ by one year on six sounds and by two years on six others. It is interesting to note that the six sounds showing a two-year spread are among those found to be most frequently misarticulated by school-age children (Van Riper and Irwin, 1958; Cairns and Williams, 1972; Irwin, Huskey, Knight, and Oltman, 1974). For these and other reasons, certain investigators feel that developmental norms should not be a crucial element in the identification and remediation of the deviant population (Winitz, 1975).

Until now, discussion has centered around phonemic normative studies which have investigated children 3 years of age or older. This concentration is not accidental; historically, few major studies have reported data on the age range below 36 months.* Some examples include the works of Olmstead (1971), Prather et al. (1975), Hare (1977), and Dyson (1979). The lack of data from children younger than 3 years is unfortunate, for even a cursory examination of child language literature shows that important phonological gains occur during these early months of life.

An example of a framework for both linguistic and phonological development has been offered by David Ingram (1976). Ingram outlined six stages of development which correspond roughly to Piaget's stages of cognitive development. Although the reader is referred to Ingram (1976) for a complete exposition of all the stages, it is important to note that the transition between the second and third stages of his outline represents an age range of 16 to 24 months, which has been relatively ignored in the literature. Two major events occur both linguistically and phonologically during this period. As pointed out by Ingram, the second stage, 12 to 18 months, is marked by a gradual stabilization of linguistic symbols. Then, in the beginnings of the third stage, 18 to 24 months, there is a rapid increase in vocabulary, which demands a more complex phonological system. The rapid development which occurs within a relatively short period of time underscores the sig-

---

*The authors wish to acknowledge the fine and laborious research of O. C. Irwin and his associates. However, much of Irwin's work involved sound acquisition research prior to the onset of true words. Winitz (1969) offers an excellent summary and discussion of Irwin's contributions.

Phonological Development in Children

nificance of this period of growth. Ironically, only a few group phonological studies have attempted to investigate this age range.

Two studies using different sampling techniques have reported group data on children younger than 30 months. Prather et al. (1975) collected samples from children within three age groups from 2 to 4 years. Prather found that children's productions of some consonant sounds occurred with higher accuracy than had been previously reported. Furthermore, recognizing the aforementioned inadequacies of investigator-determined one-word responses, Prather suggested that younger populations, that is, children 18 to 24 months, be investigated using sampling techniques which best reflect the child's language capabilities. Olmstead (1971) analyzed the spontaneous speech of 100 children, 17 of whom had a mean age of 20 months. The data were reported in categories of correct production and were similar to those reported by Templin (1957).

Both the advantages and disadvantages of using spontaneous speech samples have often been cited in the literature. Ingram (1976) noted that spontaneous speech sampling may not be appropriate for certain populations, such as the language-delayed. Moreover, spontaneous speech sampling is more time-consuming and does not guarantee a representative sampling of all the phonemes. In contrast, spontaneous sampling does yield information relative to the child's language ability (Shriberg and Kwiatkowski, 1980). It may reveal patterns of usage that are obscured by dependence on single-word test items. That is, the child may vary his production of a sound according to the linguistic and phonetic context in which it occurs. For example, Ferguson and Farwell (1975) and Ingram (1976) have argued that children may be selective in the sounds they acquire. If this is the case, then children's production of certain phonemes may be related to the importance of the phonemes. Another point, supported by Faircloth and Faircloth (1970), is that single-word elicitation may present a biased sample of the child's phoneme production ability. That is, they argue that differences in intelligibility occur when a word produced in isolation was compared with the same word produced in conversation. Finally, in view of the suggestion by Prather et al. for developing appropriate methods of testing very young populations, spontaneous speech sampling offers an alternative for uniformly testing a wide range of ages. This is especially important for research which compares data from different age groups or for longitudinal investigations.

DISTINCTIVE FEATURE RESEARCH

Since the appearance of Jakobson, Fant, and Halle's book, *Preliminaries to Speech Analysis,* in 1952, speech/language pathology has attempted to integrate some of the ideas from the theoretical or speculative study of linguistics with more specific data-based empirical research. This research can be seen as having branched in three directions. Two of these trends, as previously noted, have been concerned with the application of distinctive feature theory to both normal and deviant populations. The third direction has been toward the development of new distinctive feature systems for specific purposes, such as clinical application. The following discussion will touch upon some of the major distinctive feature systems and will survey some of the studies which have examined "normal" populations.

Distinctive feature theory assumes that the phoneme, sometimes described as the minimal segment of oral language, can be further dissected into discrete, identifiable properties or features. Moreover, these properties may define the articulatory, acoustic, and/or perceptual boundaries of each phoneme (Singh, 1976). It can be said that the features of a phoneme serve two fundamental purposes in learning: they identify a specific phoneme both in terms of what it is and in terms of what it is not. Thus, the developing child who comes to understand the linguistic significance of /s/ has the potential for understanding not only that /s/ is an unvoiced, coronal consonant but that it is not /z/, /θ/, or /ð/. In a broad sense, then, to know the distinctive features of /s/ is also to potentially know what /s/ is not.

Distinctive feature theory also assumes that the phonemes of a language can be described by a finite number of features. For example, the universal feature system of Jakobson, Fant, and Halle (1952) has 12 features which are capable of describing all phonemes in all languages. Naturally, some phonemes in a given language are considered similar because they share many of the same features. In contrast, others may be considered very different because they have few features in common. In addition, the dissimilarity between two phonemes may be quantified by the number of features by which the two phonemes differ. It should be noted that such quantifications assume some kind of equality among features. This may not in fact be the case, as some features differ in their linguistic and perceptual importance within a given language (Singh, 1976).

A departure from the relatively abstract systems of Chomsky and Halle (1968) and Jakobson et al. (1952) can be found in the more clinically oriented works of Singh, Woods, and Becker (1972), Ladefoged (1971), and Irwin and Wong (1977). Ladefoged devised a system with 26 features, all of which offered concrete descriptions of phonetic surface events. Singh et al. (1972) were interested in determining the perceptual importance of features within an original binary system. The features of the system were determined experimentally and were designed to represent a "system that is 'truly' a function of the perceptual responses of listeners" (Singh, 1976, p. 71). They weighted the features in decreasing order of listener importance as follows: Place of Articulation, Nasality, Sibilancy, Voicing, and Plosiveness. The investigators admitted that not all subjects conformed to this rank order. Finally, a multiple-graded 10-feature system was developed by Irwin and Wong (1977). This system is capable of describing both vowels and consonants, as well as some distortions.

The works of Jakobson et al. and Chomsky and Halle represent a relatively different type of system from those of Singh et al., Ladefoged, and Irwin and Wong. Specifically, the goals of the former include the universal application of the features to all languages for linguistic analysis. In contrast, the systems of Ladefoged (1971), Singh et al. (1972), and Irwin and Wong

(1977) have language-specific application and attempt to provide practical descriptive tools for examining phonetic production and perception. This is not to say that the two types of systems are mutually exclusive in terms of their research applications. Instead, the distinction noted above highlights the efforts of professionals in speech pathology to close the often noted gap between the theoretical field of linguistics and the practically oriented field of empirical language research. Indeed, Crystal (1972), Walsh (1974), Ingram (1976), and Blache (1978) have all referred to this gap and have emphasized the need for developing alternative systems for experimental purposes.

Surprisingly, only a few studies have described normal phonological development in terms of distinctive features. Menyuk (1968) investigated phone production of Japanese children and compared the results with the data of Wellman et al. (1931). Examining the phone for the presence of the Jakobson et al. (1952) features of Gravity, Diffuseness, Stridency, Nasality, Continuancy, and Voicing, Menyuk concluded that there was similar feature acquisition across languages. In addition, the features relevant to place of articulation presented the greatest difficulty for both groups. Another study with goals similar to those of the Menyuk study was that of Prather et al. (1975). Prather's study included children aged 2 to 4 years. Using both plus and minus feature specifications of the Jakobson system, Prather et al. concluded that their study and Menyuk's demonstrated similar patterns of feature acquisition. Unfortunately, Menyuk's and Prather's studies lacked information regarding how mastery of a feature was determined (Winitz, 1969). Moreover, Menyuk confounded her data by comparing the development of children from two different age groups and at different stages of development. For this reason, Prather et al. (1975) suggested that future investigations examine more discrete age levels at specific stages of development.

A rather unusual distinctive feature investigation which is described by Singh (1976) was performed by Weiner and Bernthal. These experimenters evaluated the elicited speech of 250 subjects for the presence of modified Chomsky-Halle features. This study's uniqueness lies in the fact that the observers were trained to identify the presence of features within the utterances. Thus, the typical conversion from phonemic transcriptions of speech to features correctly produced was avoided. These authors arbitrarily assigned a high difficulty rating to those feature specifications exceeding a 10 percent error rate. They concluded that fricative production had the highest difficulty rating of the three phonetic groups. Moreover, as noted by Singh (1976), those features which rated "high" in difficulty for two of the three classes of sounds were + voice, − anterior, + high, and + coronal. The features − anterior, + high, and + coronal are place features. This conclusion is in agreement with other findings (Menyuk, 1968; Van Riper and Irwin, 1958).

Finally, Hodson and Paden (1978) studied the feature competencies of 60 normal American English-speaking 4-year-olds. They found that the most common misarticulations resulted from inappropriate use of the features Coronal and High. They also reported that the features Sonorant, Strident, Continuant, and Anterior were well established by these subjects.

CONCLUSION

The research cited in this review represents a few of the numerous alternatives available for investigating normal phonological development using phonemic and distinctive feature analysis. This review has attempted to trace some of the methodological trends and issues involved in phonemic and distinctive feature research. With respect to methodological issues, the types of populations investigated, the methods of data collection and organization, and the applicability of theoretical and clinically oriented feature systems were reviewed. An apparent gap in early developmental data (specifically, before 24 months) was noted, and a need for investigation of discrete age levels was indicated. It was shown that arbitrary mastery criteria obscure certain aspects of development for both phonemic and distinctive feature analysis. The lack of data based upon conversational testing was demonstrated.

In reference to trends of research, it was shown that researchers are beginning to realize the importance of developing new systems which are useful in the clinical setting. However, because of the lack of developmental data based on conversational testing at discrete age levels, the more abstract systems (e.g., Chomsky and Halle) need further experimental testing to help determine their usefulness in obtaining normative data.

The present study attempts to reflect the conclusions of this review. The authors have attempted to develop a new system which is clinically practical while at the same time demonstrating the applicability of one abstract system to normative research. In addition, conversational sampling at discrete age levels, as well as presentation of the data without imposing mastery criteria, will certainly offer the reader a more complete picture of the developmental process.

2   Methodology   Seok P. Wong and John V. Irwin

SUBJECTS

Subjects were 100 children, 10 girls and 10 boys at each of five age levels: 1.5, 2, 3, 4, and 6 years. Each subject satisfied, as appropriate for age level, the following general criteria: parental declaration of normal birth and developmental history, no known organic deviations, no history of speech-language therapy, acceptable pure tone hearing, and normal dentofacial structures. Children were from middle class, Caucasian families. Subject criteria for each age level are presented more specifically in the appropriate chapters.

INVESTIGATORS

Each of five investigators, all graduate students in the Department of Audiology and Speech Pathology at Memphis State University, collected the language samples at one of five assigned age levels. In ascending order of age group tested, investigators were Leslie Paschall (1.5), Gayle Hare (2), Patricia Larkins (3), Cynthia Bassi (4), and Electa Harmon (6). Each examiner had completed basic courses in language development, phonetics, and phonology at the time of data collection.

COLLECTION OF LANGUAGE SAMPLE

In each instance, the language sample was spontaneous. The examiner was an active participant in nonstructured exchanges with the subject. Data were collected in two tape-recorded sessions at 18 months and in one tape-

Entry Type	Dummy Entry Data

/s, z/ Morpho-logical Function

ROOT			POS.				PL.

Adult Form

S	A	M	'S		C	OA	T	S

IPA

S	æ	M	Z		K	O	T	S

Articulatory Errors

					d		—	—

Subject No. 0 0 1 2
Utterance No. 0 0 2 7

FIGURE 2.1 Data entry system

recorded session at each of the four older ages. Data entry was accomplished from tape. Specific techniques of eliciting speech, instrumentation, place of meeting, and other factors varied somewhat by age group. These details are given in the relevant chapters. All data, including reliability, were drawn from randomly determined central portions of the recorded sessions.

DATA ENTRY

Data were coded for computer processing by subject and utterance in conformity with the data entry system displayed in Figure 2.1, using the dummy utterance "Sam's coats." Selected morphologic functions of /s, z/ are coded in row one. The adult form of the utterance appears in row two. A broad, IPA transcription appears in row three. Three articulatory errors, one substitution of /d/ for /k/ and two omissions for /t, s/ respectively, are coded in row four. Rows two, three, and four are coded as described in all applications of this program.

Row one may be used optionally to code up to 20 linguistic or other characteristics of any phoneme entered. Root word, possessive, and plural are indicated in the example; in addition, third person singular, contractions, and superlatives were also entered. In actual practice, data in rows one, three, and four are coded by number rather than by symbols as shown in Figure 2.1.

The computer program associated with this data entry system was developed by Irwin and Wong (1977). The program generates various error outputs to permit tests of the accuracy of data entry.

THE TWO DISTINCTIVE FEATURE SYSTEMS

The 22 vowellike phonemes and 25 consonants incorporated in the computer program are treated in two distinctive feature systems: the Irwin-Wong feature system, a traditionally based, scaled articulatory system with 10 features and 38 specifications; and an extended version of the Chomsky-Halle system, with 13 features and 26 specifications.

The Irwin-Wong System

The Irwin-Wong distinctive feature system is specific to English. The system encompasses 24 consonants plus the glottal stop, 15 vowels, four phonemic diphthongs, and three syllabics. The system employs 10 phonetic features, of which two are binary and eight are scaled. The term *specification* is used in this monograph to identify scale points within a feature. In general, scale points may be assumed to be roughly ordinal, but cannot be interpreted as precisely linear. The notation used to indicate a particular specification within a feature is, for example, Motion-2 to indicate specification 2 of the feature Motion.

As Singh (1976) has noted, only a limited number of attributes need be utilized to discriminate a large number of phonemes. Singh continues:

> Such attributes are called the distinctive features. Distinctive features are the physical (articulatory or acoustic) and psychological (perceptual) realities of the phoneme. In other words, each phoneme can be described and differentiated in terms of: 1) articulatory features, namely, the place of articulation, the manner of articulation, and voicing; 2) acoustic features, namely, frequency, intensity, and duration of speech sound; and 3) perceptual features, which are the result of the auditory discrimination between the phonemes (p. 5).

In terms of Singh's threefold classification, the Irwin-Wong system is essentially articulatory. The features reflect traditional descriptions of the production of English speech sounds as manifested in the writings of Wise (1958), Thomas (1958), and Gleason (1962). In particular, the treatment of the vowels reflects the description of Wise. Each of the 10 features is used for both vowels and consonants. Obviously, however, some of the features are more discriminating for vowels than for consonants, and vice versa.

The Irwin-Wong distinctive feature matrix for vowels, diphthongs, and syllabics appears as Table 2.1. The distinctive feature matrix for consonants appears as Table 2.2. Each of the 10 features will now be described.

Oronasal (4 specifications)

This feature is concerned with the primary cavity utilized in air-sound flow. In many distinctive feature systems, as for example the Chomsky-Halle system (1968), nasality is treated as a binary feature. That is, the velopharyngeal valve is either open (nasal) or closed (oral). This binary representation does not lend itself to such clinical distinctions as partial nasality and denasality, distinctions that are frequently needed by speech-language pathologists. In the Irwin-Wong system, therefore, a four-point scaling for the oronasal feature is employed. In a roughly ordinal arrangement, from complete orality to complete nasality, the scale points are:

1. *Oral.* The velopharyngeal valve is closed; the air-sound stream is transmitted through the oral cavity. This production is typical in English of all sounds except the syllabics /m̩, n̩/ and the three consonants /m, n, ŋ/.

2. *Partial Nasalization.* The velopharyngeal valve is at least slightly open in the production of an English vowel or consonant that is normally produced with the velopharyngeal value closed. The perceptual effect, particularly for vowels, is that of a nasalized sound. Clinically, the condition is described as hypernasality.

3. *Partial Oralization.* The nasal cavity is at least partly obstructed in the production of a nasal consonant /m, n, ŋ/ or nasal syllabics /m̩, n̩/. Clinically, this condition is described as hyponasality or denasality.

4. *Nasal.* The oral passageway is closed and the air-sound stream is transmitted through the nasal passageways. In English, nasalization is characteristic only of the consonants /m, n, ŋ/ and of the nasal syllabics /m̩, n̩/.

0. *Not Relevant.* This specification means generally that the feature under consideration is not pertinent to the vowel or consonant being described. The oronasal scale, however, is applicable to each of the sounds described.

Motion (5 specifications)

This feature describes the relative stability of the target posture. Each specification indicates the primary movement characteristic of the target posture.

1. *Forward Glide.* In this specification, the highest arched portion of the tongue moves in an anterior or ventral direction during the production of the

TABLE 2.1 English Vowels, Phonemic Diphthongs, and Syllabics by Irwin-Wong Features as Stored for Computer Processing

		Vowels															Diphthongs				Syllabics		
	No.	1	2	3	4	5	6	7	8	9	10	11	12	13	14	15	21	22	23	24	31	32	33
Feature	IPA	i	ɪ	e	ɛ	æ	ɝ	ɜ	ɚ	ə	ʌ	ɑ	ɔ	o	u	ʊ	aɪ	aʊ	ɔɪ	ɪu	n̩ᵃ	l̩	m̩ᵃ
Oronasal		1	1	1	1	1	1	1	1	1	1	1	1	1	1	1	1	1	1	1	4	1	4
Motion		4	4	4	4	4	4	4	4	4	4	4	4	4	4	4	1	2	1	2	4	4	4
Fusion		1	1	1	1	1	1	1	1	1	1	1	1	1	1	1	1	1	1	1	1	1	1
Lateral		3	3	3	3	3	3	3	3	3	3	3	3	3	3	3	3	3	3	3	3	1	3
Labial		2	2	2	2	2	3	2	3	2	2	2	3	3	3	3	2	2	3	3	2	2	4
Tenseness		2	1	2	1	1	2	2	1	1	1	1	1	2	2	1	2	2	2	2	1	1	1
Vertical		3	3	2	2	1	2	2	2	2	2	1	1	2	3	3	1	1	1	3	3	3	2
Place		4	4	4	4	4	5	5	5	5	6	6	6	6	6	6	6	6	6	6	4	4	1
Laryngeal		3	3	3	3	3	3	3	3	3	3	3	3	3	3	3	3	3	3	3	3	3	3
Closure		2	2	2	2	1	2	1	2	1	1	1	1	2	2	1	1	1	1	2	4	2	4

ᵃ/n̩/ and /m̩/ differ from /n/ and /m/ only in perceived sonority.

sound. In English, the diphthongs /ɔɪ, aɪ/ are characterized by this type of movement.

2. *Backward Glide.* In this specification, the highest arched portion of the tongue moves in a posterior or dorsal direction during the production of the sound. The English diphthongs /aʊ, ɪu/ are characterized by glides in this direction.

3. *Dynamic.* This specification implies that movement of the articulators is a characteristic of the phoneme. For example, in the English phonemes /l, r, j, w/, the tongue is an essential organ of movement. In /w/, movement of the lips and the back tongue are important. In /h/, the important movement is a glide from the open glottis to a narrowed glottis plus a possible movement of the tongue to a following vowel position.

4. *Static.* In this specification, a relatively fixed posture without buildup of intraoral pressure is indicated. This specification is characteristic of the vowels, the syllabics, the eight continuant consonants, and the three nasal consonants.

5. *Plosive.* The essential elements are the closure of the air-sound passageway, the building up of pressure within the passageway, and abrupt or sudden release of the impounded air. This specification is characteristic of the six plosives, the two affricates, and the glottal stop.

0. *Not Relevant.* One of the five movement specifications is relevant to each of the phonemes of English and to the glottal stop.

Fusion (2 specifications)

This feature describes the stop-continuant juncture as manifested in the affricates /tʃ, dʒ/.

1. *Minus Affricate.* This specification denotes that the plosive and continuant elements are not blended into a perceptual unit. Except for the two affricates, this specification is characteristic of English phonemes.

TABLE 2.2 English Consonants by Irwin-Wong Features as Stored for Computer Processing

		Consonants																								
	No.	41	42	43	44	45	46	47	48	49	50	51	52	53	54	55	56	57	58	59	60	61	62	63	64	65
Feature	IPA	k	g	t	d	p	b	f	v	θ	ð	s	z	ʃ	ʒ	tʃ	dʒ	m	n	ŋ	l	r	h	w	j	ʔ
Oronasal		1	1	1	1	1	1	1	1	1	1	1	1	1	1	1	1	4	4	4	1	1	1	1	1	1
Motion		5	5	5	5	5	5	4	4	4	4	4	4	4	4	5	5	4	4	4	3	3	3	3	3	5
Fusion		1	1	1	1	1	1	1	1	1	1	1	1	1	1	2	2	1	1	1	1	1	1	1	1	1
Lateral		3	3	3	3	3	3	3	3	3	3	3	3	3	3	3	3	3	3	3	1	3	3	3	3	3
Labial		2	2	2	2	4	4	1	1	2	2	1	1	3	3	3	3	4	2	2	2	3	2	3	2	2
Tenseness		1	1	1	1	1	1	1	1	1	1	2	2	2	2	1	1	1	1	1	1	1	1	1	1	1
Vertical		3	3	3	3	2	2	2	2	2	2	2	2	2	2	3	3	2	3	3	3	2	0	2	3	0
Place		6	6	4	4	1	1	2	2	3	3	4	4	5	5	5	5	1	4	6	4	4	7	1	5	7
Laryngeal		1	3	1	3	1	3	1	3	1	3	1	3	1	3	1	3	3	3	3	3	3	2	3	3	4
Closure		4	4	4	4	4	4	3	3	3	3	3	3	3	3	4	4	4	4	4	2	2	1	2	2	1

2. *Plus Affricate*. This specification indicates the blending of two phonemes into a perceptual unit as in /tʃ, dʒ/.

0. *Not Relevant*. Fusion is relevant to each of the phonemes, including the glottal stop, treated in this system.

Lateral (3 specifications)

This feature describes the flow, if any, of the air-sound stream around the tongue blade.

1. *Bilateral*. This specification means that the tongue blocks a midsagittal portion of the oral passageway but that the air-sound stream may pass freely on both sides of the tongue. The only sounds of English that normally manifest this specification are /l, l̮/.

2. *Unilateral*. In this specification, the tongue again blocks a portion of the midsagittal oral passageway, but in this instance, the air-sound stream may escape on only one side of the tongue. The sole phoneme in English for which this specification may be regarded as an acceptable standard is /l̮/, but the difference between specifications bilateral and unilateral may not be perceptually distinct. Indeed, the production of a unilateral /l/ should be regarded as a relatively minor variation.

3. *Nonlateral*. In this specification, the midsagittal section of the air-sound passageway is either completely blocked as in /t, k/, at least partially constricted as in /s/, or relatively open as in the vowels. In English, this specification is characteristic of all the phonemes with the exception of /l, l̮/.

0. *Not Relevant*. This feature is relevant to all sounds included in the system.

Labial (4 specifications)

This feature describes the posture of the lips.

1. *Spread*. In this specification, the sound is made with the angles of the mouth open and slightly retracted. This type of lip position is typical of /f, v/.

2. *Neutral*. The lips are open but not retracted and not rounded. This position is characteristic, for example, of the English vowel /æ/ and the English consonant /k/.

3. *Rounded*. The mouth is open and the lips are somewhat pursed. This specification is characteristic of such phonemes as /u, ʃ/.

4. *Closed*. The lips are completely closed. In oral stops, as /b, p/, intraoral pressure is built up. In the nasal continuant /m/, no increase in intraoral pressure occurs.

0. *Not Relevant*. This feature is relevant for all sounds included in the system.

Tenseness (2 specifications)

This feature describes the relative tension, degree of frication, and period of holding of the primary target posture.

1. *Lax.* The phoneme, whether vowel or consonant, is made with reduced tension, definiteness, and maintenance of the posture. The feature is characteristic of vowels such as /ɪ/ and of all consonants except the sibilants /s, z, ʃ, ʒ/.

2. *Tense.* In this specification, production is characterized by increased tension and definiteness, and prolongation of the posture. It is characteristic of such vowels as /i, u/ and, as noted, the four sibilants.

0. *Not Relevant.* This feature is generally of greater importance for English vowels than for English consonants. But the tense/lax distinction is drawn for each sound in the system.

Vertical (3 specifications)

This feature describes the height of the oral target posture relative to selected horizontal planes in the oral cavity.

1. *Low.* The sound is produced with the oral target posture at or below a horizontal plane through the lower alveolar ridge. An example is the vowel /a/.

2. *Mid.* The sound is produced with the oral target posture between horizontal planes through the upper and lower alveolar ridges. Examples are the vowel /ɛ/ and the consonant /z/

3. *High.* The sound, as the vowel /i/, is produced with the oral target posture at or above a horizontal plane through the upper alveolar ridge.

0. *Not Relevant.* The basic target posture does not primarily involve the oral cavity, as in /h, ʔ/.

Place (7 specifications)

This feature describes the site of the basic target posture in the oral and pharyngeal cavities.

1. *Bilabial.* The essential articulatory posture is between the upper and lower lips. Examples are /b, p, m/.

2. *Labiodental.* The essential articulatory posture is between the lower lip and the upper incisors. Examples are /f, v/.

3. *Linguadental.* The essential articulatory posture is between the front tongue and the upper incisors. Examples are the phonemes /θ, ð/.

4. *Lingua-alveolar.* The essential articulatory posture is between the front tongue and the upper alveolar ridge. Examples are /s, z/.

5. *Linguapalatal.* The essential articulatory posture is between the tongue and the hard palate. Examples in English are the phonemes /ʃ, ʒ/.

6. *Linguavelar.* The essential articulatory posture is between the back tongue and the velum. Examples in English are /k, g, ŋ/.

7. *Glottal.* The essential articulatory posture is at the glottis, as in /h, ʔ/.

0. *Not Relevant.* This feature is relevant to all sounds included in the system.

Laryngeal (4 specifications)

This feature describes the degree of closure at the glottis.

1. *Voiceless*. The vocal bands are relatively open; the airstream can pass between them without generating any audible sound. The unvoiced consonants of English are examples of this degree of glottal closure.

2. *Whisper*. The membranous bands are closed sufficiently to produce turbulence as the airstream escapes between them. The resulting aperiodic pulse and airstream may be used to generate whispered versions of all the sounds of English, including the vowels and voiced consonants. Voicing is, of course, lost.

3. *Voice*. The approximation of the vocal bands is close enough that the escaping airstream generates periodic pulsations. In English, this specification is characteristic of the vowels, diphthongs, and syllabics, plus all of the voiced consonants.

4. *Stopped*. The vocal bands are tightly approximated. In this position, pressure may be built up beneath the bands and then suddenly released. This specification is characteristic in English only of the glottal stop /ʔ/.

0. *Not Relevant*. The glottal feature is relevant for all sounds included in the system.

Closure (4 specifications)

This feature describes the degree of openness of the oral passageway, regardless of whether the basic articulatory posture is oral or glottal.

1. *Open*. The degree of closure in the oral passageway is slight; the escaping air-sound stream does not produce oral turbulence. This mode of production is characteristic of the low vowels of English such as /a/.

2. *Approximation*. The oral passageway is somewhat closed but, again, not to a degree that produces audible frication. This specification is characteristic of the mid and high vowels of English and of the four phonemes /l, r, w, j/.

3. *Constriction*. The degree of closure in or at the oral passageway is great enough to result in turbulence. This mode of production is characteristic of such English consonants as /f, v/.

4. *Occlusion*. The degree of oral obstruction is complete, either during the pressure build-up phase, as in oral stops and affricates, or during the central phase of the sound, as in the English nasals.

0. *Not Relevant*. This feature is used to describe each phoneme in the system.

Feature/Degree Differences

Analyzing phonemes in terms of distinctive features allows for an analysis of substitution errors by a measure of the "distance" between the target sound and the substituted sound. In the Irwin-Wong system this "distance" is expressed through counts of differences in features and in specifications, termed feature/degree differences. For example, /d/ and /t/ differ from each other in this system in only one feature (glottal). The phoneme /d/ has a glottal specification of 1, which indicates voicing; the phoneme /t/, a glottal specification of 3, which indicates devoicing. The difference in glottal specification between /d/ and /t/ is thus two degrees. The feature/degree difference between /d/ and /t/ in the Irwin-Wong system is expressed as 1/2 (one feature but two degrees within the feature). In the Irwin-Wong articulatory based feature system, the smaller the number of feature/degree differences between two phonemes, the more similarly the two sounds are produced. In the Chomsky-Halle system, the same concept is expressed in feature difference alone, as the system is binary.

The Extended Chomsky-Halle System

In order to facilitate use of the computerized system of analysis, the Chomsky-Halle system (1968) was arbitrarily extended in two ways: (1) The system was extended—perhaps inappropriately—to certain English sounds not included in the original description. This extension made possible the processing of each of the 22 vowellike and 25 consonant sounds for which the computer program had been designed. (2) The features Voice, Continuant, Nasal, and Strident were included in vowel summaries, and the features Round and Tense were included in consonant summaries. The purpose of extending these features was to enable the computer program to make distinctive feature difference counts when subjects replaced vowels with consonants or consonants with vowels. The number of such replacements was typically so small that the practical consequences of the second extension are not great, except possibly in the 1.5 year corpus, at which age level some cross-substitutions did occur. Because the Chomsky-Halle system is binary, degree differences are not computed; only feature differences are relevant.

The extended Chomsky-Halle matrices for vowels and consonants appear as Tables 2.3 and 2.4 respectively. A description of each feature follows.

Vocalic

Plus vocalic means that the constriction in the oral cavity is not greater than that required for the high vowels /i, u/, and the vocal cords are so positioned that spontaneous voicing occurs. Minus vocalic sounds are characterized by the absence of one or both of these stipulations. Vocalic sounds include the voiced liquids /l, r/ and the voiced vowellike sounds. Nonvocalic sounds include nasal consonants, obstruents, and glides.

Consonantal

Plus consonantal means that the sound is made with a radical obstruction— at least as narrow as is characteristic of the fricatives—in the midsagittal region of the oral cavity. Minus consonantal refers to a lack of such constriction. Consonantal sounds include the liquids and both nasal and nonnasal consonants.

High

Plus high indicates that the body of the tongue is elevated above the neutral position; minus high, that the tongue is not so raised. High sounds include /i, k/; nonhigh, /ɛ, ə/.

Back

Plus back indicates that the body of the tongue retracts from the neutral position. Minus back means that this retraction does not occur. Back sounds include /u, k/; nonback sounds, /i, f/.

Low

Plus low means that the body of the tongue is lowered below the neutral position. Minus low indicates that this lowering does not take place. Representative low sounds are /æ, ɔɪ/; representative nonlow sounds, /ɛ, ə/.

Anterior

Plus anterior means that the sound is produced farther forward in the mouth than /ʃ/. Sounds produced at the /ʃ/ position or farther back in the mouth are nonanterior. Anterior sounds include /p, f, d/; nonanterior sounds, /ʒ, k/.

TABLE 2.3 English Vowels, Phonemic Diphthongs, and Syllabics by Chomsky-Halle Features as Extended and Stored for Computer Processing

		Vowels															Diphthongs				Syllabics		
	No.	1	2	3	4	5	6	7	8	9	10	11	12	13	14	15	21	22	23	24	31	32	33
Feature	IPA	i	ɪ	e	ɛ	æ	ɝ	ɜ	ɚ	ə	ʌ	ɑ	ɔ	o	u	ʊ	aɪ	aʊ	ɔɪ	ɪu	n̩[a]	l̩	m̩[a]
Vocalic		2	2	2	2	2	2	2	2	2	2	2	2	2	2	2	2	2	2	2	1	2	1
Consonantal		1	1	1	1	1	1	1	1	1	1	1	1	1	1	1	1	1	1	1	2	2	2
High		2	2	1	1	1	1	1	1	1	1	1	1	1	2	2	1	1	1	2	1	1	1
Back		1	1	1	1	1	1	1	1	1	2	2	2	2	2	2	2	2	2	1	1	1	1
Low		1	1	1	1	2	1	1	1	1	1	2	1	1	1	1	2	1	2	1	1	1	1
Anterior		1	1	1	1	1	1	1	1	1	1	1	1	1	1	1	1	1	1	1	2	2	2
Coronal		1	1	1	1	1	2	1	2	1	1	1	1	1	1	1	1	1	1	1	2	2	1
Round		1	1	1	1	1	1	2	1	2	1	1	2	2	1	2	1	1	2	2	0	0	0
Tense		2	1	2	1	1	2	2	1	1	1	1	1	2	2	1	2	2	2	2	0	0	0
Voice		2	2	2	2	2	2	2	2	2	2	2	2	2	2	2	2	2	2	2	2	2	2
Continuant		1	1	1	1	1	1	1	1	1	1	1	1	1	1	1	1	1	1	1	1	2	1
Nasal		1	1	1	1	1	1	1	1	1	1	1	1	1	1	1	1	1	1	1	2	1	2
Strident		1	1	1	1	1	1	1	1	1	1	1	1	1	1	1	1	1	1	1	1	1	1

[a]/n̩/ and /m̩/ differ from /n/ and /m/ only in perceived sonority.

Coronal

Plus coronal sounds are made with the blade of the tongue raised from the neutral position. Minus coronal sounds are made with the blade in a neutral position. Examples of coronal sounds are /t, z/ and of noncoronal sounds are /k, ŋ/.

Round

Plus round indicates a narrowing of the lip orifice. Minus round sounds are produced without such narrowing. The sounds /o, u/ are round; the sounds /ɪ, ɛ/, nonround.

Tense

Plus tense indicates that the sound is produced deliberately, accurately, and distinctly. Minus tense sounds are produced with relative rapidity and lack of distinctness. The vowel /i/ is tense; the vowel /ɪ/, lax.

Voice

Plus voice means that, during the production of the sound, the larynx produces periodic vibration. Minus voice means that the bands are opened sufficiently to prevent periodic vibration, although turbulence may be created. Such cognates as /z, s/, /d, t/, and /g, k/ represent this contrast.

TABLE 2.4 English Consonants by Chomsky-Halle Features as Extended and Stored for Computer Processing

		Consonants																							
No.		41	42	43	44	45	46	47	48	49	50	51	52	53	54	55	56	57	58	59	60	61	62	63	64	65
Feature	IPA	k	g	t	d	p	b	f	v	θ	ð	s	z	ʃ	ʒ	tʃ	dʒ	m	n	ŋ	l	r	h	w	j	ʔ
Vocalic		1	1	1	1	1	1	1	1	1	1	1	1	1	1	1	1	1	1	1	2	2	1	1	1	1
Consonantal		2	2	2	2	2	2	2	2	2	2	2	2	2	2	2	2	1	1	2	1	1	1	2	2	1
High		2	2	1	1	1	1	1	1	1	1	1	1	1	1	1	1	1	1	2	1	1	1	2	1	1
Back		2	2	1	1	1	1	1	1	1	1	1	1	1	1	1	1	1	1	1	1	1	2	1	1	2
Low		1	1	1	1	1	1	1	1	1	1	1	1	1	1	1	1	1	1	1	1	1	2	1	1	2
Anterior		1	1	2	2	2	2	2	2	2	2	2	2	1	1	1	1	2	2	1	2	1	1	1	1	1
Coronal		1	1	2	2	1	1	1	1	2	2	2	2	2	2	2	2	1	2	1	2	2	1	1	1	1
Round		0	0	0	0	0	0	0	0	0	0	0	0	0	0	0	0	0	0	0	0	0	0	2	1	1
Tense		0	0	0	0	0	0	0	0	0	0	0	0	0	0	0	0	0	0	0	0	0	0	1	1	0
Voice		1	2	1	2	1	2	1	2	1	2	1	2	1	2	1	2	2	2	2	2	2	1	2	2	1
Continuant		1	1	1	1	1	1	2	2	2	2	2	2	2	2	1	1	1	1	1	2	2	2	2	2	2
Nasal		1	1	1	1	1	1	1	1	1	1	1	1	1	1	1	1	2	2	2	1	1	1	1	1	1
Strident		1	1	1	1	1	1	2	2	1	1	2	2	2	2	2	2	1	1	1	1	1	1	1	1	1

0 = not relevant.
1 = binary feature not present.
2 = binary feature present.

Continuant

Plus continuant indicates partial constriction of the vocal tract; the flow of air is not completely blocked. Complete interruption of the flow of air does occur in minus continuant. In the extension of this feature to vowels, the absence of partial constriction is also coded as minus continuant. The fricatives are examples of continuant consonants; the plosives, nasals, and affricates represent noncontinuant consonants.

Nasal

Plus nasal describes a production in which the velopharyngeal valve is sufficiently open to permit the air-sound stream to be directed through the nose. If the velopharyngeal valve is closed, the production is described as minus nasal. The nasal consonants and the two nasal syllabics are plus nasal. In English, the remaining consonants and vowellike sounds are nonnasal.

Strident

Plus strident indicates that the airstream is directed over a rough surface in such a way as to produce an audible noise. In minus strident sounds, the airstream does not produce this noise. The fricatives, with the exception of /θ, ð/, and the affricates are strident. The other sounds are nonstrident.

RELIABILITY

Inter- and intraexaminer* reliability were established for each age group for both (1) utterance selection** and (2) phonemic transcription. For both types of measures, interexaminer percentages of agreement were greater than 90 percent; intraexaminer reliability was greater than 96 percent. Subject reliability was not examined.

DATA PROCESSING

Storage

As indicated in Figure 2.1, input data are stored by subject and utterance for each sample. But, in addition, two distinctive feature matrices—the Irwin-Wong (1977) system and the extended version of the Chomsky-Halle (1968) system—are stored permanently. Each matrix includes the 22 vowellike and 25 consonant sounds described in English. Within the limits of each distinctive feature system, distortions may be added to either matrix as may be necessary for any subject.

*Intraexaminer reliability was not established for the six year group.
**The reliability of utterance selection was not tested for the six year group.

Retrieval

The Irwin-Wong program permits retrieval of data in either or both of two basic outputs: *utterance outputs* and *summary tables*. *Utterance outputs* typically present the consecutive utterances of an individual subject. Utterance outputs may, however, be organized across or within subjects by any selected characteristic or set of characteristics: for example, utterances that demonstrate plural /s, z/, omission of final /d/, or English words beginning with /tr/ and /dr/. *Summary tables* are organized by individual subject or any coded combination of subjects. For example, subjects may be combined by age, race, sex, sociolinguistic status, or area of disability.

For each utterance, the utterance output includes the adult English form, the IPA transcription, the error status (if any) of each phoneme, and the feature characteristics of both correct and incorrect phonemes by both feature systems. In addition, for the present study, the morphologic functions of /s, z/ are shown. A sample utterance output appears as Table 2.5. Data by individual utterances are not reported in this work, however.

Six major types of summary tables were produced; each type will be discussed in turn. As noted above, such summary tables could be produced for one subject or for any selected group of subjects. "Table 1," then, was produced a total of 115 times for this particular study: once for each of 100 subjects and three times (boys, girls, and total) for each of five age groups.

Computer Output Table 1

This first of six working tables (which are not included in this work) presents the distribution of the 47 phonemes entered for analysis by individual phoneme and by the major categories of phonemes. The categories summarized are: (1) 22 vowellike sounds, broken down into three subsets of 15 vowels, four diphthongs, and three syllabics; and (2) 25 consonants. Thus, for the 6-year-old sample, /ð/ was entered 196 times and made up 4 percent of the 5,187 phonemes summarized. /ð/ was produced correctly 128 times, for 65 percent of the /ð/ production and 3 percent of the total distribution. /ð/ was produced in error 68 times, for 35 percent of the /ð/ production and 1 percent of the total distribution. The errors consisted of 24 omissions, 44 substitutions, and no distortions. A similar pattern of data is given for each phoneme and phoneme category. As footnotes to Computer Output Table 1, lists are provided of (1) any phonemes not entered, (2) phonemes 100 percent correct, (3) phonemes not 100 percent correct, and (4) phonemes used as additions.

Computer Output Table 2

This table summarizes the occurrences of each phoneme by any coded linguistic or other function. The distribution of each phoneme is summarized by number of correct and incorrect productions. Error productions are further tabulated by error type. Thus, the number of unmarked (not specifically coded) and marked (specifically coded) occurrences for each classification is listed. Finally, for marked occurrences, the function and number of each occurrence is given. Thus, for the 4-year-old corpus, /s/ was produced correctly 571 times and was marked in each instance. That is, /s/ was correctly produced as a plural form 26 times, as a possessive form once, as a third person singular verb form 27 times, as part of a contraction 43 times, as a superlative form once, and as part of a word root 473 times. Similar information is given for the error productions of /s/.

TABLE 2.5 Sample Utterance Output

Utterance 32	And	I	got	some	swings		and	a	slide
Marker				09	09	01			09
Error	90						90		79
Phoneme	055844	21	421143	511057	5163025952		055844	10	51602144
A. Oronasal	1 4-1	1	1 1 1	1 1 4	1 1 1 4 1		1 4-1	1	1 1 1 1
B. Motion	4 4-5	1	5 4 5	4 4 4	4 3 4 4 4		4 4-5	4	34 3 1 5
C. Fusion	1 1-1	1	1 1 1	1 1 1	1 1 1 1 1		1 1-1	1	1 1 1 1
D. Lateral	3 3-3	3	3 3 3	3 3 3	3 3 3 3 3		3 3-3	3	13 1 3 3
E. Labial	2 2-2	2	2 2 2	1 2 4	1 3 2 2 1		2 2-2	2	21 2 2 2
F. Tenseness	1 1-1	2	1 1 1	2 1 1	2 1 1 1 2		1 1-1	1	12 1 2 1
G. Vertical	1 3-3	1	3 1 3	2 2 2	2 2 3 3 2		1 3-3	2	32 3 1 3
H. Place	4 4-4	6	6 6 4	4 6 1	4 1 4 6 4		4 4-4	6	4 4 6 4
I. Laryngeal	3 3-3	3	3 3 1	1 3 3	1 3 3 3 3		3 3-3	3	1 3 3 3
J. Closure	1 4-4	1	4 1 4	3 1 4	3 2 2 4 3		1 4-4	1	23 2 1 4
A. Vocalic	2 1-1	2	1 2 1	1 2 1	1 1 2 1 1		2 1-1	2	21 2 2 1
B. Consonantal	1 2-2	1	2 1 2	2 1 2	2 1 1 2 2		1 2-2	1	2 2 1 2
C. High	1 1-1	1	2 1 1	1 1 1	1 2 2 2 1		1 1-1	1	1 1 1 1
D. Back	1 1-1	2	2 2 1	1 2 1	1 2 1 2 1		1 1-1	2	1 1 2 1
E. Low	2 1-1	2	1 2 1	1 1 1	1 1 1 1 1		2 1-1	1	1 1 2 1
F. Anterior	1 2-2	1	1 1 2	2 1 2	2 1 1 1 2		1 2-2	1	2 2 1 2
G. Coronal	1 2-2	1	1 1 2	2 1 1	2 1 1 1 2		1 2-2	1	2 2 1 2
H. Round	1 0-0	1	0 1 0	0 1 0	0 2 1 0 0		1 0-0	1	0 0 1 0
I. Tense	1 0-0	2	0 1 0	0 1 0	0 1 1 0 0		1 0-0	1	0 0 2 0
J. Voice	2 2-2	2	2 2 1	1 2 2	1 2 2 2 2		2 2-2	2	1 2 2 2
K. Continuant	1 1-1	1	1 1 1	2 1 1	2 2 1 1 2		1 1-1	1	2 2 1 1
L. Nasal	1 2-1	1	1 1 1	1 1 2	1 1 1 2 1		1 2-1	1	1 1 1 1
M. Strident	1 1-1	1	1 1 1	2 1 1	2 1 1 1 2		1 1-1	1	12 1 1 1

Utterance: Adult model as interpreted by investigator.
Marker: /s/ (51) in *some, swings,* and *slide* is part of basic word (09). /z/ (52) in *swings* has plural (01) function.
Error: /d/ (44) in each *and* is omitted (90). The /s/ (51) of *slide* is replaced by a distortion of /s/ (79).
Phoneme: Broad transcription of adult model. Each pair of digits represents a phoneme. Thus *and* is transcribed as /æ/ (05), /n/ (58), and /d/ (44), and *I* as /aɪ/ (21).
Features: The Irwin-Wong (A–J) and Chomsky-Halle (A–M) features for correct rendering of the adult model are shown. Specifications are aligned with second digit of each phoneme. Omissions (90) are indicated with a minus sign (−) before each specification. Replacement features, in this instance (79), appear before standard feature. Thus, in Chomsky-Halle, Strident (2) is replaced by Strident (1) and Vocalic (1) is replaced by Vocalic (2).

Phonological Development in Children

Computer Output Table 3

This table provides the same information as Computer Output Table 2 but is organized by phoneme classifications and by total sample. Thus, of the 8,073 consonants produced correctly in the 4-year-old corpus, 7,729 (89 percent) were unmarked and 974 (11 percent) were marked. Of the 974 marked consonants, in this instance either /s/ or /z/, 140 expressed plurality; 24, possession; 140, third person singular; 94, contractions; 1, superlative; and 575, part of a word root.

Computer Output Tables 4 and 4A

Computer Tables 4 and 4A summarize, for the Irwin-Wong and Chomsky-Halle systems respectively: (1) the number of possible occurrences of each feature in each system; (2) the number and percent right; (3) the number and percent wrong; and (4) the replacement(s) for each error specification by specification, number, and percent. In the Chomsky-Halle system, which is binary, the replacement for any error is typically the other specification. Thus, for Subject No. 111 in the 3-year-old corpus, of 1,403 possible occurrences of + back, the nine error occurrences were replaced by nine productions of − back. But in the Irwin-Wong system, which is graded, of the 77 possible occurrences of Place-3, the 70 error occurrences were replaced 10 times by Place-2 and 60 times by Place-4.

Computer Output Tables 5 and 5A

These tables summarize the replacements for error productions by phoneme, the number of times each replacement is used, and the difference(s) in specifications between target phoneme and error phoneme. For the 6-year-old data, /ɪ/ is replaced once by /i/, which has a feature difference of one in the Chomsky-Halle system, and five times by /æ/, which has a Chomsky-Halle difference of two.

Computer Output Tables 6 and 6A

For each misarticulated phoneme, these tables summarize the mean feature/degree differences (Irwin-Wong) and feature differences (Chomsky-Halle) by each replacement phoneme, both for the number of error occurrences of each phoneme and for the total number of occurrences. Thus, for the 2-year-old corpus, using Chomsky-Halle data from Computer Output Table 6A, the mean feature difference per error for the four replacements for /ð/ was 1.06, and the mean feature difference per total occurrence was .94 features.

DESIGN

Using descriptive statistics, the data are reported at age level by phoneme and by distinctive feature set. Trends across age levels are reported in the summary chapter. To a limited extent, inferential statistics are employed in the summary chapter to facilitate the interpretation of possible effects of age, sex, phoneme, and phoneme type.

Phoneme Selection: Descriptive Statistics

The basic presentation of data in this study is descriptive. Thus, there is a chapter on each of the individual age groups (Chapters 3 through 7). The summary chapter, Chapter 8, includes the descriptive summary of the data both by phoneme and distinctive feature. For these presentations, it was planned to use the data from each of the 46 different phonemes included in the study. The actual distribution of the 22 vowellike phonemes and of the 24 consonants will be presented in Chapter 8.

The brief treatment of the morphological functions of /s, z/ is based, of course, on all occurrences of these two sounds.

Phoneme Selection: Inferential Statistics

Certain of the planned analyses would not be adversely affected by the unequal frequency of occurrence of different phonemes. Among the planned comparisons were an examination of the relative frequency of vowels and consonants and an examination of the relative percentage of correct productions by female and male speakers. For these analyses, it was planned to use data from each of the 46 phonemes.

For more detailed comparisons, however, it was recognized from the work of Dewey (1923) and Denes (1963) that many of the phonemes could not be expected to occur frequently enough in the speech of small children to be included in the statistical analysis. It was further planned to limit detailed comparisons to the consonants, both because of the assumed more rapid development of the vowels and because of the heavy emphasis in intervention on problems involving consonants. Indeed, consonant acquisition has been more studied than vowel acquisition; this monograph is consistent with this trend.

The major planned comparisons were to be concerned with the mean percents correct of (1) voiced and unvoiced cognates, (2) voiced and unvoiced plosives and fricatives, (3) manner of production, and (4) place of constriction. Table 2.6 presents the 24 English consonants recorded in this work, classified by voicing, manner of articulation, and place of constriction. Of these 24 consonants, it was planned, primarily on the basis of the work of Dewey and Denes, to eliminate the following phonemes from this series of analyses:

Fricatives: /ʃ/ and /ʒ/ to be dropped because of the expected low occurrence of the /ʒ/, generally regarded as the most infrequent sound of English. In addition, /h/ to be dropped, partly because it does not have a voiced equivalent, thus making it unlike the other fricatives, and partly because it is the only phoneme made at the glottis.

TABLE 2.6 Traditional Classification of 24 Consonants by Manner, Voicing, and Place of Constriction

| | Manner | | | | | | | | | | | |
| | Fricatives | | Plosives | | Affricates | | Nasals | | Liquids | | Glides | |
	u	v	u	v	u	v	u	v	u	v	u	v
Bilabial			p	b			—	m			—	w
Labiodental	f	v										
Linguadental	θ	ð										
Alveolar	s	z	t	d			—	n	—	l,r		
Palatal	ʃ[a]	ʒ[a]			tʃ[a]	dʒ[a]					—	j[a]
Velar			k	g			—	ŋ				
Glottal	h[a]	—										

[a]To be dropped from a series of four inferential analyses involving selected consonant characteristics.

Affricates: Both affricates /tʃ/ and /dʒ/ to be dropped because of the expected low frequency of occurrence of both phonemes.

Glides: The glide /j/ to be dropped because of its anticipated low frequency of occurrence.

For each of the planned analyses, then, the available phonemes are as follows:

1. Unvoiced vs. voiced cognate pairs: /p – b, t – d, k – g, f – v, θ – ð, s – z/.

2. Unvoiced and voiced plosives in relation to unvoiced and voiced fricatives: plosives /p, b, t, d, k, g/ and fricatives /f, v, θ, ð, s, z/.

3. Classification by manner: plosives /p, b, t, d, k, g/; fricatives /f, v, 0, ð, s, z/; nasals /m, n, ŋ/; and liquids and glides /l, r, w/. Because affricates were dropped and liquids and glides were combined, only four manner groups remained.

4. Classification by place: bilabials /p, b, m, w/; labiodentals /f, v/; linguadentals /θ, ð/; alveolars /s, z, t, d, n, l, r/; and velars /k, g, ŋ/. As indicated in Table 2.6, all palatal and glottal phonemes were dropped.

3   Development at 18 Months   Leslie Paschall

METHOD

Subjects

Number

Spontaneous speech samples obtained from 10 white females and 10 white males aged 16 to 18 months were analyzed for acquisition of phonemes and distinctive features. A corpus of utterances acquired during two one-hour sessions was broadly transcribed in phonetics from audiotape recordings of each subject.

Criteria

To be included in this study, each child was required to be no younger than 16 months and no older than 18 months at the test date. Each child was also required to demonstrate the following: an unremarkable medical history (i.e., no known gross intellectual, neurological, or physiological difficulties); normal hearing for at least one ear; and consistent use of some intelligible words for communication. Information pertaining to both the child's medical history and approximate vocabulary size was obtained during the initial telephone contact with the parent. No child whose vocabulary contained fewer than five words was included in the study. Normal hearing for at least one ear was established by employing a hearing evaluation screening test adopted from Northern and Downs (1974). More specifically, each parent was asked the following questions concerning the child's hearing capabilities: (1) Do you have any reason to be concerned about your child's hearing? (2) When your child is asleep in his or her room, does he or she stir or awaken when you come in and make noise or talk? Each child's parent answered no to the first question and yes to the second, and gave two specific examples of awakening her child as described above.

The examiner then obtained orienting responses using an audiometer calibrated to produce tones at 40 dB SPL for a modified sound field presentation. More specifically, the earphone of the audiometer was held approximately 12 inches from the child's ear and out of his or her peripheral vision. The child was first conditioned to produce an orienting response. After a conditional response was obtained, the child was required to produce an orienting response on at least one of the presentations at each frequency. All testing was performed with the child positioned in his or her high chair and with his or her mother sitting in front of him or her, distracting him or her with a toy. The examiner stood behind the subject and presented the tones. Each correct orienting response was reinforced by the mother. To avoid incorrect reinforcement, the examiner cued the mother to reinforce responses. All calibrations of the audiometer were performed in a sound-treated room in which the actual testing conditions were simulated (i.e., position of the child relative to the mother and the examiner).

Data Collection

Setting and Participants

All sessions were conducted in the children's homes and in a room where they frequently played. Besides the examiner, only one parent—usually the mother—was present during each testing session. The two sessions lasted one hour each and were scheduled no more than five days apart. No two sessions were scheduled for the same day.

Before each session the parent was briefed on what to expect and how the session must be conducted in order to obtain a spontaneous speech sample. Specifically, each parent was instructed: to avoid eliciting imitative responses, asking the child direct questions, and giving the child specific commands, such as "Come play with this toy"; to reinforce the child's utterances; to indirectly encourage the child to interact with the toys by modeling play behavior; and to respond appropriately to any child-initiated instructions. The examiner demonstrated and role-played with the parent until the parent appeared to understand how to implement these instructions. In addition, each parent was told that clarification of the child's utterances might be requested throughout the session.

Equipment

A Pioneer Model 2121 stereo cassette recorder and two Shure Model 555 microphones were used to record the sessions. The recording levels were adjusted to obtain a peak that centered about 0 dB VU (± 5 dB VU) for each child's speech, and the distance from subject to microphone was three to four feet. The microphones were connected to separate channels and placed on opposite sides of the child's immediate play area. This microphone placement allowed the child to move about more freely without readjusting the microphones' position or the recording level. High quality BASF and TDK recording tape was used.

Modes of Stimulation

The selection of various materials (toys, pictures, etc.) to stimulate speech was based on the particular words in each child's vocabulary, as well as on the parent's statement that certain items had elicited speech in the past. Thus, no standard set of stimulus materials was used for all the subjects. The examiner required each parent to compile a relatively complete list of words in the child's vocabulary and reviewed the list with the parent before a session began. This enabled the examiner to select items from the list—usually toys—which had the greatest potential for eliciting speech. These items were then randomly distributed in brightly colored bags and placed in the play area before the child was brought in for testing.

Corpus

During each session, both the orthographic form and the nonlinguistic context were recorded for each of the subject's utterances. If the examiner could not determine what the child was saying, the parent was asked to clarify the utterance. After the testing session, the list of utterances was reviewed with the parent and compared with the previously compiled vocabulary list. The parent was also asked to judge if the child's verbal performance during the session was fairly representative of the child's abilities. In doing this, the examiner was better able to determine if the corpus during a given session accurately reflected the child's language ability. Finally, the examiner reviewed the orthographic transcriptions with each parent in order to determine what, if any, variant adult phonemic speech the child had been exposed to. A variant adult phonemic form was defined as any consistent adult phonemic production of a lexical item whose phonetic transcription varied from the standard transcription and/or whose origin could be traced to learned colloquialisms used within a given family. To illustrate, some parents reported that their children had only been exposed to the lexical item "Daddy" in the phonemic form /dædæ/, a variation of the standard form /dædi/. In such a case, if the child's production of "Daddy" were /dædæ/ and the reported adult variant form were the same, then the child's production was considered correct. In like manner, the child's phonemic approximations of the same lexical item were compared with the adult variant form. Specific colloquialisms used within a given family were generally nicknames for relatives, pets, favorite toys, and so forth, that the child had been taught.

A broad phonetic transcription was later made of the intelligible speech that was audiorecorded during each one-hour session. In order to increase the variety of each child's sample, all repeated utterances were marked as such and eliminated from the corpus to be prepared for computer analysis. An intelligible utterance was considered a repetition only if preceded by an utterance that was both intelligible and phonemically identical. Thus, two phonemically identical utterances separated by unintelligible speech were not considered to be repetitive. The final corpus size entered for computer analysis was determined by the number of nonrepetitive intelligible utterances occurring during two one-hour testing sessions for each subject. Finally, no imitations, whether solicited or unsolicited, were entered for analysis.

Reliability

In order to establish both inter- and intrajudge reliability, the percent of agreement between the investigator and an independent observer was determined for (1) the selection of utterances for analysis, and (2) phonetic transcriptions of utterances from the audiotapes. A randomly chosen 10 percent of each subject's recorded sample was used in computing reliability.

For the selection of utterances for analysis, the percentages of inter- and intrajudge agreement were:

Interjudge reliability	91.2%
Intrajudge reliability (examiner)	97.0%
Intrajudge reliability (observer)	91.0%

For transcribing utterances from the audiotapes, the percentages of inter- and intrajudge agreement were:

Interjudge reliability	91.3%
Intrajudge reliability (examiner)	97.0%
Intrajudge reliability (observer)	90.7%

All inter- and intrajudge percentages of agreement were at least 90.7.

RESULTS

Phoneme Distribution by Individual Sounds

A total of 12,775 phonemes was entered for phonemic analysis; a mean of 639 phonemes was analyzed for each subject. The number of phonemes entered for analysis for any one subject ranged from 33 to 2,232. That is, one subject's sample comprised 0.2 percent of the group total, while another's represented 17 percent.

For the group, the distribution of vowellike phonemes and consonantal phonemes was 43 percent and 57 percent respectively. No individual subject's vowellike/consonantal distribution varied from the group's by more than 4 percent.

The percentages of frequency distribution for individual phonemes are compiled in Table 3.1. The distribution range for vowellike phonemes was 0 to 6 percent. The most frequently occurring phonemes were /ɪ, æ, ɑ, o/, each comprising 4 percent, and /i/ which comprised 6 percent. Four vowellike

TABLE 3.1 Percentage of Occurrence of Individual Vowellike and Consonant Sounds Based on Total Phoneme Sample (N = 12,775)

Phonemic Category	% of Distribution	Phoneme
Vowellike	0*	/ɜ, ɔɪ, n̩, m̩/
	1	/ɛ, ɝ, ɚ, u, ʊ, aʊ, ɪu, l̩/
	2	/ə, ʌ/
	3	/e, ɔ, aɪ/
	4	/ɪ, æ, ɑ, o/
	5	—
	6	/i/
Consonant	0	/v, ʒ, dʒ, j, ʔ/
	1	/f, θ, ð, z, tʃ, ŋ, w, ʃ/
	2	/g, h/
	3	/p, s, n, r/
	4	/d, m, l/
	5	/t/
	6	—
	7	/k/
	8	—
	9	—
	10	—
	11	/b/

*< .5 percent

sounds /ɜ, ɔɪ, n̩, m̩/ were essentially absent in the children's speech: each made up less than 0.5 percent of the total distribution.

The distribution range for consonants was 0 to 11 percent. The consonants occurring most frequently were /k, b/, which represented 7 and 11 percent respectively of the phonemic sample. The consonants /d, m, l/ each comprised 4 percent; /t/ comprised 5 percent. Five consonants were essentially absent in the children's speech: /v, ʒ, dʒ, j, ʔ/ made up less than 0.5 percent of the distribution.

Percentage of Correct Production by Phoneme

Vowellike Sounds

The percentages of correct production of individual vowels are compiled in Table 3.2. The level of correct production for all vowellike phonemes was 59 percent. Individual subjects' mean levels of correct production for all vowels ranged from 23 to 71 percent.

The level of correct production of individual vowels, based on all 20 subjects, ranged from 0 to 81 percent. The vowel /ɑ/ was produced with the greatest accuracy (81 percent); two others (/ʊ, i/) occurred with greater than 75 percent accuracy. Nine vowels (/ɪ, ʌ, ə, u, o, ɔ, æ, aʊ, ɔɪ/) occurred with 50 to 75 percent accuracy, and eight (/e, ɛ, ð, ɝ, aɪ, l̩, n̩/) occurred with less than 50 percent accuracy. In all, 60 percent of the vowels were produced correctly at least half of the time. Only one vowellike sound, /n̩/, was never produced correctly.

Consonants

The percentages of correct production for individual consonants are presented in Table 3.3. The level of correct production for all consonants was 50 percent. Individual subjects' mean levels of correct production for all consonants ranged from 30 to 60 percent.

The level of correct production of the 23 individual consonants, based on group data, ranged from 0 to 90 percent. The /b/ phoneme was produced with the greatest accuracy (90 percent); only one other phoneme was produced correctly more than three-quarters of the time: /m/, with 84 percent accuracy. Seven consonants (/j, h, f, d, n, w, p/) occurred with greater than 50 but less than 75 percent accuracy, and 15 (/g, k, t, tʃ, v, dʒ, s, ð, l, ŋ, ʃ, r, z, θ, ʒ/) occurred with less than 50 percent accuracy. In all, 39 percent of all consonants that occurred were produced with greater than 50 percent accuracy. The /θ/ phoneme was never produced correctly.

TABLE 3.2   Percentage of Correct Production of Individual Vowellike Sounds Based on Total Occurrence of Each Phoneme

Sounds	Phoneme	% Correct Production	No. of Correct Occurrences/ No. of Total Occurrences
Vowels	/ɑ/	81	364/452
	/ʊ/	77	127/164
	/i/	76	602/797
	/ɪ/	73	349/479
	/ʌ/	73	214/292
	/ə/	60	147/244
	/u/	59	87/147
	/o/	58	266/462
	/ɔ/	53	232/436
	/æ/	50	242/484
	/e/	46	155/337
	/ɛ/	35	56/162
	/ɚ/	3	4/131
	/ɝ/	2	2/97
Diphthongs	/aʊ/	62	81/130
	/ɔɪ/	60	18/30
	/aɪ/	47	170/361
	/ɪu/	40	56/141
Syllabics	/l̩/	27	26/96
	/n̩/	0	0/6
	/m̩/	—	0/0
Total		59	3,198/5,448

Error Type Distribution

Vowellike Sounds

The error type distributions for all vowels are presented in Table 3.4. Error-productions made up 41 percent of all vowel productions; 35 percent of all vowel productions were substitution errors and 6 percent were omission errors. Vowel additions were rarely observed in the children's speech.

With the exception of the vowels /i, ə, n̩/, most of the error distributions of individual vowels were consistent with the total group distribution: the individual vowel distributions repeatedly showed relatively lower percentages of omission errors and higher percentages of substitution errors. To illustrate, there were no omission errors for /ɪu, ɔ, ɔɪ, aʊ, ʌ, ʊ, or ɑ/; the level of substitution errors ranged from 19 to 60 percent for these sounds. Vowels /i, ə/ both had essentially equal percentages of omission and substitution errors. One vowel, /n̩/, showed a higher percentage of omission errors.

TABLE 3.3 Percentage of Correct Production of Individual Consonants Based on Total Occurrence of Each Phoneme

Phoneme	% Correct Production	No. of Correct Occurrences/ No. of Total Occurrences
/b/	90	1,238/1,370
/m/	84	438/524
/j/	71	12/17
/h/	68	168/247
/f/	67	95/142
/d/	63	355/567
/n/	63	235/375
/w/	63	50/79
/p/	56	228/409
/g/	49	141/289
/k/	47	403/865
/t/	36	217/609
/tʃ/	22	21/96
/v/	13	5/40
/dʒ/	9	5/58
/s/	8	27/333
/ð/	5	4/75
/l/	4	19/452
/ŋ/	3	3/94
/ʃ/	2	2/106
/r/	2	6/329
/z/	1	2/138
/θ/	0	0/113
/ʒ/	0	0/0
/ʔ/	0	0/0
Total	50	3,674/7,327

Consonants

Omissions were the most common type of error in the production of consonants. More specifically, the level of production error for all consonants was
50 percent: 27 percent omissions, 17 percent substitutions, and 6 percent
distortions. Of the 23 consonants observed, 13 had error distributions that
were consistent with the group total (i.e., they showed relatively higher percentages of omissions).

These group totals, however, tend to mask the patterns revealed in Table
3.5, where the categories fall into four categories according to error type
distribution: (1) essentially equal frequencies of omissions and substitutions,
with few or no distortions; (2) greater frequency of omissions than substitutions, with few or no distortions; (3) greater frequency of substitutions than
omissions, with few or no distortions; and (4) a much higher frequency of
distortions than either omissions or substitutions.

TABLE 3.4   Error Type Distribution (Percent Omissions and Percent Substitutions)
for Each Vowellike Sound

Category	Vowellike Sound	% Omissions	% Substi- tutions	No. of Errors/ No. of Occurrences
Essentially Equal Distri- bution Between Error Types	/i/	12	12	195/797
	/ə/	21	19	97/244
Greater Frequency of Omissions	/n̩/	83	17	6/6
Greater Frequency of Substitutions	/ɪu/	0	60	85/141
	/ɔ/	0	46	204/436
	/ɔɪ/	0	40	12/30
	/aʊ/	0	38	49/130
	/ʌ/	0	26	78/292
	/ʊ/	0	23	37/164
	/ɑ/	0	19	88/452
	/ɝ/	2	97	95/97
	/aɪ/	1	52	191/361
	/æ/	1	49	242/484
	/e/	2	52	182/337
	/o/	3	39	196/462
	/u/	3	38	60/147
	/ɪ/	7	20	130/479
	/ɛ/	14	52	106/162
	/l̩/	24	49	70/96
	/ɚ/	39	58	127/131

TABLE 3.5 Error Type Distribution (Percent Omissions and Percent Substitutions) for Each Consonant

Category	Consonant	% Omissions	% Substitutions	% Distortions	No. of Errors/ No. of Occurrences
Essentially Equal	/k/	24	29	0	462/865
Distribution Between	/g/	27	24	0	148/289
Error Types (Ex-	/b/	5	5	0	132/1,370
cluding Distortion)	/θ/	46	53	1	113/113
Greater Frequency	/t/	46	18	0	392/609
of Omissions	/d/	25	13	0	212/567
	/m/	11	5	0	86/524
	/n/	31	6	0	140/375
	/ŋ/	79	18	0	91/94
	/l/	81	15	0	433/452
	/r/	72	26	0	323/329
	/h/	26	6	0	79/247
	/w/	24	13	0	29/79
	/j/	29	0	0	5/17
Greater Frequency	/p/	15	28	0	181/409
of Substitutions	/f/	4	24	0	47/142
	/v/	30	57	0	35/40
	/ð/	16	79	0	71/75
	/dʒ/	28	53	10	53/58
Greater Frequency	/s/	25	9	58	306/333
of Distortions	/z/	32	7	60	136/138
	/ʃ/	4	18	76	104/106
	/tʃ/	3	27	48	75/96

Note. The following sounds were not entered: /ʒ/, /m̩/.

Correct Production of Distinctive Features

Irwin-Wong Distinctive Feature System

The analysis of phonemes using the Irwin-Wong distinctive feature system yielded a body of data that consisted of 127,750 feature specifications.

Examination of the mean percentages for each of the 10 Irwin-Wong feature sets revealed that all sets were produced with at least 85 percent correctness so far as the group data were concerned. All but two sets, Vertical and Place, had mean levels of correct production of at least 90 percent, and three feature sets, Oronasal, Fusion, and Lateral, were produced with 99 percent accuracy. The rank order (high to low) of feature sets in terms of correct use was: Lateral, Oronasal, and Fusion; Laryngeal; Motion; Labial and Tenseness; Closure; Vertical; and Place. Table 3.6 provides specific percentages and numbers of specifications analyzed for each set.

Using data based on group totals, the percentages of correct production for each specification within each Irwin-Wong feature set were obtained. These percentages and the number of occurrences of the specifications are also included in Table 3.6. Only one of the 10 feature sets, Oronasal (which had a set mean of 99 percent correct production), had essentially correct production (95 percent) of each feature specification. In some cases, individual specifications were produced with far less accuracy than the set as a whole. For example, Place had a mean percent correct of 85, but Place-3 was only 36 percent correct.

TABLE 3.6   Correct Usage of Irwin-Wong Feature Sets and Feature Specifications by Percent and Number Based on Total Sample

Feature Set	Feature Specification	% Correct	No. of Correct Occurrences/ No. of Total Occurrences
Oronasal	0	—	0/0
	1	100	11,722/11,776
	2	—	0/0
	3	—	0/0
	4	95	945/999
	Set Mean	99	12,667/12,775
Motion	0	—	0/0
	1	49	190/391
	2	51	137/271
	3	93	1,041/1,124
	4	94	6,352/6,726
	5	98	4,161/4,263
	Set Mean	93	11,881/12,775
Fusion	0	—	0/0
	1	100	12,601/12,621
	2	61	94/154
	Set Mean	99	12,695/12,775

TABLE 3.6 *Continued*

Feature Set	Feature Specification	% Correct	No. of Correct Occurrences/ No. of Total Occurrences
Lateral	0	—	0/0
	1	80	439/548
	2	—	0/0
	3	100	12,216/12,227
	Set Mean	99	12,655/12,775
Labial	0	—	0/0
	1	86	561/653
	2	97	7,337/7,543
	3	69	1,566/2,276
	4	98	2,255/2,303
	Set Mean	92	11,719/12,775
Tenseness	0	—	0/0
	1	98	9,479/9,696
	2	73	2,252/3,079
	Set Mean	92	11,735/12,775
Vertical	0	94	233/247
	1	83	1,570/1,893
	2	87	4,693/5,383
	3	92	4,815/5,252
	Set Mean	89	11,311/12,775
Place	0	—	0/0
	1	98	2,343/2,382
	2	66	121/182
	3	36	68/188
	4	82	4,224/5,164
	5	59	440/749
	6	90	3,493/3,863
	7	94	233/247
	Set Mean	85	10,922/12,775
Laryngeal	0	—	0/0
	1	80	2,134/2,673
	2	94	233/247
	3	98	9,617/9,855
	4	—	0/0
	Set Mean	94	11,984/12,775
Closure	0	—	0/0
	1	94	2,665/2,840
	2	82	3,071/3,726
	3	76	717/947
	4	96	5,069/5,262
	Set Mean	90	11,522/12,775
Total for All Sets		93	119,091/127,750

The individual differences from group means for correct use of feature sets are shown in Table 3.7. The group mean percent of correct production for all sets was 93; no individual subject's percent of correct production for all sets varied from the group mean by more than 5 percent. Moreover, no individual subject varied more than 19 percent from the group means for individual feature sets. In three feature sets (Oronasal, Fusion, and Lateral), no individual subject varied from the group mean by more than 3 percent. The feature sets with the greatest individual variations from the group mean were Tenseness and Labial.

Chomsky-Halle Distinctive Feature System

The analysis of phonemes using the Chomsky-Halle feature system yielded a body of data that consisted of 166,075 feature specifications.

All feature sets within the Chomsky-Halle system were produced with at

TABLE 3.7 Comparison of Individual Subjects with Group Means by Percentage of Correct Usage of Irwin-Wong Feature Sets

Subject Number	Oronasal	Motion	Fusion	Lateral	Labial
1	99	92	100	99	93
2	99	97	100	96	83
3	98	86	98	100	92
4	100	97	100	100	93
5	100	98	100	100	91
6	100	94	100	100	92
7	99	93	100	99	95
8	100	93	98	99	91
9	99	91	99	99	91
10	99	95	100	100	96
11	100	82	100	99	86
12	98	96	99	100	88
13	100	85	99	100	94
14	98	95	99	98	92
15	100	95	100	99	92
16	99	90	100	97	90
17	100	92	100	97	92
18	99	89	100	100	98
19	100	100	100	100	79
20	99	96	99	99	89
Range of % for Individual	98–100	82–100	98–100	96–100	79–98
Group Mean	99	93	99	99	92

least 90 percent accuracy. Based on group data, the mean percent of correct production for all sets was 95 percent. The rank order (high to low) of these feature sets, in terms of correct use, was: Nasal and Strident; Vocalic; Consonant; Anterior and Continuant; Coronal; Voice; Low; High, Back, and Round; and Tense. Table 3.8 provides specific percentages and numbers of specifications analyzed for each set.

The individual differences from group means for use of feature sets are shown in Table 3.9. No individual subject's mean percent of correct production for *all* sets varied from the group mean by more than 3 percent. In addition, no single subject varied more than 19 percent from any of the group means for any individual set. For three feature sets (Nasal, Strident, Vocalic), no individual mean varied from the group mean by more than two percentage points. The feature sets with the greatest individual variation from the group mean were Tense and Round.

Text continued on p. 44

Tenseness	Vertical	Place	Laryngeal	Closure	Overall
93	93	81	93	91	94
85	80	77	87	79	88
85	84	81	93	86	90
94	93	89	95	92	95
96	93	91	91	98	96
90	90	89	86	94	93
96	90	87	92	91	94
89	87	84	91	87	92
86	87	86	94	87	92
93	88	86	97	88	94
73	86	90	100	86	90
93	90	92	92	93	94
93	80	75	99	83	91
96	84	82	93	86	92
91	88	88	96	91	94
92	87	84	96	88	92
91	86	89	95	87	93
91	93	93	96	95	95
97	94	91	94	97	95
94	92	84	96	94	94
73–97	80–94	75–93	86–100	79–98	88–96
92	89	85	94	90	93

TABLE 3.8 Correct Usage of Modified Chomsky-Halle Feature Sets and Feature Specifications by Percent and Number Based on Total Sample

Feature Set	Feature Specification	% Correct	No. of Correct Occurrences/ No. of Total Occurrences
Vocalic	0	—	0/0
	1	99	6,497/6,552
	2	98	6,072/6,223
	Set Mean	98	12,569/12,775
Consonantal	0	—	0/0
	1	99	5,648/5,689
	2	95	6,727/7,086
	Set Mean	97	12,375/12,775
High	0	—	0/0
	1	94	8,881/9,443
	2	87	2,902/3,332
	Set Mean	92	11,783/12,775
Back	0	—	0/0
	1	92	8,125/8,833
	2	91	3,578/3,942
	Set Mean	92	11,703/12,775
Low	0	—	0/0
	1	95	10,682/11,201
	2	83	1,313/1,574
	Set Mean	94	11,995/12,775
Anterior	0	—	0/0
	1	97	7,326/7,526
	2	94	4,960/5,249
	Set Mean	96	12,286/12,775
Coronal	0	—	0/0
	1	99	9,072/9,194
	2	85	3,055/3,581
	Set Mean	95	12,127/12,775

TABLE 3.8 *Continued*

Feature Set	Feature Specification	% Correct	No. of Correct Occurrences/ No. of Total Occurrences
Round	0	—	0/0
	1	93	3,616/3,886
	2	70	1,092/1,556
	Set Mean	92	11,693/12,775
Tense	0	95	6,985/7,333
	1	93	2,733/2,940
	2	69	1,738/2,502
	Set Mean	90	11,456/12,775
Voice	0	—	0/0
	1	84	2,466/2,920
	2	98	9,617/9,855
	Set Mean	95	12,083/12,775
Continuant	0	—	0/0
	1	98	10,429/10,608
	2	84	1,828/2,167
	Set Mean	96	12,257/12,775
Nasal	0	—	0/0
	1	100	11,722/11,776
	2	95	945/999
	Set Mean	99	12,667/12,775
Strident	0	—	0/0
	1	100	11,835/11,862
	2	82	751/913
	Set Mean	99	12,586/12,775
Total for All Sets		95	157,480/166,075

TABLE 3.9 Comparison of Individual Subjects with Group Means by Percentage of Correct Usage of Modified Chomsky-Halle Feature Sets

Subject Number	Vocalic	Consonantal	High	Back	Low	Anterior	Coronal
1	96	96	92	92	97	94	93
2	100	96	91	84	88	94	88
3	97	97	92	87	92	97	95
4	98	98	92	92	94	96	96
5	100	100	98	93	96	100	100
6	100	100	95	90	92	100	99
7	98	94	91	91	94	96	95
8	99	97	91	89	93	95	94
9	100	98	92	89	94	96	93
10	99	99	94	94	95	98	98
11	99	99	99	91	82	99	99
12	100	98	96	96	91	97	97
13	99	98	97	94	93	98	98
14	99	94	89	87	90	93	93
15	99	98	92	93	93	96	96
16	97	95	89	88	96	95	94
17	96	96	92	94	95	96	95
18	100	99	97	96	97	99	98
19	100	100	97	94	82	100	100
20	98	98	92	95	97	96	94
Range of % for Individual	96–100	94–100	89–99	84–96	82–97	93–100	88–100
Group Mean	98	97	92	92	94	96	95

Phonological Development in Children

Round	Tense	Voice	Continuant	Nasal	Strident	Overall
93	90	93	96	99	98	95
91	81	87	95	99	99	92
91	84	93	95	98	98	94
90	91	95	100	100	100	95
96	96	91	100	100	100	98
92	90	86	100	100	100	96
91	91	94	94	99	100	95
92	86	92	96	100	97	94
92	86	94	95	99	97	94
97	93	97	97	99	99	97
84	71	100	97	100	100	94
85	91	94	98	98	99	95
94	91	99	90	100	99	96
92	92	95	92	98	99	93
94	90	97	96	100	98	96
89	89	96	96	99	97	94
91	89	96	96	100	98	95
97	91	96	98	99	100	97
76	97	94	100	100	100	95
92	93	96	98	99	98	96
76–97	71–97	86–100	90–100	98–100	97–100	92–98
92	90	95	96	99	99	95

Replacement Characteristics

Irwin-Wong Distinctive Feature System

The error productions for each vowel and consonant were analyzed for the different replacements made, for the frequency of each replacement, and for the feature/degree difference for each replacement. Table 3.10 presents the results of this analysis. Mean feature/degree differences were also calculated for each phoneme; the results are presented in Table 3.11.

TABLE 3.10 Error Productions by Replacement, Frequency of Replacement, and Feature/Degree Differences of Replacement as Specified in Irwin-Wong System

Phonetic Classification	Phoneme in Error	Replacement 1	Replacement 2	Replacement 3	Replacement 4	Replacement 5
Vowels	/i/	/e/:25–1/1ᵃ	/ɪ/:23–1/1	/ɑ/:10–4/6	/ɛ/:7–2/2 /u/:7–2/3 /æ/:7–3/4	/ə/:5–4/4
	/ɪ/	/i/:36–1/1	/ɑ/:29–3/5	/ɛ/:12–1/1	/ʌ/:11–3/4	/e/:4–2/2 /æ/:4–2/3
	/e/	/ɪ/:40–2/2	/æ/:28–3/3	/ɛ/:27–1/1 /ʌ/:27–3/4	/ɑ/:23–4/5	/aɪ/:12–4/7
	/ɛ/	/ɪ/:20–1/1	/æ/:18–2/2	/ə/:14–2/2	/ʌ/:12–2/3	/aɪ/:5–5/8
	/æ/	/ɑ/:102–1/2	/ʌ/:43–2/3	/ɪ/:21–2/3	/aɪ/:20–3/6	/ɛ/:13–2/2 /e/:13–3/3
	/ɝ/	/u/:49–4/4	/u/:12–2/2 /ə/:12–3/3 /ʌ/:12–4/4	/ɑ/:5–5/5		
	/ɚ/	/u/:23–3/3	/ə/:22–2/2	/l/:8–4/5	/u/:7–3/3	/ʌ/:4–3/3
	/ə/	/ɪ/:11–3/3	/æ/:10–2/2	/ɑ/:8–2/2	/ʌ/:4–1/1 /u/:4–5/5	/e/:3–3/3 /i/:3–4/4
	/ʌ/	/u/:33–2/2	/ɑ/:16–1/1	/æ/:6–2/3	/ɔ/:4–2/2 /ɛ/:4–2/3	/o/:3–3/3 /aɪ/:3–3/5
	/ɑ/	/ʌ/:54–1/1	/ə/:13–2/2	/æ/:5–1/2	/ɔ/:3–1/1 /aʊ/:3–2/3 /aɪ/:3–2/4	/ɛ/:2–3/4 /o/:2–4/4
	/ɔ/	/ɑ/:115–1/1	/ʌ/:43–2/2	/o/:18–3/3	/ə/:7–3/3	/aʊ/:6–3/4
	/o/	/ʌ/:67–3/3	/ɑ/:26–4/4	/ə/:20–4/4	/u/:18–3/3	/ɔ/:14–3/3
	/u/	/ɪ/:16–3/4	/ʊ/:11–2/2	/ʌ/:6–4/4	/ɪu/:5–1/2 /i/:5–2/3	/ɑ/:4–4/5
	/ʊ/	/ʌ/:19–2/2	/u/:10–2/2	/ɪ/:3–3/4		
Diphthongs	/aɪ/	/ɑ/:133–2/4	/ʌ/:22–3/5	/æ/:13–3/6	/ə/:10–4/6	/ɛ/:5–5/8
	/aʊ/	/ɑ/:19–2/3	/æ/:12–3/5	/ʌ/:6–3/4	/aɪ/:3–1/1	/ɛ/:2–5/7
	/ɔɪ/	/u/:4–3/6	/ɔ/:3–2/4	/o/:2–3/5 /ʌ/:2–4/6		
	/ɪu/	/u/:46–1/2	/ɪ/:19–4/6	/i/:10–3/5	/ə/:5–6/7	/ʌ/:2–5/6
Syllabics	/l/	/ʊ/:13–4/6	/ə/:7–4/5 /u/:7–4/6	/ʌ/:5–4/6 /ɑ/:5–4/7 /o/:5–5/7	/v/:4–6/11	

Note: A replacement must have occurred more than once to be included in this table.

ᵃThat is, the replacement /e/, which occurred 25 times, is removed from /i/ by a feature/degree difference of 1/1.

TABLE 3.10 *Continued*

Phonetic Classification	Phoneme in Error	Replacement 1	Replacement 2	Replacement 3	Replacement 4	Replacement 5
Consonants	/k/	/g/:121–1/2	/ʔ/:52–4/10	/d/:41–2/4	/t/:18–1/2	/m/:7–6/14
	/g/	/k/:52–1/2	/d/:7–1/2	/ʔ/:3–4/8	/n/:2–3/6	
	/t/	/d/:47–1/2	/ʔ/:33–4/12	/k/:12–1/2	/p/:4–3/6	/g/:2–2/4
						/ɪ/:2–3/5
						/n/:2–3/6
						/b/:2–4/8
						/w/:2–6/11
	/d/	/t/:23–1/2	/b/:21–3/6	/n/:9–2/4	/ʔ/:5–4/10	/g/:3–1/2
						/h/:3–5/12
						/w/:3–5/9
	/p/	/b/:99–1/2	/t/:5–3/6	/d/:3–4/8	/m/:2–3/6	
					/k/:2–3/8	
					/ʔ/:2–5/16	
	/b/	/p/:29–1/2	/m/:12–2/4	/w/:11–3/5	/dʒ/:4–4/7	/d/:3–3/6
						/ə/:3–4/10
	/f/	/b/:21–5/8	/v/:3–1/2	/ʃ/:2–3/5		
			/s/:3–3/5			
			/p/:3–4/6	/t/:2–5/6		
				/w/:2–5/7		
				/h/:2–6/12		
	/v/	/g/:15–5/8	/b/:7–4/6			
	/θ/	/d/:35–5/6	/f/:5–2/2	/ə/:3–3/6	/h/:2–5/10	
			/t/:5–4/4	/k/:3–4/6		
				/r/:3–5/6		
	/ð/	/d/:53–4/4	/t/:2–5/6			
			/b/:2–4/6			
	/s/	/s/:172–1/1	/ʃ/:18–1/1	/t/:15–5/5	/g/:3–7/9	/ts/:2–6/6
					/h/:3–7/11	/d/:2–6/7
	/z/	/s/:74–3/4	/ʃ/:9–2/3	/b/:3–5/9	/s/:2–1/2	
	/ʃ/	/ʃ/:47–1/2	/s/:28–1/2	/ʊ/:9–6/6	/k/:8–6/6	/ts/:4–7/7
	/tʃ/	/ts/:32–2/2	/t/:14–3/3	/dz/:10–3/4	/k/:5–3/3	/s/:3–6/7
					/d/:5–4/5	
	/dʒ/	/d/:12–3/3	/ɔ/:7–5/8	/dz/:6–3/3	/g/:5–3/3	/o/:3–6/7
	/m/	/b/:17–2/4				
	/n/	/ŋ/:7–0/0	/ə/:5–4/8	/ɪ/:4–2/5	/d/:3–2/4	/m/:2–3/6
	/ŋ/	/ʔ/13–6/12	/ʌ/:2–1/2			
			/ɔ/:2–4/9			
	/l/	/w/:20–4/7	/j/:13–2/3	/ə/:6–5/6	/ḷ/:5–1/1	/ɑ/:3–5/8
				/n/:6–4/8	/k/:5–5/10	
	/r/	/w/:57–1/3	/ə/:10–4/4	/ɪ/:7–3/3	/b/:3–4/8	/ʊ/:2–4/5
						/g/:2–5/5
	/h/	/n/:6–6/14	/p/:3–6/16			
			/d/:3–5/12			
	/w/	/b/:7–3/5	/h/:2–5/11			

Vowels

As shown in Table 3.10, vowels in error showed a relatively large range of different sound replacements. Examination of those vowels which made up at least half of the vowel distribution (/i, ɪ, æ, ɑ, o/), for example, revealed a range of 8 to 14 different sound replacements. The most frequent replacements for these vowels were /e, i, ɑ, ʌ, ʌ/ respectively. The range of feature/degree differences between the vowels in error and their replacements was 1/1 to 6/11.

Certain vowels showed relatively high numbers of replacements by a single vowel. The vowel /ɑ/ was the most frequent replacement for the vowels /aɪ, æ, ɔ/. Error vowellike sounds tended to be replaced by phonemes which had correct production percentages that exceeded those of the phonemes being replaced. These replacement phonemes generally accounted for more than half of the error phoneme's total replacements.

For the vowels which occurred most frequently (/i, ɪ, æ, ɑ, o/) mean feature differences ranged from 1.37 for /ɑ/ to 3.24 for /o/. Note that /ɑ/, the vowel with the highest percent of correct production (81 percent), had the lowest mean feature/degree difference from the target phoneme, regardless of how the mean was computed. Moreover, the vowels /ɛ, ɝ, ɚ, ŋ/, which had percentages of correct production of less than 5 percent and which comprised less than 2 percent of the total distribution, had a mean feature difference range from 2.14 for /ɛ/ to 3.63 for /ɝ/. Examination of the mean feature differences based on total errors showed that most of the vowels (60 percent) had mean feature differences of greater than two and less than three. Finally, the syllabic phoneme /l̩/ had the highest mean feature difference based on total errors (4.21).

Consonants

Like the vowellike sounds, the consonants in error showed a relatively large range in the number of different sounds with which they were replaced (1 to 9). Specifically, /m/ with 1 had the fewest and /f/ with 9 had the most. In contrast to the vowel group, no group of consonants showed relatively high numbers of replacements by a single consonant.

As was the case with the vowels, error consonant sounds also tended to be replaced more than 50 percent of the time by phonemes which had the correct production percentages exceeding those of the error consonants. The consonants demonstrating this pattern were the following: /k, p, f, v, θ, ð, m, l, r, w/.

Comparison of consonant and vowel mean feature/degree differences showed that consonants generally had higher mean differences when computed on total errors. The ranges for consonant error were 1.95 to 5.18 for feature differences and 1.77 to 13.93 for degree differences. In comparison, for vowels, means ranged from 1.77 to 4.21 for feature differences and 1.59 to 6.38 for degree differences.

TABLE 3.11 Mean Feature/Degree Difference Values by Phoneme as Specified in Irwin-Wong System

Phonetic Classification	Phoneme in Error	Number of Errors	Number of Occurrences	$\bar{X}$ Feature Difference Based on Errors	$\bar{X}$ Feature Difference Based on Occurrences	$\bar{X}$ Degree Difference Based on Errors	$\bar{X}$ Degree Difference Based on Occurrences
Vowels	/i/	98	797	2.19	.27	2.86	.35
	/ɪ/	98	479	1.96	.40	2.76	.56
	/e/	176	337	2.57	1.34	3.07	1.61
	/ɛ/	84	162	2.14	1.11	2.65	1.38
	/æ/	235	484	1.77	.86	2.87	1.39
	/ɝ/	94	97	3.63	3.52	3.64	3.53
	/ɜ/	—	—	—	—	—	—
	/ɚ/	76	131	2.83	1.64	3.00	1.74
	/ə/	46	244	2.67	.50	2.74	.52
	/ʌ/	77	292	2.00	.53	2.35	.62
	/ɑ/	87	452	1.37	.26	1.59	.31
	/ɔ/	202	436	1.64	.76	1.80	.83
	/o/	181	462	3.24	1.27	3.59	1.41
	/u/	56	147	2.82	1.07	3.63	1.38
	/ʊ/	37	164	2.24	.51	2.41	.54
Diphthongs	/aɪ/	189	361	2.41	1.26	4.52	2.37
	/aʊ/	49	130	2.84	1.07	4.31	1.62
	/ɔɪ/	12	30	2.92	1.17	5.33	2.13
	/ɪu/	85	141	2.39	1.44	3.74	2.26
Syllabics	/n̩/	1	6	3.00	.50	1.33	8.00
	/l̩/	47	96	4.21	2.06	6.38	3.13
Consonants	/k/	251	865	2.09	.61	4.59	1.33
	/g/	70	289	1.50	.36	2.93	.71
	/t/	112	609	2.39	.44	5.80	1.07
	/d/	73	567	2.41	.31	4.88	.63
	/p/	118	409	1.46	.42	3.05	.88
	/b/	65	1,370	2.05	.10	3.98	.19
	/f/	41	142	4.39	1.27	6.93	2.00
	/v/	23	40	4.74	2.72	7.48	4.30
	/θ/	61	113	4.46	2.41	5.66	3.05
	/ð/	59	75	4.07	3.20	4.22	3.32
	/s/	222	333	1.62	1.08	1.77	1.18
	/z/	92	138	2.18	1.46	3.28	2.19
	/ʃ/	100	106	2.33	2.20	3.11	2.93
	/tʃ/	72	96	2.78	2.08	3.07	2.30
	/dʒ/	37	58	3.73	2.38	4.68	2.98
	/m/	26	524	2.65	.13	5.58	.28
	/n/	24	375	2.29	.15	4.79	.31
	/ŋ/	17	94	5.18	.94	10.47	1.89
	/l/	68	452	3.72	.56	6.26	.94
	/r/	86	329	1.95	.51	3.59	.94
	/h/	14	247	5.71	.32	13.93	.79
	/w/	10	79	3.60	.46	6.60	.84
Total		3,571	12,758	2.42	.68	3.62	1.01

Chomsky-Halle Distinctive Feature System

Table 3.12 analyzes the errors made on vowels and consonants according to the phoneme replacement, the frequency of replacement, and the feature difference of the replacement.

For diphthongs, the feature differences for most frequent replacements ranged from 1 to 3; for vowels, from 1 to 5. The syllabic /ļ/ showed a higher

TABLE 3.12   Error Productions by Replacement, Frequency of Replacement, and Feature Differences of Replacement as Specified in Modified Chomsky-Halle System

Phonetic Classification	Phoneme in Error	Replacement 1	Replacement 2	Replacement 3	Replacement 4	Replacement 5
Vowels	/i/	/e/:25–1[a]	/ɪ/:23–1	/ɑ/:10–4	/ɛ/:7–1 /u/:7–2 /æ/:7–3	/ə/:5–3
	/ɪ/	/i/:36–1	/ɑ/:29–3	/ɛ/:12–1	/ʌ/:11–2	/e/:4–2 /æ/:4–2
	/e/	/ɪ/:40–2	/æ/:28–2	/ɛ/:27–1 /ʌ/:27–2	/ɑ/:23–3	/aɪ/:12–2
	/ɛ/	/ɪ/:20–1	/æ/:18–1	/ə/:14–1	/ʌ/:12–1	/aɪ/:5–3
	/æ/	/ɑ/:102–1	/ʌ/:43–2	/ɪ/:21–2	/aɪ/:20–2	/ɛ/:13–1 /e/:13–2
	/ɝ/	/ʊ/:49–5	/u/:12–3 /ə/:12–3 /ʌ/:12–3	/ɑ/:5–4		
	/ɚ/	/ʊ/:23–4	/ə/:22–2	/ļ/:8–5	/u/:7–4	/ʌ/:4–2
	/ə/	/ɪ/:11–2	/æ/:10–2	/ɑ/:8–3	/ʌ/:4–2 /u/:4–4	/e/:3–2 /i/:3–3
	/ʌ/	/ʊ/:33–2	/ɑ/:16–1	/æ/:6–2	/ɔ/:4–1 /ɛ/:4–1	/o/:3–2 /aɪ/:3–2
	/ɑ/	/ʌ/:54–1	/ə/:13–3	/æ/:5–1	/ɔ/:3–1 /aʊ/:3–2 /aɪ/:3–2	/ɔ/:2–2 /o/:2–3
	/ɔ/	/ɑ/:115–2	/ʌ/:43–1	/o/:18–1	/ə/:7–1	/aʊ/:6–2
	/o/	/ʌ/:67–2	/ɑ/:25–3	/ə/:20–2	/ʊ/:18–2	/ɔ/:14–1
	/u/	/ɪ/:16–2	/ʊ/:11–2	/ʌ/:6–2	/ɪu/:5–1 /i/:5–1	/ɑ/:4–3
	/ʊ/	/ʌ/:19–2	/u/:10–2	/ɪ/:3–2		
Diphthongs	/aɪ/	/ɑ/:133–1	/ʌ/:22–2	/æ/:13–2	/ə/:10–4	/ɛ/:5–3
	/aʊ/	/ɑ/:19–2	/æ/:12–3	/ʌ/:6–1 /ɪ/:6–3	/aɪ/:3–1	/ɛ/:2–2
	/ɔɪ/	/u/:4–3	/ɔ/:3–2	/u/:4–3	/o/:2–1 /ʌ/:2–3	
	/ɪu/	/u/:46–1	/ɪ/:19–3	/i/:10–2	/ə/:5–3	/ʌ/:2–3

Note. A replacement must have occurred more than once to be included in this table.

[a]That is, the replacement /e/, which occurred 25 times, is removed from /i/ by a feature difference of 1.

Phonological Development in Children

TABLE 3.12 *Continued*

Phonetic Classification	Phoneme in Error	Replacement 1	Replacement 2	Replacement 3	Replacement 4	Replacement 5
Syllabics	/l/	/ʊ/:13–8 /u/:7–8	/ə/:7–6	/ʌ/:5–7 /ɑ/:5–7 /o/:5–8	/v/:4–3	
Consonants	/k/	/g/:121–1	/ʔ/:52–7	/d/:41–5	/t/:18–4	/m/:7–5
	/g/	/k/:52–1	/d/:7–4	/ʔ/:3–8	/n/:2–5	
	/t/	/d/:47–1	/ʔ/:33–7	/k/:12–4	/p/:4–1	/g/:2–2 /ɪ/:2–2 /n/:2–5 /b/:2–8 /w/:2–9
	/d/	/t/:23–1	/b/:21–1	/n/:9–1	/ʔ/:5–8	/g/:3–4 /h/:3–6 /w/:3–8
	/p/	/b/:99–1	/t/:5–1	/d/:3–2	/m/:2–2 /k/:2–3 /ʔ/:2–6	
	/b/	/p/:29–1	/m/:12–1	/w/:11–7	/dʒ/:4–4	/d/:3–1 /ə/:3–5
	/f/	/b/:21–3	/v/:3–1 /s/:3–2 /p/:3–1	/ʃ/:2–3 /ts/:2–3 /t/:2–4 /w/:2–4 /h/:2–8		
	/v/	/g/:15–5	/b/:7–2			
	/θ/	/d/:35–2	/f/:5–1 /t/:5–2	/ə/:3–3 /k/:3–5 /r/:3–8	/h/:2–4	
	/ð/	/d/:53–1	/t/:2–2 /b/:2–2			
	/s/	/s/:172–0	/ʃ/:18–2	/t/:15–2	/g/:3–5 /h/:3–7	/ts/:2–3 /d/:2–3
	/z/	/s/:74–1	/ʃ/:9–3	/b/:3–3	/s/:2–1	
	/ʃ/	/ʃ/:47–0	/s/:28–2	/t/:9–4	/k/:8–4	/ts/:4–1
	/tʃ/	/ts/:32–0	/t/:14–3	/dz/:10–1	/k/:5–3 /d/:5–4	/s/:3–3
	/dʒ/	/d/:12–3	/ɔ/:7–8	/dz/:6–0	/g/:5–3	/o/:3–8
	/m/	/b/:17–1				
	/n/	/ŋ/:7–0	/ə/:5–7	/ɪ/:4–8	/d/:3–1	/m/:2–1
	/ŋ/	/ʔ/:13–9	/ʌ/:2–6 /ɔ/:2–4			
	/l/	/w/:20–8	/j/:13–7	/ə/:6–3 /n/:6–6	/l̩/:5–0 /k/:5–7	/ɑ/:3–8
	/r/	/w/:57–7	/ə/:10–5	/ɪ/:7–6	/b/:3–4	/ʊ/:2–7 /g/:2–5
	/h/	/n/:6–7	/p/:3–4 /d/:3–6			
	/w/	/b/:7–7	/h/:2–6			

TABLE 3.13   Mean Feature Difference Values as Specified in Modified Chomsky-Halle System

Phonetic Classification	Phoneme in Error	Number of Errors	Number of Occurrences	$\bar{X}$ Feature Difference Based on Errors	$\bar{X}$ Feature Difference Based on Occurrences
Vowels	/i/	98	797	1.94	.24
	/ɪ/	98	479	1.83	.37
	/e/	176	337	1.93	1.01
	/ɛ/	84	162	1.33	.69
	/æ/	235	484	1.64	.80
	/ɝ/	94	97	4.10	3.97
	/ɚ/	76	131	3.36	1.95
	/ə/	46	244	2.43	.46
	/ʌ/	77	292	1.78	.47
	/ɑ/	87	452	1.48	.29
	/ɔ/	202	436	1.73	.80
	/o/	181	462	2.24	.88
	/u/	56	147	2.23	.85
	/ʊ/	37	164	2.08	.47
Diphthongs	/aɪ/	189	361	1.44	.75
	/aʊ/	49	130	2.20	.83
	/ɔɪ/	12	30	2.42	.97
	/ɪu/	85	141	1.78	1.07
Syllabics	/n̩/	1	6	8.00	1.33
	/l̩/	47	96	6.89	3.38
Consonants	/k/	251	865	3.40	.99
	/g/	70	289	2.01	.49
	/t/	112	609	3.64	.67
	/d/	73	567	2.33	.30
	/p/	118	409	1.31	.38
	/b/	65	1,370	2.46	.12
	/f/	41	142	3.00	.87
	/v/	23	40	4.13	2.38
	/θ/	61	113	2.66	1.43
	/ð/	59	75	1.19	.93
	/s/	222	333	.68	.46
	/z/	92	138	1.51	1.01
	/ʃ/	100	106	1.38	1.30
	/tʃ/	72	96	1.42	1.06
	/dʒ/	37	58	4.35	2.78
	/m/	26	524	1.92	.10
	/n/	24	375	4.04	.26
	/ŋ/	17	94	8.06	1.46
	/l/	68	452	5.94	.89
	/r/	86	329	6.43	1.68
	/h/	14	247	5.93	.34
	/w/	10	79	6.90	.87
Total		3,571	12,758	2.38	.67

feature difference from its most frequent replacement (8) than did any other vowel or diphthong.

Consonants showed a wider range of feature replacements than did the vowels; feature differences for the most frequent replacements ranged from 1 to 9 (/ŋ/ replaced by /ʔ/).

Table 3.13 shows the mean feature differences between error phonemes and their replacements.

DISCUSSION

This investigation provides information regarding the spontaneous speech of 20 children aged 16 to 18 months. The data collected have been analyzed according to phoneme and distinctive feature acquisition. The developmental period investigated in this study has received little attention in previous group phoneme and distinctive feature acquisition research. Thus, the data presented here are relatively new.

Phoneme Acquisition

Vowels

A total of 5,448 vowels was collected for analysis. These vowels constituted approximately 43 percent of the 12,725 total phonemes collected. The vowels were produced with 59 percent accuracy. For the group as a whole, vowel errors were typically of the substitution type.

Dewey (1923) reported that adult English consisted of approximately 38 percent vowels and 62 percent consonants. Denes (1963) reported similar percentages of vowels and consonants in adult speech (39 percent and 61 percent respectively). Hare (1977) found that the speech of children 21 to 24 months of age closely approximated Dewey's and Denes' vowel/consonant ratios. The present data show that children 16 to 18 months old are also beginning to approximate the adult ratios with a vowel/consonant ratio of 43/57. These data are also similar to Hare's in that both age groups had low percentages of individual variation from the group mean. That is, in each study, no individual child's vowel/consonant ratio varied from its group mean by more than 4 percent.

The above percentages were based on the total occurrence of target phonemes rather than attempted productions. Thus, omission errors are not accounted for in the 43/57 ratio. Analysis of attempted productions as well revealed a different vowel/consonant ratio: for the group, the children's actual speech consisted of 49 percent vowels and 51 percent consonants.

Until Hare's (1977) study, developmental data concerning vowel production had not been reported in depth. Three studies (Wellman et al., 1931; Poole, 1934; and Templin, 1957) found that virtually all vowels were present by age 3. Winitz (1969) elected not to discuss vowel acquisition, citing that, for the most part, vowels are acquired early and are generally not found to be defective. Thus a reader may be left with the impression that children may begin their speech development by pronouncing vowels correctly. And, indeed, Hare's (1977) data showed a relatively high percentage (88 percent) of correct vowel production in the spontaneous speech of 21 to 24 month old children. The present data for younger children, however, show a much lower percentage of correct vowel production (59 percent) than Hare's. The level of correct vowel production for 17 of the 20 individual children ranged from 49 to 72 percent. Hare (1977) reported a variability range of 15 percent for individual subject's vowel production. The two studies may indicate that the period of development between the age ranges of 16 to 18 and 21 to 24 months is one in which children make rapid gains in vowel production and begin to demonstrate less individual variation. However, conclusive data concerning this suggestion may be better obtained from longitudinal studies.

Finally, with the exception of the vowellike sounds /ɚ, u, ɔ, aɪ/, both studies showed the same set of seven vowels (/ɪ, æ, u, e, o, ɑ, i/) constituting half of the vowel distribution. These similarities suggest that children in this stage of development may be demonstrating early patterns of vowel production preference. This idea is further supported by the fact that with the exception of /æ, e/, all of the aforementioned vowels had relatively high correction production percentages when compared to the group mean on vowellike sounds. Similar findings were reported for consonants by Ferguson and Farwell (1975)—children showed selectivity in the sound patterns of words which they acquire. That is, the children preferred words that contained consonants which they produced frequently and accurately. The data presented here do not provide information pertaining to vowel production in specific word forms. However, the vowel frequency/accuracy relationship evidenced in these data suggest that further research in this area may demonstrate whether children in this age range also show selective use of certain vowels.

Consonants

A total of 7,327 consonants was analyzed for this study, of which 3,674 or 50 percent were produced correctly. Individual consonants accounted for 0 to 11 percent of the total distribution. Correct production, based on total occurrence of each phoneme, ranged from 0 to 90 percent. Finally, approximately 46 percent of the consonant errors observed were omissions.

The distribution range for this study closely paralleled that of Hare's (1977) study. Although Hare reported a smaller consonant distribution range (0 to 7 percent) than the range reported here, many of the sounds found to account for at least 4 percent of the total distribution were the same in both studies: /d, m, t, k, b/. Furthermore, the consonant /b/ was the most frequently produced consonant in both studies, and the consonants /v, ʒ, dʒ, j, ʔ/ essentially did not occur in the sample drawn from either group.

Similarly high percentages of correct production were observed in both studies for the consonants /b, m/. These consonants have typically been classified as being among the first consonants mastered (Wellman et al., 1931; Templin, 1957; Poole, 1934; and Sander, 1972).

The sounds /θ, ʒ, ð, z/, which have been classified as late developing phonemes, had low percentages of correct production in this study. If Sander's (1972) 51 percent correct production mastery level were imposed on these data, approximately one third of the consonants would be considered acquired by age 18 months.

Distinctive Feature Analysis

Irwin-Wong Distinctive Feature System

The analysis of spontaneous speech utilizing the Irwin-Wong distinctive feature system revealed that all feature sets were produced with at least 93 percent accuracy. The least accurate feature set was Place. Previous studies utilizing the Irwin-Wong feature system have consistently reported Place-3 as the least accurate of all the feature specifications (Hare, 1977; Bassi, 1979). Hare reported that Place was produced with 93 percent accuracy, but that Place-3 was produced with only 18 percent accuracy. The present investigation showed a 36 percent correct production for Place-3 and 85 percent correct for the feature set as a whole. Closure-3 was also reported as occurring with relatively low levels of accuracy (Hare, 1977); Closure-3 was produced with 76 percent accuracy in this study.

The percentages of correct production for these specifications reflect the apparent difficulty of the phonemes which have been reported to occur with only 75 percent accuracy in children 6 years old or older (Templin, 1957). Place-3 applies only to consonants /θ, ð/.

The specifications which occurred with relatively less accuracy also occurred less frequently. This finding helps to explain why the feature set as a whole may still be produced with a relatively high degree of accuracy. Thus, Place-3 was only 36 percent correct. But its relatively low frequency of occurrence (188 times) in relation to the other specifications of the set (12,587 times) allows the set total percent of correct use to be 85 percent.

Analysis of error sound productions for feature/degree differences from the target phonemes indicated a wide range of feature/degree differences for the most frequent replacements. Generally, no consistent error patterns in terms of feature/degree differences were revealed. For example, the most frequent vowel replacements did not seem to be characterized by a lower number of feature/degree differences than did the most frequent consonant replacements. However, the range of feature/degree differences for consonants was slightly higher than that for vowels. The most frequent consonant replacements were not generally characterized by a small number of feature/degree differences, but in a few cases the most frequent replacement did tend to differ from the target phoneme by only one feature. For example, the consonant /b/ was replaced most frequently by /p/. In the Irwin-Wong system, /b/ and /p/ differ by one feature and two degrees. Other consonants demonstrating this minimal difference pattern of replacement were /d – t/

and /g – k/. This finding with respect to plosives tends to agree with other investigators' reports that frequent errors in children's speech are accounted for by a substitution that differs by one feature (Cairns and Williams, 1972; Menyuk, 1968). The present data, however, must be interpreted with caution, as not all consonant replacements displayed this pattern.

Chomsky-Halle Distinctive Feature System

The analysis utilizing the extended Chomsky-Halle feature system indicated that all features, as a group, were produced with 95 percent accuracy. The least accurate feature was Tense. Other features demonstrating less than 94 percent accuracy were High, Back, and Round.

The number of feature differences between the target and its replacements was computed both for vowellike sounds and for consonants. No major differences between the two groups were demonstrated by these data. The vowellike replacements did not have a significantly higher or lower feature difference than did the consonant replacements. However, it should be noted that the consonants, as a group, showed a wider range of feature replacements than did the vowellike group.

Examination of replacements using the Chomsky-Halle system yields essentially the same information derived from the Irwin-Wong analysis. In general, more frequent replacements were not systematically characterized by lower feature differences. Naturally, the frequency with which individual phonemes occurred as replacements remained the same for both analyses.

METHOD

Subjects

Ten white females and 10 white males ranging in age from 21 to 24 months were selected as subjects for this study. These children had no known gross intellectual, neurological, or physiological handicapping conditions. In order to establish adequate hearing for normal speech and language development, each subject passed all items in a hearing evaluation screening procedure adapted from Northern and Downs (1974). This informal screening was conducted in each child's home before the actual data collection session was begun.

Subjects met a criterion that established their level of linguistic development as within Brown's Stage I (1973); that is, each child's mean length of utterance (MLU) fell within a range of 1.0 to 2.0 morphemes. For each subject, mean length of utterance in morphemes was based on a corpus of 100 utterances obtained during the data collection session, and was computed according to the scoring conventions of Brown (1973) and Siegel (1974).

Data Collection

Setting

Each child was seen in his/her home environment for one session, which generally lasted from one and one-half to two hours. Observation of subjects took place in an area where the child customarily played (e.g., playroom, den, bedroom). Each child's mother was present during the entire sampling session.

Equipment

Equipment consisted of a UHER audiotape recorder (Model 4000 Report-L) and a portable microphone which was kept within a distance of two to three feet of the child. Five-inch reel-to-reel Scotch brand magnetic tapes (Catalogue No. RB-1/4-5), recorded at a speed of one and seven-eighths inches per second, were used. At the initiation of each recording session, the examiner adjusted the recording volume to obtain a peak that centered circa 0 dB VU (± 5 dB VU) for the child's speech.

Stimulus Materials

The examiner provided the same set of toys (contained in a box) and picture books as stimulus materials during each session. Several of each child's own favorite toys, selected by the mother prior to the beginning of each sampling session, were used as additional stimulus materials.

Collecting the Sample

Children's utterances were recorded during three conditions: Condition I, free play with the child's own toys; Condition II, free play with the set of toys provided by the examiner; and Condition III, looking (with parent) at the picture books provided by the examiner. A similar number of utterances was collected during each condition, comprising a language sample of approximately 250 utterances for each subject. Siegel's (1974) criteria for designating vocal response units were used in defining the occurrence of an utterance.

At the beginning of each session, the examiner casually interacted with the mother and child until the child seemed comfortable with the examiner's presence. During this time, the examiner reviewed the purpose of the study and explained the sampling procedures which would be used. The mothers were instructed to encourage their children to interact with a variety of stimulus items during each sampling condition by use of indirect prompts, such as "Hey, look what I found" or "I wonder what else is in the box." The importance of allowing the child to "talk on his/her own" in order to obtain spontaneous utterances for calculating MLU was explained, and the mothers were instructed to refrain from asking direct questions or requesting the child to imitate. General examples of appropriate and inappropriate responses were provided by the examiner. Once the mothers were familiar with the sampling procedures, the hearing screening was administered to each subject. Immediately prior to the beginning of the recorded session, the mothers read a written summary of the examiner's oral explanation of the sampling procedure and instructions.

During the actual recording session, the examiner wrote both the adult form (in English) and the nonlinguistic context of the child's utterances on numbered recording forms. This supplemental information was referred to later, during phonetic transcription of the audiotapes. Mothers typically vol-

unteered responses such as "He wants the _____" or "That's her word for
_____" to aid in determining the adult forms of the child's utterances.

As stated, language samples were collected for two purposes: (1) to determine that MLU fell within the criterion range of 1.0 to 2.0 morphemes; and
(2) to provide a representative phonetic sample for analysis. In order to obtain a sample of sufficient length and variety to serve both purposes, the
examiner counted only the first occurrence of a consecutively repeated utterance. Consecutive repetitions of the utterance were indicated by placing
an "R" beside the original utterance. For example:

Adult Form	Nonlinguistic Context
1. table	putting cup on table
2. cup R R	as cup falls to floor
3. where cup	looking under table
4. table	looking under table

Once 65 numbered utterances had been collected during a sampling condition, the investigator changed the stimulus materials. Only the materials appropriate to each sampling condition were available to the child during that
time. For example, the child's own toys were put away before presentation
of the box which contained the examiner's toys. Similarly, this set of toys
was made inaccessible to the child before presentation of the picture books.
The sampling session was terminated after a total of 195 numbered utterances had been collected (65 numbered utterances for each of the three
conditions).

Preparing the Sample for Analysis

Broad phonetic transcription in IPA of each subject's sample was made from
the audiotape recording within four days of the actual home visit. All of the
child's utterances (including repetitions) were phonetically transcribed, and
the information regarding adult form and nonlinguistic context was trans-
ferred to another set of forms used for phonetic transcription. So, for each
subject, a written record of the child's utterances in IPA, the adult forms of
the utterances in English, and the nonlinguistic context of each utterance
were obtained.

While listening to the audiotapes for each subject, the examiner marked
the transcript for four kinds of utterances that were excluded from analysis
(Siegel, 1974). (1) If a child's utterance was in response to a direct question or
request for imitation, it was not considered spontaneous and was eliminated
from the sample. (2) Utterances which were not recognizable as words or
word approximations were excluded. For example, an utterance was excluded if it elicited a response from the mother such as "I don't know what
she's saying" or "I don't know what he wants." (3) Utterances which were
defined as noncommunicative were also eliminated from the sample used for
phonemic analysis. These utterances consisted of grunts, noises, or speech
sounds ("aah," "haha") which did not serve as affirmation, negation, or in-

terrogation. (4) Finally, utterances for which the listener could not decide on a phonetic transcription were excluded. If, after a total of three playings of an utterance, the listener could not decide on a consistent transcription, the utterance was discarded. Repeated listening past this point was felt to be unreliable. This type of utterance occurred relatively infrequently.

After a written transcript had been completed for each subject, a mean length of utterance in morphemes, based on a corpus of 100 utterances, was computed according to the scoring conventions of Brown (1973) and Siegel (1974). The corpus consisted of the first 50 scorable utterances from each of Conditions I and II that occurred after the initial five utterances in each condition. (Utterances from Condition III were not included in calculating MLU. It was the investigator's impression that the activity of looking at pictures may have tended to elicit one-word naming responses from the subjects. An MLU based on utterances obtained under those circumstances might have underestimated the child's level of language development.) As noted previously, MLUs were computed for each subject in order to establish a prerequisite level of language development between 1.0 and 2.0 morphemes.

Once MLU had been calculated and found to fall within the criterion range, each transcript was prepared for phonemic analysis. The transcript was marked for first occurrences of utterances that were consecutively repeated in identical phonemic form. If there were intervening instances of speech between identical phonemic repetitions of an utterance, both occurrences of the utterance were included. If there were phonemic variations on utterances which had the same adult form, all utterances were included in the phonemic analysis. For example, the italicized forms below were included in the corpus used for phonemic analysis.

Child's Utterance	Adult Form	Nonlinguistic Context
bebi	baby	taking doll out of blanket
bebi	baby	,,
bebi	baby	,,
bot	boat	pointing to puzzle piece of boat
bo	boat	picking up puzzle piece
bebi	baby	handing doll to mother

The first 60 acceptable utterances in each of Conditions I, II, and III constituted the total corpus of 180 utterances which was analyzed for each subject.

Data Entry and Analysis

The articulatory distinctive feature system developed and computerized by Irwin and Wong (1977) was implemented in the analysis of the subjects' samples. The adult forms of the subjects' utterances were phonetically transcribed and then numerically coded according to the numbers designated for individual phonemes in the Irwin and Wong system. Any differences between the child's production of a word and the adult form were regarded as errors and were also assigned code numbers.

The computer program generated analyses for individual subjects as well as for the total group of 20 subjects. For purposes of this study, results obtained for the total group are generally presented. The results yielded information pertaining to the subjects' correct/incorrect use of sounds in terms of phonemes, the Irwin-Wong system of distinctive features, and the modified Chomsky-Halle system of distinctive features.

Reliability

In order to establish reliability of the data, inter- and intrajudge agreement were determined for the investigator and an independent observer. Reliability was determined both for application of the scoring procedures for selecting utterances for analysis and for phonetic transcription of utterances from the audiotapes. A representative sample (10 percent, i.e., at least 18 utterances) of each subject's recorded sample was used in computing reliability. For selecting utterances for analysis, the percentages of inter- and intrajudge agreement were:

Interjudge reliability	91.8%
Intrajudge reliability (for examiner)	100.0%
Intrajudge reliability (for observer)	92.9%

For transcribing utterances from the audiotapes, the percentages of inter- and intrajudge agreement were:

Interjudge reliability	92.2%
Intrajudge reliability (for examiner)	98.0%
Intrajudge reliability (for observer)	96.5%

As indicated, all inter- and intrajudge percentages of agreement were greater than or equal to 91.8 percent.

RESULTS

Phoneme Distribution by Individual Sounds

The frequency distribution of the individual vowellike and consonant sounds is presented in Table 4.1. The frequency distribution (based on all phonemes) for individual vowel sounds ranged from 0 to 6 percent. The frequency distribution for individual consonant sounds ranged from 0 to 7 percent. So, some phonemes were essentially not used in the children's speech; other phonemes accounted for up to 7 percent of the children's speech. The vowel sounds which occurred with relatively greater frequency (i.e., at least 4 percent of the total phoneme sample) were /i, ɑ, e, o/. The consonant sounds which occurred with relatively greater frequency were /b, t, k, m, n, d, r/.

TABLE 4.1 Percentage of Occurrence of Individual Vowellike and
Consonant Sounds Based on Total Phoneme Sample (N = 14,711)

Phoneme Category	% of Distribution	Phoneme
Vowellike	0	/ɜ, ɪu, n̩, l̩, m̩/
	1	/ɛ, ɝ, ɚ, ɔ, ʊ, aʊ, ɔɪ/
	2	/ə, ʌ, aɪ/
	3	/ɪ, æ, u/
	4	/e, o/
	5	/ɑ/
	6	/i/
Consonant	0	/v, θ, ʒ, dʒ, ŋ, j, ʔ/
	1	/f, z, ʃ, tʃ, w/
	2	/ð, h/
	3	/g, p, s, l/
	4	/d, r/
	5	/k, m, n/
	6	/t/
	7	/b/

TABLE 4.2 Percentage of Correct Production of Individual
Vowellike Sounds Based on Total Occurrence of Each Phoneme

Sounds	Phoneme	% Correct Production	No. of Correct Occurrences/ No. of Total Occurrences
Vowels	/u/	99	381/386
	/ʌ/	99	310/314
	/ɑ/	97	688/707
	/ɔ/	97	149/154
	/i/	96	856/889
	/æ/	96	442/459
	/ʊ/	93	149/161
	/o/	91	488/539
	/e/	89	463/522
	/ɛ/	89	182/204
	/ə/	86	221/258
	/ɪ/	84	380/452
	/ɝ/	45	49/109
	/ɚ/	27	25/93
	/ɜ/	0	0/0
Diphthongs	/ɪu/	100	1/1
	/aʊ/	99	170/172
	/aɪ/	98	338/345
	/ɔɪ/	97	83/86
Syllabics	/n̩/	73	11/15
	/l̩/	50	24/48
	/m̩/	0	0/0
Total		91	5,410/5,914

Phonological Development in Children

Percentage of Correct Production by Phoneme

Vowellike Sounds

The group mean percentage of correct production for all vowellike sounds was 91 percent. Mean percentages of correct production for all vowellike sounds for individual subjects ranged from 77 to 96 percent. Table 4.2 displays the group mean percentages of correct production for individual vowellike sounds. Of the 21 vowellike sounds which appeared, only 4 sounds (/ɝ, ɚ, n̩, l̩/) occurred with less than 84 percent accuracy.

Consonants

The group mean percentage of correct production for all consonant sounds was 63 percent. Individual subjects' mean percentages of correct production for all consonant sounds ranged from 36 to 77 percent. Table 4.3 shows the

TABLE 4.3 Percentage of Correct Production of Individual Consonants Based on Total Occurrence of Each Phoneme

Phoneme	% Correct Production	No. of Correct Occurrences/ No. of Total Occurrences
/b/	97	1,032/1,067
/m/	97	714/739
/w/	94	143/152
/h/	78	206/263
/n/	75	516/691
/ŋ/	74	39/53
/k/	71	546/772
/g/	71	270/381
/p/	66	305/464
/f/	65	136/208
/d/	64	414/648
/t/	55	481/879
/j/	55	29/53
/s/	54	267/493
/dʒ/	53	30/57
/ʃ/	43	61/143
/tʃ/	35	64/184
/z/	33	56/171
/l/	27	116/437
/r/	20	129/645
/v/	7	1/15
/θ/	2	1/49
/ð/	1	3/233
/ʒ/	0	0/0
/ʔ/	0	0/0
Total	63	5,559/8,797

group mean percentages of correct production for individual consonant sounds. Of the 23 consonant sounds that appeared, /b/, /m/, and /w/ occurred with at least 94 percent accuracy. Correct production of /h/, /n/, /ŋ/, /k/, and /g/ ranged between 71 and 78 percent. Sounds ranging from 53 to 66 percent accuracy were /p/, /f/, /d/, /t/, /j/, /s/, and /dʒ/. The remaining sounds, /ʃ/, /tʃ/, /z/, /l/, /r/, /v/, /θ/, and /ð/, occurred with less than 43 percent accuracy.

Error Type Distribution

Vowellike Sounds

Table 4.4 presents the mean distribution of error types for each vowellike sound. For most vowellike sounds, error productions were fairly evenly distributed between omissions and substitutions; that is, the difference between percent of omissions and percent of substitutions was less than or equal to 4 percent. The error type distributions for the following sounds were exceptions to this pattern; that is, there was at least a 10 percent difference between percent of omissions and percent of substitutions. Omission errors for /ə/ and /n̩/ occurred relatively more frequently, and substitution errors for /e/, /ɜ˞/, and /ə˞/ occurred relatively more frequently.

TABLE 4.4 Error Type Distribution (Percent Omissions and Percent Substitutions) for Each Vowellike Sound

Category	Vowellike Sound	% Omissions	% Substitutions	No. of Errors/ No. of Occurrences
Essentially Equal Distribution Between Error Types	/i/	2	1	33/889
	/ɪ/	7	9	72/452
	/ɛ/	7	4	22/204
	/æ/	1	3	17/459
	/ʌ/	0	1	4/314
	/ɑ/	0	2	19/707
	/ɔ/	0	3	5/154
	/o/	4	5	51/539
	/u/	0	1	5/386
	/ʊ/	2	6	12/161
	/aɪ/	1	1	7/345
	/aʊ/	0	1	2/172
	/ɔɪ/	0	3	3/86
	/l̩/	27	23	24/48
Greater Frequency of Omissions	/ə/	13	2	37/258
	/n̩/	20	7	4/15
Greater Frequency of Substitutions	/e/	1	11	59/552
	/ɜ˞/	3	36	60/109
	/ə˞/	5	65	68/93

Phonological Development in Children

Consonants

Table 4.5 presents the mean distribution of error types for each consonant sound. Three patterns of error type distribution for consonant sounds were revealed: (1) essentially equal distribution between error types (i.e., ≤ 8 percent difference between percent of omissions and percent of substitutions); (2) relatively greater frequency of omissions (i.e., ≥ 10 percent difference between percent of omissions and percent of substitutions); and (3) relatively greater frequency of substitutions (i.e., ≥ 10 percent difference between percent of substitutions and percent of omissions).

Correct Production of Distinctive Features

Irwin-Wong Distinctive Feature System

All 10 of the feature sets which constitute the Irwin-Wong articulatory feature system occurred with mean percentages of accuracy ranging between 93 and 100 percent. The rank order (high to low) of feature sets in terms of correct use was: Lateral; Oronasal and Fusion; Tenseness; Motion, Labial,

TABLE 4.5   Error Type Distribution (Percent Omissions and Percent Substitutions) for Each Consonant

Category	Consonant	% Omissions	% Substitutions	No. of Errors/ No. of Occurrences
Essentially Equal Distribution Between Error Types	/k/ 41	14	15	226/772
	/g/ 42	18	11	111/381
	/t/ 43	27	19	398/879
	/b/ 46	1	2	35/1,067
	/f/ 47	17	17	72/208
	/θ/ 49	45	53	48/49
	/m/ 57	2	1	25/739
	/w/ 63	5	1	9/152
Greater Frequency of Omissions	/d/ 44	23	13	234/648
	/v/ 48	53	40	14/15
	/s/ 51	32	14	226/493
	/n/ 58	25	1	175/691
	/ŋ/ 59	25	2	14/53
	/l/ 60	64	9	321/437
	/r/ 61	51	28	516/645
	/h/ 62	19	3	57/263
	/j/ 64	30	15	24/53
Greater Frequency of Substitutions	/p/ 45	10	24	159/464
	/ð/ 50	10	88	230/233
	/z/ 52	16	51	115/171
	/ʃ/ 53	9	48	82/143
	/tʃ/ 55	4	61	120/184
	/dʒ/ 56	0	47	27/57

and Vertical; Laryngeal and Closure; Place. The overall mean for correct use of all sets was 97 percent. The mean percentages of correct use for all of the feature sets are presented in Table 4.6.

Table 4.6 also presents the mean percentages for correct use of feature specifications. Of the 35 specifications which appeared in all the feature sets, 11 occurred with less than 95 percent accuracy. The rank order (high to low) of the mean percentages of correct use of these 11 feature specifications was:

Feature Set Specification	Percent Correct
Motion-2	93
Vertical-2	93
Lateral-1	89
Labial-1	89
Labial-3	86
Place-2	84
Laryngeal-1	84
Closure-3	75
Place-5	70
Fusion-2	44
Place-3	18

TABLE 4.6 Correct Usage of Irwin-Wong Feature Sets and Feature Specifications by Percent and Number Based on Total Sample

Feature Set	Feature Specification	% Correct	No. of Correct Occurrences/ No. of Total Occurrences
Oronasal	0	—	0/0
	1	100	13,149/13,213
	2	—	0/0
	3	—	0/0
	4	99	1,480/1,498
	Set Mean	99	14,629/14,711
Motion	0	—	0/0
	1	98	423/431
	2	99	171/173
	3	93	1,443/1,550
	4	96	7,757/8,105
	5	98	4,381/4,452
	Set Mean	96	14,175/14,711
Fusion	0	—	0/0
	1	100	14,461/14,470
	2	44	106/241
	Set Mean	99	14,567/14,711

TABLE 4.6 *Continued*

Feature Set	Feature Specification	% Correct	No. of Correct Occurrences/ No. of Total Occurrences
Lateral	0	—	0/0
	1	89	433/485
	2	—	0/0
	3	100	14,213/14,226
	Set Mean	100	14,646/14,711
Labial	0	—	0/0
	1	89	788/887
	2	99	8,754/8,844
	3	86	2,340/2,710
	4	99	2,257/2,270
	Set Mean	96	14,139/14,711
Tenseness	0	—	0/0
	1	99	10,760/10,855
	2	95	3,657/3,856
	Set Mean	98	14,417/14,711
Vertical	0	97	256/263
	1	98	1,893/1,923
	2	93	5,970/6,418
	3	98	5,994/6,107
	Set Mean	96	14,113/14,711
Place	0	—	0/0
	1	99	2,409/2,422
	2	84	188/223
	3	18	50/282
	4	95	6,242/6,553
	5	70	626/897
	6	97	3,956/4,071
	7	97	256/263
	Set Mean	93	13,727/14,711
Laryngeal	0	—	0/0
	1	84	2,692/3,192
	2	97	256/263
	3	98	11,057/11,256
	4	—	0/0
	Set Mean	95	14,005/14,711
Closure	0	—	0/0
	1	99	2,886/2,919
	2	94	4,250/4,530
	3	75	988/1,312
	4	99	5,892/5,950
	Set Mean	95	14,016/14,711
Total for All Sets		97	142,434/147,110

Table 4.7 provides a comparison of individual mean percentages of correct use for feature sets with the group mean percentages. No individual subject varied more than 6 percent from any group mean percentage. For 6 of the 10 feature sets, the range of individual percentages around the group mean was not greater than 5 percent. For example, the group mean for correct use of the feature set Motion was 97 percent. The range of individual percentages of correct use for this feature set only extended from 94 to 99 percent. Four feature sets were characterized by greater ranges of individual variability, from 6 to 10 percent: Vertical, Place, Labial, Laryngeal.

Chomsky-Halle Distinctive Feature System

All 13 of the feature sets which make up the Chomsky-Halle system occurred with mean percentages of accuracy ranging between 95 and 99 percent. The rank order (high to low) of feature sets in terms of correct use was: Vocalic, Low, and Nasal; Consonant, Back, Anterior, and Strident; Coronal, Round,

TABLE 4.7 Comparison of Individual Subjects with Group Means by Percentage of Correct Usage of Irwin-Wong Feature Sets

Subject Number	Oronasal	Motion	Fusion	Lateral	Labial
1	100	99	98	100	96
2	100	97	99	99	96
3	99	97	99	99	96
4	99	97	97	99	95
5	99	97	95	100	90
6	99	95	98	100	95
7	100	99	98	100	95
8	100	96	100	100	97
9	100	98	100	100	96
10	100	98	100	100	99
11	100	97	100	100	99
12	100	97	99	100	97
13	100	98	99	100	98
14	99	95	99	99	94
15	99	94	100	98	95
16	99	98	100	100	96
17	99	96	100	100	97
18	100	94	100 ′	100	98
19	100	97	100	100	96
20	99	97	100	99	98
Range of % for Individual	99–100	94–99	95–100	98–100	90–99[a]
Group Mean	99	97	99	100	96

[a]Variability > 5 percent.

Tense, and Continuant; High; and Voice. The overall mean for correct use of all sets was 98 percent. The mean percentages of correct use for each of the Chomsky-Halle feature sets are included in Table 4.8.

The mean percentages for correct use of the feature specifications in each Chomsky-Halle feature set are also presented in Table 4.8. Of the 29 specifications which appeared, 5 occurred with less than 95 percent accuracy. The rank order (high to low) of the mean percentages of correct use of these feature specifications was:

Feature Set Specification	Percent Correct
High-2	92
Coronal-2	92
Voice-1	86
Continuant-2	85
Strident-2	81

Text continued on p. 70

Tenseness	Vertical	Place	Laryngeal	Closure	Overall
98	98	96	97	97	98
99	96	93	90	96	96
98	98	96	97	96	98
97	95	91	89	96	96
96	96	91	90	94	95
97	95	90	95	93	96
100	98	95	98	96	98
99	96	93	99	94	97
99	96	95	96	95	97
98	96	96	98	97	98
99	96	95	98	95	100
97	94	92	97	94	97
98	97	95	98	97	98
95	92	95	91	94	95
97	92	91	90	93	95
99	98	97	98	97	98
98	96	95	98	95	97
99	94	93	97	93	97
98	97	92	96	95	97
99	97	95	96	98	98
95–100	92–98[a]	90–97[a]	89–99[a]	93–98	95–100
98	96	94	95	98	97

TABLE 4.8 Correct Usage of Modified Chomsky-Halle Feature Sets and Feature Specifications by Percent and Number Based on Total Sample

Feature Set	Feature Specification	% Correct	No. of Correct Occurrences/ No. of Total Occurrences
Vocalic	0	—	0/0
	1	100	7,715/7,730
	2	98	6,835/6,981
	Set Mean	99	14,550/14,711
Consonantal	0	—	0/0
	1	100	6,303/6,319
	2	97	8,132/8,392
	Set Mean	98	14,435/14,711
High	0	—	0/0
	1	98	10,778/11,027
	2	92	3,374/3,684
	Set Mean	96	14,152/14,711
Back	0	—	0/0
	1	98	10,242/10,488
	2	97	4,107/4,223
	Set Mean	98	14,349/14,711
Low	0	—	0/0
	1	99	12,756/12,851
	2	98	1,827/1,860
	Set Mean	99	14,583/14,711
Anterior	0	—	0/0
	1	97	8,280/8,554
	2	99	6,069/6,157
	Set Mean	98	14,349/14,711
Coronal	0	—	0/0
	1	99	9,721/9,816
	2	92	4,486/4,895
	Set Mean	97	14,207/14,711

TABLE 4.8 *Continued*

Feature Set	Feature Specification	% Correct	No. of Correct Occurrences/ No. of Total Occurrences
Round	0	97	8,402/8,655
	1	97	4,577/4,705
	2	97	1,316/1,351
	Set Mean	97	14,295/14,711
Tense	0	97	8,402/8,655
	1	97	2,930/3,007
	2	96	2,941/3,049
	Set Mean	97	14,273/14,711
Voice	0	—	0/0
	1	86	2,974/3,455
	2	98	11,057/11,256
	Set Mean	95	14,031/14,711
Continuant	0	—	0/0
	1	100	11,744/11,801
	2	85	2,475/2,910
	Set Mean	97	14,219/14,711
Nasal	0	—	0/0
	1	100	13,149/13,213
	2	99	1,480/1,498
	Set Mean	99	14,629/14,711
Strident	0	—	0/0
	1	100	13,407/13,440
	2	81	1,033/1,271
	Set Mean	98	14,440/14,711
Total for All Sets		98	186,512/191,243

Table 4.9 provides a comparison of individual mean percentages of correct use for feature sets with the group mean percentages of correct use. No individual varied more than 6 percent from any group mean percentage. For 9 of the 13 feature sets, the range of individual percentages around the group means was not greater than 5 percent. For example, the group mean for correct use of the feature set Consonantal was 98 percent. The range of individual percentages of correct use for this feature set only extended from 96 to 100 percent. Four feature sets were characterized by greater ranges of individual variability, from 6 to 10 percent: Anterior, High, Strident, Voice.

TABLE 4.9 Comparison of Individual Subjects with Group Means by Percentage of Correct Usage of Modified Chomsky-Halle Feature Sets

Subject Number	Vocalic	Consonantal	High	Back	Low	Anterior	Coronal
1	100	100	97	100	99	98	99
2	99	98	96	98	100	97	97
3	99	99	97	97	100	99	97
4	98	96	92	95	97	94	95
5	100	99	93	98	99	94	96
6	100	99	95	97	99	96	96
7	98	97	96	98	100	98	96
8	99	98	98	98	100	99	97
9	100	99	98	99	99	98	98
10	98	98	96	97	98	99	98
11	99	98	99	99	99	100	97
12	100	99	96	96	99	98	96
13	99	99	96	97	100	98	97
14	100	99	97	98	98	98	98
15	97	97	93	95	98	96	94
16	99	98	98	99	100	99	97
17	99	99	97	97	99	98	96
18	99	98	98	99	99	99	98
19	100	99	97	98	100	97	96
20	97	96	96	96	100	98	96
Range of % for Individual	97–100	96–100	92–99[a]	95–100	97–100	94–100[a]	94–99
Group Mean	99	98	96	98	99	98	97

[a]Variability > 6 percent.

Replacement Characteristics

Irwin-Wong Distinctive Feature System

The counts of feature/degree differences from the target phoneme for all the vowellike and consonant sounds for which substitution errors occurred appear in Table 4.10, according to the Irwin-Wong feature system. Replacement sounds that were substituted for each phoneme are arranged by decreasing frequency of occurrence (left to right). For example, eight different phonemes were substituted for /t/. The most frequently appearing error was the d/t substitution, accounting for 145 of 164 substitution errors.

Text continued on p. 74

Round	Tense	Voice	Continuant	Nasal	Strident	Overall
99	98	97	99	100	98	99
97	97	90	96	100	99	97
97	97	97	98	99	99	98
97	94	89	97	99	97	96
97	97	90	96	99	93	96
98	98	95	94	99	96	97
96	96	98	97	100	98	98
97	97	99	95	100	99	98
98	97	96	97	100	99	98
98	96	98	99	99	100	98
98	98	98	96	100	100	99
97	97	97	97	100	99	98
97	97	98	99	100	99	98
97	96	91	96	99	97	97
96	97	91	94	99	98	96
97	98	98	98	99	99	98
98	98	98	97	99	98	98
98	98	97	94	100	99	98
98	98	96	97	100	99	98
96	96	96	98	99	99	97
96–99	94–98	89–99[a]	94–99	99–100	93–100[a]	96–99
97	97	95	97	99	98	98

TABLE 4.10 Error Productions by Replacement, Frequency of Replacement, and Feature/Degree Differences of Replacement as Specified in Irwin-Wong System

Phonetic Classification	Phoneme in Error	Replacement 1	Replacement 2	Replacement 3	Replacement 4	Replacement 5
Vowels	/i/	/e/:10–1/1[a]	/ɪ/:2–1/1	/ə/:1–4/4		
	/ɪ/	/i/:32–1/1	/ə/:3–3/3	/æ/:2–2/3	/e/:1–2/2	/ʌ/:1–3/4
	/e/	/i/:25–1/1	/æ/:15–3/3	/ɑ/:6–4/5	/ə/:4–3/3	/aɪ/:4–4/7
	/ɛ/	/i/:7–2/2	/ɑ/:1–3/4			
	/æ/	/ɑ/:5–1/2	/i/:4–3/4	/aɪ/:2–3/6	/ɪ/:1–2/3	/ɛ/:1–2/2
	/ɝ/	/ʊ/:26–4/4	/ʊə/:18–3/3	/ə/:4–3/3	/i/:3–3/3	/ʌ/:2–4/4
	/ə/	/ɝ/:1–2/2	/aɪ/:2–4/6	/i/:1–4/4		
	/ʌ/	/i/:1–4/5	/e/:1–3/4	/æ/:1–2/3	/ɑ/:1–1/1	
	/ɑ/	/ʌ/:8–1/1	/o/:5–4/4	/æ/:3–1/2		
	/ɔ/	/ə/:2–3/3	/æ/:1–2/3	/o/:1–3/3	/aʊ/:1–3/4	
	/o/	/ɑ/:13–4/4	/ə/:4–4/4	/ɔɪ/:4–3/5	/i/:3–3/4	/æ/:1–5/6
	/u/	/i/:3–2/3	/ʌ/:1–4/4			
	/ʊ/	/u/:4–2/2	/i/:2–4/5	/æ/:1–3/5	/ʌ/:1–2/2	/ɑ/:1–2/3
Diphthongs	/aɪ/	/ɑ/:2–2/4	/æ/:1–3/6	/ʌ/:1–3/5	/aʊ/:1–1/1	
	/aʊ/	/ə/:1–4/5	/ʌ/:1–3/4			
	/ɔɪ/	/o/:3–3/5				
Syllabics	/n̩/	/θ/:1–4/8				
	/l̩/	/ɝ/:6–4/5	/ə/:4–4/5	/u/:1–4/6		
Consonants	/k/	/g/:48–1/2	/t/:26–1/2	/d/:23–2/4	/ʔ/:15–4/10	/l/:4–5/10
	/g/	/k/:26–1/2	/d/:10–1/2	/ʔ/:4–4/8	/t/:3–2/4	
	/t/	/d/:145–1/2	/k/:4–1/2	/b/:4–4/8	/ʔ/:4–4/12	/n/:3–3/6
	/d/	/t/:44–1/2	/g/:14–1/2	/n/:12–2/4	/l/:6–3/6	/w/:4–5/9
	/p/	/b/:86–1/2	/m/:18–3/6	/t/:4–3/6	/k/:1–3/8	/g/:1–4/10
	/b/	/m/:9–2/4	/p/:8–1/2	/d/:2–3/6	/f/:2–5/8	/w/:1–3/5
	/f/	/p/:12–4/6	/v/:6–1/2	/t/:4–5/6	/s/:4–2/3	/d/:3–6/8
	/v/	/b/:4–4/6	/f/:1–1/2	/s/:1–3/5		
	/θ/	/f/:13–2/2	/s/:7–3/3	/d/:2–5/6	/t/:1–4/4	/v/:1–3/4
	/ð/	/d/:194–4/4	/t/:7–5/6	/s/:3–4/5	/n/:2–4/6	
	/s/	/d/:34–6/7	/t/:16–5/5	/z/:4–1/2	/h/:4–7/12	/f/:3–2/3
	/z/	/s/:81–1/2	/t/:3–6/7	/d/:3–5/5	/θ/:1–4/5	
	/ʃ/	/s/:47–2/3	/d/:11–7/8	/t/:4–6/6	/tʃ/:3–5/5	/dʒ/:2–6/7
	/tʃ/	/d/:61–4/5	/t/:37–3/3	/k/:5–3/3	/dʒ/:4–1/2	/s/:3–7/8
	/dʒ/	/d/:24–3/3	/ʃ/:2–6/7	/tʃ/:1–1/2		
	/m/	/b/:9–2/4	/p/:1–3/6	/h/:1–7/18		
	/n/	/d/:3–2/4	/t/:1–3/6	/b/:1–5/10		
	/ŋ/	/s/:1–7/11				
	/l/	/w/:18–4/7	/j/:8–2/3	/m/:6–7/14	/n/:6–4/8	/d/:1–3/6
	/r/	/w/:103–1/3	/θ/:73–4/4	/ʊə/:4–3/4	/ʊ/:2–4/5	/ʌ/:1–4/5
	/h/	/b/:7–6/16				
	/w/	/r/:1–1/3				
	/j/	/m/:4–6/13	/l/:2–2/3	/t/:1–4/7	/h/:1–4/7	

[a]That is, the replacement /e/, which occurred 10 times, is removed from /i/ by a feature/degree difference of 1/1.

Replacement 6	Replacement 7	Replacement 8	Replacement 9	Replacement 10	Replacement 11
/ɑ/:1–3/5 /ɪ/:2–2/2					
/ə/:1–2/2 /u/:2–2/2	/ɑ/:1–5/5	/o/:1–1/1			
/ʌ/:1–3/3	/ɔ/:1–3/3	/u/:1–1/1			
/s/:2–6/7	/h/:1–5/10				
/dʒ/:2–4/5 /ʔ/:2–4/10 /ʔ/:1–5/16	/p/:1–3/6 /k/:1–2/4	/f/:1–5/6			
/b/:3–5/8	/n/:2–6/10	/k/:1–5/8	/tʃ/:1–6/9		
/n/:1–5/8	/ʔ/:1–5/12				
/g/:2–7/9	/ʃ/:2–2/3	/k/:1–6/7	/θ/:1–3/3	/tʃ/:1–7/8	/l/:1–7/9
/z/:1–3/5 /ʃ/:2–5/5	/n/:1–7/10 /ʒ/:1–6/7				
/s/:1–7/9 /b/:1–4/8	/n/:1–5/10				

A final set of calculations was based upon the sum of feature/degree differences of all the substitution errors which occurred for each phoneme in Table 4.10. Table 4.11 presents the mean number of feature/degree differences for each vowellike and consonant sound, as specified in the Irwin-Wong feature system. Two types of "mean errors" in terms of feature and degree differences were computed. First, mean numbers of feature and degree differences were computed based on only the number of substitution errors which occurred for each sound. Then, mean numbers of features and degree differences were computed based on all occurrences of the phoneme, both correct and incorrect (including omissions and distortions as well as substitutions). These calculations are presented by phoneme categories (vowels, diphthongs, syllabics, and consonants) in Table 4.11.

A comparison of errors made on all vowellike sounds with those made on all consonant sounds reveals similar mean number of feature and degree differences, when only error productions are considered.

	$\bar{X}$ Feature Difference	$\bar{X}$ Degree Difference
Vowellike	2.67	3.02
Consonant	2.65	3.88

However, when means are based on all phoneme occurrences, greater differences in mean numbers of feature and degree differences are obtained.

	$\bar{X}$ Feature Difference	$\bar{X}$ Degree Difference
Vowellike	.15	.17
Consonant	.43	.63

These means reflect the relatively greater frequency of consonant sounds in the subjects' speech as well as the higher frequency of errors for consonant sounds compared to vowel sounds.

Chomsky-Halle Distinctive Feature System

Counts of feature differences from the target phoneme for all the vowellike and consonant sounds for which substitution errors occurred appear in Table 4.12, according to the Chomsky-Halle feature system. Because the Chomsky-Halle system is binary and does not include feature degrees as does the Irwin-Wong system, only mean numbers of feature differences have been computed. Replacement sounds substituted for each phoneme are arranged by decreasing frequency of occurrence from left to right. The number of occurrences of a replacement sound and the count of feature differences from the target phoneme appear as follows in Table 4.12:

Phoneme in Error	Replacement 1
/t/	/d/:145–1

Text continued on p. 78

Phonological Development in Children

TABLE 4.11 Mean Feature/Degree Difference Values as Specified in Irwin-Wong System

Phonetic Classification	Phoneme in Error	Number of Errors	Number of Occurrences	$\bar{X}$ Feature Difference Based on Errors	$\bar{X}$ Feature Difference Based on Occurrences	$\bar{X}$ Degree Difference Based on Errors	$\bar{X}$ Degree Difference Based on Occurrences
Vowels	/i/	13	889	1.23	.02	1.23	.02
	/ɪ/	40	452	1.32	.12	1.45	.13
	/e/	56	522	2.25	.24	2.57	.28
	/ɛ/	8	204	2.13	.08	2.25	.09
	/æ/	14	459	2.07	.06	3.21	.10
	/ɝ/	57	109	3.46	1.81	3.46	1.81
	/ɚ/	63	93	2.25	1.53	2.25	1.53
	/ə/	4	258	3.50	.05	4.50	.07
	/ʌ/	4	314	2.50	.03	3.25	.04
	/ɑ/	17	707	2.18	.05	2.82	.07
	/ɔ/	5	154	2.80	.09	3.20	.10
	/o/	28	539	3.61	.19	4.04	.21
	/u/	4	386	2.50	.03	3.25	.03
	/ʊ/	9	161	2.56	.14	3.11	.17
Diphthongs	/aɪ/	5	345	2.20	.03	4.00	.06
	/aʊ/	2	172	3.50	.04	4.50	.05
	/ɔɪ/	3	86	3.00	.10	5.00	.17
Syllabics	/n̩/	1	15	4.00	.27	8.00	1.17
	/l̩/	11	48	4.00	.92	5.09	.59
Consonants	/k/	119	772	1.82	.28	3.82	.59
	/g/	43	381	1.35	.15	2.70	.30
	/t/	164	879	1.26	.23	2.55	.48
	/d/	83	648	1.57	.20	3.13	.40
	/p/	111	464	1.48	.35	3.05	.73
	/b/	22	1,067	2.05	.04	3.86	.08
	/f/	36	208	3.83	.66	5.69	.99
	/v/	6	15	3.33	1.33	5.17	2.07
	/θ/	26	49	2.85	1.51	3.35	1.78
	/ð/	206	233	4.03	3.57	4.10	3.63
	/s/	69	493	5.26	.74	6.23	.87
	/z/	88	171	1.34	.69	2.31	1.19
	/ʃ/	69	143	3.36	1.62	4.30	2.08
	/tʃ/	113	184	3.64	2.23	4.25	2.61
	/dʒ/	27	57	3.15	1.49	3.26	1.54
	/m/	11	739	2.55	.04	5.45	.08
	/n/	5	691	2.80	.02	5.60	.04
	/ŋ/	1	53	7.00	.13	11.00	.21
	/l/	41	437	4.12	.39	7.49	.70
	/r/	184	645	2.30	.66	3.48	.99
	/h/	7	263	6.00	.16	16.00	.43
	/w/	1	152	1.00	.01	3.00	.02
	/j/	8	53	4.50	.68	9.00	1.36
Total All Phonemes		1,784	14,711	2.62	.32	3.67	.45

TABLE 4.12 Error Productions by Replacement, Frequency of Replacement, and Feature Differences of Replacement as Specified in Modified Chomsky-Halle System

Phonetic Classification	Phoneme in Error	Replacement 1	Replacement 2	Replacement 3	Replacement 4	Replacement 5
Vowels	/i/	/e/:10–1[a]	/ɪ/:2–1	/ə/:1–3		
	/ɪ/	/i/:32–1	/ə/:3–2	/æ/:5–2	/e/:1–2	/ʌ/:1–2
	/e/	/i/:25–1	/æ/:15–2	/ɑ/:6–3	/ə/:4–2	/aɪ/:4–2
	/ɛ/	/i/:7–2	/ɑ/:1–2			
	/æ/	/ɑ/:5–1	/i/:4–3	/aɪ/:2–2	/ɪ/:1–2	/ɛ/:1–1
	/ɝ/	/ʊ/:26–5	/ʊə/:18–4	/ə/:4–3	/i/:3–2	/ʌ/:2–3
	/ɚ/	/ə/:50–2	/ɑ/:3–3	/ʊə/:3–3	/æ/:2–2	/u/:2–4
	/ə/	/aɪ/:2–4	/i/:1–3	/ɚ/:1–2		
	/ʌ/	/i/:1–3	/e/:1–2	/æ/:1–2	/ɑ/:1–1	
	/ɑ/	/ʌ/:8–1	/o/:5–3	/æ/:3–1		
	/ɔ/	/ə/:2–1	/æ/:1–3	/o/:1–1	/aʊ/:1–2	
	/o/	/ɑ/:13–3	/ə/:4–2	/ɔɪ/:4–1	/i/:3–3	/æ/:1–4
	/u/	/i/:3–1	/ʌ/:1–2			
	/ʊ/	/u/:4–2	/i/:2–3	/æ/:1–4	/ʌ/:1–2	/ɑ/:1–3
Diphthongs	/aɪ/	/ɑ/:2–1	/æ/:1–2	/ʌ/:1–2	/aʊ/:1–1	
	/aʊ/	/ə/:1–3	/ʌ/:1–1			
	/ɔɪ/	/o/:3–1				
Syllabics	/n̩/	/ə/:1–7				
	/l̩/	/ɚ/:6–5	/ə/:4–6	/u/:1–8		
Consonants	/k/	/g/:48–1	/t/:26–4	/d/:23–5	/ʔ/:15–1	/l/:4–7
	/g/	/k/:26–1	/d/:10–4	/ʔ/:4–8	/t/:3–5	
	/t/	/d/:145–1	/k/:4–4	/b/:4–2	/ʔ/:4–7	/n/:3–2
	/d/	/t/:44–1	/g/:14–4	/n/:12–1	/l/:6–2	/w/:4–8
	/p/	/b/:86–1	/m/:18–2	/t/:4–1	/k/:1–3	/g/:1–4
	/b/	/m/:9–1	/p/:8–1	/d/:2–1	/f/:2–3	/w/:1–7
	/f/	/p/:12–2	/v/:6–1	/t/:4–3	/s/:4–1	/d/:3–4
	/v/	/b/:4–2	/f/:1–1	/s/:1–2		
	/θ/	/f/:13–2	/s/:7–1	/d/:2–2	/t/:1–1	/v/:1–3
	/ð/	/d/:194–1	/t/:7–2	/s/:3–2	/n/:2–2	
	/s/	/d/:34–3	/t/:16–2	/z/:4–1	/h/:4–5	/f/:3–1
	/z/	/s/:81–1	/t/:3–3	/d/:3–2	/θ/:1–2	
	/ʃ/	/s/:47–2	/d/:11–5	/t/:4–4	/tʃ/:3–1	/dʒ/:2–2
	/tʃ/	/d/:61–4	/t/:37–3	/k/:5–3	/dʒ/:4–1	/s/:3–3
	/dʒ/	/d/:24–3	/ʃ/:2–2	/tʃ/:1–1		
	/m/	/b/:9–1	/p/:1–2	/h/:1–6		
	/n/	/d/:3–1	/t/:1–2	/b/:1–2		
	/ŋ/	/s/:1–8				
	/l/	/w/:18–8	/j/:8–7	/m/:6–4	/n/:6–3	/d/:1–2
	/r/	/w/:103–7	/ə/:73–5	/ʊə/:4–6	/ʊ/:2–7	/ʌ/:1–6
	/h/	/b/:7–5				
	/w/	/r/:1–7				
	/j/	/m/:4–7	/l/:2–7	/t/:1–8	/h/:1–5	

[a]That is, the replacement /e/, which occurred 10 times, is removed from /i/ by a feature difference of 1.

Phonological Development in Children

Replacement 6	Replacement 7	Replacement 8	Replacement 9	Replacement 10	Replacement 11
/ɑ/:1–3 /ɪ/:2–2					
/ə/:1–2 /u/:2–3 /ʊ/:2–4	/ɑ/:1–4 /i/:1–3	/o/:1–3			
/ʌ/:1–2	/ɔ/:1–1	/u/:1–2			
/s/:2–6	/h/:1–5				
/dʒ/:2–4 /ʔ/:2–8 /ʔ/:1–6	/p/:1–1 /k/:1–5	/f/:1–3			
/b/:3–3	/n/:2–5	/k/:1–5	/tʃ/:1–4		
/n/:1–3	/ʔ/:1–6				
/g/:2–7	/ʃ/:2–2	/k/:1–6	/θ/:1–1	/tʃ/:1–3	/l/:1–3
/z/:1–3 /ʃ/:2–1	/n/:1–6 /ʒ/:1–2				
/s/:1–3 /b/:1–4	/h/:1–6				

Like Table 4.11 for the Irwin-Wong system, Table 4.13 presents the mean number of feature differences for each vowellike and consonant sound as specified in the Chomsky-Halle system. Means were first calculated based only on the number of substitution errors which occurred for each sound and then based on all occurrences (correct and incorrect) of each sound. Phonemes are grouped in phonetic categories (vowels, diphthongs, syllabics, and consonants). The differences between means based only on error productions and means based on all occurrences in the Chomsky-Halle system, as in the Irwin-Wong system, are due to the relatively greater frequency of consonant sounds in the subjects' speech as well as the higher frequency of errors for consonant sounds compared to vowel sounds.

The mean feature differences obtained for the Chomsky-Halle system were generally very similar to those obtained for the Irwin-Wong system. For example, the following sets of mean feature differences for phonemic subgroups in each system are comparable.

	$\bar{X}$ Feature Differences Based on Number of Errors	$\bar{X}$ Feature Differences Based on Number of Occurrences
Vowels		
Irwin-Wong	2.62	.15
Chomsky-Halle	2.45	.14
Diphthongs		
Irwin-Wong	2.70	.04
Chomsky-Halle	1.40	.02
Syllabics		
Irwin-Wong	4.00	.76
Chomsky-Halle	5.75	1.10
Vowellike		
Irwin-Wong	2.67	.15
Chomsky-Halle	2.54	.14
Consonants		
Irwin-Wong	2.65	.43
Chomsky-Halle	2.72	.44

The means computed for all vowellike and consonant sounds are essentially equal in each system.

DISCUSSION

Phonemic Acquisition

The findings of this investigation overwhelmingly supported the view that important phonological gains are being made even in the early stages of the language acquisition process (Ingram, 1976). The high group percentages of

TABLE 4.13 Mean Feature Difference Values as Specified in
Modified Chomsky-Halle System

Phonetic Classification	Phoneme in Error	Number of Errors	Number of Occurrences	$\bar{X}$ Feature Difference Based on Errors	$\bar{X}$ Feature Difference Based on Occurrences
Vowels	/i/	13	889	1.15	.02
	/ɪ/	40	452	1.22	.11
	/e/	56	522	1.66	.18
	/ɛ/	8	204	2.00	.08
	/æ/	14	459	1.86	.06
	/ɝ/	57	109	4.19	2.19
	/ɚ/	63	93	2.24	1.52
	/ə/	4	258	3.25	.05
	/ʌ/	4	314	2.00	.03
	/ɑ/	17	707	2.00	.05
	/ɔ/	5	154	1.60	.05
	/o/	28	539	2.46	.13
	/u/	4	386	1.25	.01
	/ʊ/	9	161	2.56	.14
Diphthongs	/aɪ/	5	345	1.40	.02
	/aʊ/	2	172	2.00	.02
	/ɔɪ/	3	86	1.00	.03
Syllabics	/n̩/	1	15	7.00	.47
	/l̩/	11	48	5.64	1.29
Consonants	/k/	119	772	3.50	.54
	/g/	43	381	2.63	.30
	/t/	164	879	1.31	.24
	/d/	83	648	2.13	.27
	/p/	111	464	1.25	.30
	/b/	22	1,067	1.45	.03
	/f/	36	208	2.39	.41
	/v/	6	15	1.83	.73
	/θ/	26	49	1.92	1.02
	/ð/	206	233	1.06	.94
	/s/	69	493	2.78	.39
	/z/	88	171	1.11	.57
	/ʃ/	69	143	2.62	1.27
	/tʃ/	113	184	3.42	2.10
	/dʒ/	27	57	2.85	1.35
	/m/	11	739	1.55	.02
	/n/	5	691	1.40	.01
	/ŋ/	1	53	8.00	.15
	/l/	41	437	6.17	.58
	/r/	184	645	6.16	1.76
	/h/	7	263	5.00	.13
	/w/	1	152	7.00	.05
	/j/	8	53	6.88	1.04
Total All Phonemes		1,784	14,711	2.65	.32

correct use for both vowels (91 percent) and consonants (63 percent) indicated remarkable phonemic competency in children as young as 21 to 24 months.

Specific data relating to vowel and consonant sound use were generally comparable to phonemic acquisition data reported in other developmental studies. The process of vowel production has been somewhat slighted in previous acquisition studies (Wellman et al., 1931; Poole, 1934; Templin, 1957; Sander, 1972; Prather et al., 1975) because of essentially 100 percent correct use by the age groups under study—generally children older than three years. The high group mean percentage for correct use of vowels (91 percent) as compared to consonants (63 percent) found in the present study is consistent with the conclusion of prior studies that vowels are acquired before consonants (Ingram, 1976).

In looking at production of individual vowel sounds, 20 of 22 possible vowels appeared in the samples of the subjects. Of these 20 sounds, only 4 were produced with less than 84 percent accuracy (/ɜ˞, ə˞, n̩, l̩/). Percentages of correct use for the 7 vowel sounds which occurred with the greatest frequency ranged from 84 to 99 percent. These figures (from Tables 4.1 and 4.2) indicate nearly complete acquisition of the full repertoire of vowel sounds as early as 21 to 24 months.

The ordering of consonants by percentage of correct use in Table 4.3 generally parallels the ordering of sounds from "early mastery" to "late mastery" in previous studies. For example, the three consonants /b/, /m/, and /w/, which occurred with the greatest accuracy in the present study, have been classified among the first phonemes that children master. Consonant sounds such as /ð/ and /ʒ/, which appeared with the least accuracy in the present study, have been grouped among the last sounds that children acquire. However, the present data reflect consistently higher levels of correct consonant production at notably younger ages than suggested by available norms. In fact, if a mastery criterion of 50 percent were imposed upon the percentages yielded by this analysis, 15 of the 25 consonant sounds would be considered acquired by two years of age.

Joint review of Tables 4.1 and 4.3 reveals an apparent relationship between relatively higher percentages of *correct* production and relatively higher percentages of *occurrence* for consonant sounds. Of the 10 consonant sounds that occurred most frequently, 8 occurred with relatively high levels of correct use (at least 54 percent). Of the 5 consonants that occurred the most frequently, 4 were produced with at least 71 percent correct use. Generally, it appeared that consonant sounds that appeared more frequently in the children's speech were also produced more accurately.

A finding by Ferguson and Farwell (1975) may partially account for the high frequency/high accuracy relationship revealed in the present data, and may also suggest an alternative way of analyzing these data. Ferguson and Farwell described several apparent characteristics of phonological acquisition from their observation of three children. Longitudinal data were collected from the subjects from the age of about 1 year until the total recorded lexicon for each child reached at least 50 words. Ferguson and Farwell discovered a tendency in their data for children to show preferences for the kinds of words acquired. For example, one of the children acquired words with labial stops only if they began with /b/. No words beginning with /p/ were acquired for several sessions. Similarly, another child preferred /b/ words until around 2 years, when several /p/ words were acquired. The investigators suggested that children are highly selective in the sound patterns of words which they acquire, and they proposed that profitable study of either the phonetic or lexical parameter of child language acquisition could not result without a joint consideration of both aspects.

The relationship between frequency and accuracy in the present data might support the notion that children demonstrate some sort of selectivity in sound use, even at a later stage of language acquisition than that studied by Ferguson and Farwell (1975). Children did indeed seem to be using words which contained certain sounds more frequently than others. The analysis procedures implemented in the present investigation were designed to provide group norms of a quantitative nature for phonemic acquisition; hence, production in specific word forms was not accounted for. However, an analysis of individual data which traced phonemic production specific to word forms might yield additional insight into the nature of the acquisition process. This kind of individual analysis across subjects could reveal differences, for example, between one child's correct use of a sound in 10 different words and another child's correct use of a sound in the same word which occurred 10 times.

The method of sampling and reporting phoneme production used in this study revealed a significant distinction in children's use of consonant sounds which has not been obvious in other group developmental data. Norms from past studies were based on the subjects' production of certain words stipulated by the examiner. A child was given a limited and usually equal number of opportunities to either succeed or fail on production of each particular sound. In making references to these norms, one might conclude that, although the young child cannot accurately produce those sounds designated as "late emerging," the number of unsuccessful attempts of those sounds in free speech is similar to the number of successful productions of "early emerging" sounds. In the present data, the pattern of high percentages of correct use and frequency specific to particular consonant sounds indicated that the sounds which children produced most accurately were the sounds used most frequently in free speech. Frequency of production of sounds with high percentages of errors did not approach that of sounds used correctly. Thus, contrary to impressions based on test-type sampling, all consonant sounds are not of equal importance in the child's speech (Ingram, 1976).

Sander (1972) suggested that an important indicator of articulation deviance may be evident in error patterns even at the age of two or three years. Familiarity with error behaviors observed in normal children is a prerequisite to accurate judgments of deviance and/or delay by a clinician (Leonard, 1973). Tables 4.4 and 4.5 group phonemes by three patterns of error-type distribution for vowel and consonant sounds: essentially equal distribution between omissions and substitutions, greater frequency of omissions, and greater frequency of substitutions. Specific vowel sounds generally were not characterized by a greater number of omission or substitution errors. Consonant sounds, however, more obviously fell into groups characterized by more substitution or omission errors.

The group data in Tables 4.4 and 4.5 reveal general patterns, but provide no basis for explaining these error-type patterns. Group treatment of the data was insufficient to determine if error patterns: (1) were typical of all children, present to a much greater extent in some subjects than in others; and (2) were specific to certain phonemes or to some other factor, such as position in word, phonetic context, fronting, backing, weak syllable, or some other phonological process. Analyzing error patterns in individual data and then comparing findings across subjects might yield more specific and differentiated results. The complications involved in procedures of error analysis are evidence that phoneme acquisition must be regarded as a complex process, no less systematic or rule-governed than other aspects of language.

Some limitations of using standardized tests to sample language behaviors were identified by Leonard, Prutting, Perozzi, and Berkley (1978). Similarly, Ingram (1976) summarized several drawbacks of using test-type procedures to sample articulatory behavior and presented positive factors which supported the use of nonstandard methods of data collection. By obtaining spontaneous samples, several examples of a sound, rather than one, are usually available; the fact that sounds do not occur with equal frequency is accounted for; a sample of the child's production in words within his own lexicon is provided; and sound production can be viewed in conjunction with other aspects of language development.

The use of spontaneous sampling in the present study provided normative data that were more representative of children's speech production than previous norms based on production of a standard set of single words. The findings of this investigation strongly support Sander's (1972) impression that altered sampling methods might reveal that children are producing many more sounds, with higher levels of correctness, and at much younger ages than previously supposed. The acquisition ages from previous developmental studies do not appear to represent accurately the capacities of the child's phonemic system as it functions in spontaneous speech.

Distinctive Feature Acquisition

The distinctive feature analysis performed in the present study was an attempt to yield information about: (1) an articulation-based feature system—the Irwin-Wong system; (2) a linguistically developed feature system—the Chomsky-Halle system; and (3) distinctive feature theory as an account of sound acquisition in children.

Several important methodological differences exist between this investigation and previous group studies of feature acquisition (Menyuk, 1968; Olmstead, 1971; Prather et al., 1975). The age ranges and numbers of subjects have varied from study to study. Some investigators collected data through spontaneous sampling, and others obtained one-word naming responses by picture presentation. Dissimilar methods of measuring feature acquisition were used. Menyuk and Prather et al. analyzed only features in speech sounds that were produced correctly. The present investigator analyzed feature use in both correct and incorrect sound productions. Because of certain practical shortcomings in linguistically based feature systems when clinically applied (Walsh, 1974; Singh, 1976), some studies used only the articulatory features in the Chomsky-Halle system or a totally articulation-based system of features.

These various methodological differences present real limitations in comparing the findings of the present investigation with those of other feature acquisition studies. Schane (1973) suggested that it is not only difficult but perhaps meaningless to compare findings based on feature systems that are relatively abstract (Jakobson, Fant, and Halle, 1952; Chomsky and Halle, 1968) with findings based on feature systems that are relatively concrete (Ladefoged, 1971; Singh, Woods, and Becker, 1972; Irwin and Wong, 1977). Therefore, this discussion deals only with feature acquisition findings obtained in the present study, and comparison of the Irwin-Wong and Chomsky-Halle feature systems is limited to some general points.

The high levels of correct production of feature sets in both the Irwin-Wong and Chomsky-Halle systems reflect the subjects' high levels of accurate sound production in spontaneous speech. The overall mean for correct use of all sets in the Irwin-Wong system was 97 percent; no feature set was produced with less than 94 percent accuracy. The overall mean for correct use of all sets in the Chomsky-Halle system was 98 percent; no feature set was produced with less than 95 percent accuracy. Data on feature set production suggested high performance levels in 2-year-old children; however, specific information regarding an acquisition order or a continuum of difficulty for features was not revealed.

The levels of correct production for feature specifications provided more differentiated information regarding feature use. In the Irwin-Wong system, levels of correct use for feature specifications ranged from 18 to 100 percent. The 11 specifications (of a total of 35 specifications) which occurred with less than 95 percent accuracy may represent aspects of sounds which are difficult to produce, unstable, or perhaps actively emerging in the speech of young children. Those specifications which occurred with greater than 95 percent accuracy seem to have been "acquired," at least in the phonemic contexts presented in the subjects' spontaneous samples.

Levels of correct use of specifications in the Chomsky-Halle feature system ranged from 81 to 100 percent. Only 5 specifications (of a total of 29 specifications) occurred with less than 95 percent accuracy. Generally, the Irwin-Wong feature system seemed to represent more sensitively some aspects of sound production which have not yet been mastered by normal children. As Walsh (1974) proposed, an articulation-based feature system does seem to offer a more complete and detailed description of articulatory production than a linguistically based system.

A comparison of individual subjects with group means for correct feature set use revealed only small differences: no subject varied more than 6 percent from any group mean percentage for Irwin-Wong or Chomsky-Halle feature use. However, in comparing individual subjects with group means for correct use of feature specifications (individual data not included here), much greater variation was noted. For example, the Irwin-Wong feature Place-3 (primary target posture obtained by linguadental contact or approximation) was the feature specification most frequently in error, with a group mean of only 18 percent correct usage. A review of individual data indicated that two children achieved 100 percent correct use and another child achieved 80 percent correct use. In analyzing specification use, then, a group mean percentage may not be typical of individual subject performance.

The data shown in Tables 4.10 and 4.12 describe substitution errors by phoneme, frequency of error, and feature/degree differences from the target sounds. Errors on vowel sounds occurred infrequently and with no apparent patterns across subjects. Errors on consonant sounds were markedly more frequent, and a most frequent substitution was usually indicated for each consonant. For example, eight phonemes accounted for 160 errors which occurred on the /t/ sound, but 145 of those errors were accounted for by d/t substitutions. The /d/ sound was clearly the most frequent substitution for the /t/ phoneme. To a greater or lesser extent, most frequent errors were obvious for all consonant sounds. These substitutions might be viewed as acceptable errors in normal speech production of other 2-year-old children, or might be viewed as a normal but delayed pattern of behavior when observed in older children.

General distinctive feature theory and a limited amount of research of substitution errors (Cairns and Williams, 1972; Menyuk, 1968) suggest that the most frequently observed errors in children's speech are accounted for by a substituted sound which is different from the target sound by one specification. The analyses of most frequent error productions by feature/degree or feature differences from the target sound revealed no consistent pattern in the present data. Findings indicated a wide range of feature/degree or feature differences for the most frequent errors produced by the subjects: from 1/1 to 7/11 in the Irwin-Wong system and from 1 to 8 in the Chomsky-Halle system.

Conclusion

The measurement of "acquisition" in terms of phonemes and distinctive features in this study yielded some new information regarding the use of speech sounds by 21- to 24-month-old children. This investigation also demonstrated a methodology which is substantially more involved than test-type sampling but obviously more appropriate for use with young children. However, the investigator recognizes several important qualifications on the normative data obtained: (1) The mean levels of production reported represent only a small group of 20 children. (2) Generally, reporting of and/or accounting for individual differences from group means was not attempted. (3) Aspects of language clearly related to phoneme production (e.g., production in specific lexical forms) were not examined.

With public laws and public awareness mandating services for preschoolers and even younger children, the process of sound acquisition in normal children requires continued research. A more complete understanding of normal acquisition will enable clinicians to develop more accurate judgments of delayed or deviant behavior as well as to develop more expedient and successful intervention strategies.

5   Development at 3 Years   Patricia Larkins

METHOD

Subjects

Ten white females and 10 white males, 34 to 38 months of age, served as subjects for this study. These children had no known gross intellectual, neurological, or physiological handicapping conditions, and were from middle- to upper-middle-class homes.

Data Collection

Each child was seen in his home environment for one session, which typically lasted from one to one and one-half hours. Observations of subjects took place in an area in which the child customarily played. Except for very infrequent interruptions, each mother was present during the entire session.

Equipment consisted of a Sony cassette tape recorder and a portable microphone. Three sets of items were used as stimulus materials: (1) several of the child's own favorite toys as selected by the mother; (2) a uniform set of toys provided by the examiner; and (3) a set of the child's favorite picture books.

At the beginning of each session, the examiner interacted casually with the child and the mother until the child appeared comfortable in the examiner's presence. Each mother was instructed to encourage the child to interact with a variety of stimulus items during each sampling condition. The examiner gave examples of indirect prompting (e.g., "I wonder what is in the bag"). The importance of allowing the child to "talk on his own" was explained, and the mother was instructed to refrain from asking direct questions or requiring imitated productions.

Language samples consisting of approximately 200 spontaneous utterances were collected for each subject. Siegel's (1974) criteria for designating vocal response units were used in defining the occurrence of an utterance.

Children's utterances were obtained under three conditions: (1) free play with the child's own toys; (2) free play with the standard set of toys provided by the examiner; (3) looking with the mother at the child's favorite picture books. Only the stimulus materials appropriate to each sampling condition were available to the child at any one time. For example, the child's own toys were put away before presentation of the bag which contained the examiner's toys. Approximately 70 utterances were collected during each condition.

Once the actual session had begun, the examiner wrote the adult form and the nonlinguistic context of the child's utterances in English on numbered recording forms. These notations served as supplementary information during later phonetic transcription of the audiotapes.

In order to increase the variety of the sample, the examiner entered on the recording forms only the first occurrence of a repeated utterance; any utterance repeated in its entirety was not entered. Sixty acceptable utterances were drawn from each of the three conditions. Broad phonetic transcriptions of each session, using the IPA, were made from audiotape recording within four days of the home visit.

Reliability

Both inter- and intrajudge reliability were established for (1) accuracy of phonetic transcription, and (2) identification of utterances for analysis. The independent observer was selected on the basis of knowledge of basic phonetics and practical experience in phonetic transcription.

For phonetic transcription, the overall level of agreement between the investigator and the independent observer was 93 percent. The overall level of interjudge agreement for selection of utterances for phonetic analysis was 95 percent. Intrajudge reliability for the investigator was 97 percent for phonetic transcription and 100 percent for utterance selection. Intrajudge reliability for the independent observer was 96 percent for phonetic transcription and 98 percent for utterance selection.

RESULTS

Phoneme Distribution by Individual Sounds

Analyses were made for each individual child as well as for the total group of 20 subjects. A grand total of 37,989 phonemes distributed in 3,600 utterances was entered for phonemic analysis. The mean length of each utterance, expressed in phonemes, was 10.5. The mean number of phonemes per subject was 1,899.

Based on data for all subjects, the phoneme distribution by vowellike and consonant sounds was 40 percent and 60 percent, respectively.

Table 5.1 presents the frequency distribution for both the vowellike and consonant sounds. The frequency for individual vowel sounds ranged from 0 percent to 7 percent, and the frequency for individual consonant sounds ranged from 0 percent to 8 percent. Thus, some phonemes constituted essentially 0 percent of the children's speech, and no phoneme constituted more than 8 percent of the children's speech. The phonemes /ɪ/ and /t/ were the most frequently used vowel and consonant, respectively.

Percentage of Correct Production by Phoneme

Vowellike Sounds

As shown in Table 5.2, the level of correct production of each vowel was essentially 100 percent.

Consonants

Of the 24 different consonants that appeared, all but three occurred with at least 93 percent accuracy. Of these three, /r/ was 89 percent correct; /θ/, 49 percent; and /ð/, 40 percent. Table 5.3 presents the percentage of correct production of each consonant sound.

Text continued on p. 92

TABLE 5.1 Percentage of Occurrence of Individual Vowellike and Consonant Sounds Based on Total Phoneme Sample (N = 37,989)

Phoneme Category	% of Distribution	Phoneme
Vowellike	0	/ɝ, ʒ, ɔɪ, n̩, l̩/
	1	/ɔ, ʊ, ɚ, aʊ/
	2	/e, ɑ, u/
	3	/i, ɛ, æ, ʌ, o, aɪ/
	5	/ə/
	7	/ɪ/
Consonant	0	/ʒ, tʃ, dʒ, θ/
	1	/ʃ, j, f, v, ŋ/
	2	/p, g/
	3	/b, m, h, w, k, z, l/
	4	/d, s, r, ð/
	5	/n/
	8	/t/

TABLE 5.2   Percentage of Correct Production of Individual
Vowellike Sounds Based on Total Occurrence of Each Phoneme

Sounds	Phoneme	% Correct Production	No. of Correct Occurrences/ No. of Total Occurrences
Vowels	/i/	100	996/997
	/e/	100	712/712
	/ɛ/	100	1,184/1,187
	/æ/	100	1,078/1,079
	/ɝ/	100	159/159
	/ɜ/	100	6/6
	/ə/	100	1,818/1,822
	/ʌ/	100	974/975
	/ɑ/	100	643/643
	/ɔ/	100	437/437
	/o/	100	1,173/1,174
	/u/	100	744/744
	/ʊ/	100	293/293
	/ɪ/	99	2,760/2,779
	/ɚ/	99	397/400
Diphthongs	/aɪ/	100	1,126/1,126
	/aʊ/	100	329/329
	/ɔɪ/	100	41/41
Syllabics	/n̩/	100	1/1
	/l̩/	100	175/175
Total		100	15,046/15,079

TABLE 5.3   Percentage of Correct Production
of Individual Consonants Based on Total
Occurrence of Each Phoneme

Phoneme	% Correct Production	No. of Correct Occurrences/ No. of Total Occurrences
/b/	100	975/976
/ʒ/	100	1/1
/m/	100	1,272/1,273
/n/	100	1,993/1,997
/h/	100	1,326/1,327
/w/	100	1,042/1,043
/d/	99	1,418/1,431
/p/	99	760/764
/ʃ/	99	267/269
/j/	99	362/364
/k/	98	1,190/1,211
/t/	98	3,087/3,145
/s/	98	1,456/1,491
/z/	98	1,133/1,160
/f/	97	382/394
/tʃ/	97	59/61
/dʒ/	96	91/95
/ŋ/	96	454/474
/v/	96	276/288
/g/	94	695/736
/l/	93	1,138/1,227
/r/	89	1,328/1,500
/θ/	49	83/171
/ð/	40	600/1,512
Total	93	21,388/22,910

Error Type Distribution

Vowellike Sounds

Table 5.4 presents vowel sounds by error type distribution. Because of the limited number of errors on the vowels, however, no meaningful error type distribution can be reported.

Consonants

Total consonant errors were characterized by a somewhat greater percentage of substitutions (6 percent) than of omissions (1 percent). Table 5.5 presents the consonant sounds by error type distribution.

TABLE 5.4   Error Type Distribution (Percent Omissions and Percent Substitutions) for Each Vowellike Sound

Category	Vowellike Sound	% Omissions	% Substitutions	No. of Errors/ No. of Occurrences
Essentially Equal Distribution Between Error Types	/i/	0	0	1/997
	/e/	0	0	0/712
	/ɛ/	0	0	3/1,187
	/æ/	0	0	1/1,079
	/ɝ/	0	0	0/159
	/ɜ/	0	0	0/6
	/ə/	0	0	4/1,822
	/ʌ/	0	0	1/975
	/ɑ/	0	0	0/643
	/ɔ/	0	0	0/437
	/o/	0	0	1/1,174
	/u/	0	0	0/744
	/ʊ/	0	0	0/293
	/aɪ/	0	0	0/1,126
	/aʊ/	0	0	0/329
	/ɔɪ/	0	0	0/41
	/n̩/	0	0	1/1
	/l̩/	0	0	0/175
Greater Frequency of Omissions	/ɪ/	1	0	19/2,779
Greater Frequency of Substitutions	/ɚ/	0	1	3/400
Total		0	0	33/15,079

Note. The following sounds were not entered: /ɪu/, /m̩/.

TABLE 5.5   Error Type Distribution (Percent Omissions and Percent Substitutions) for Each Consonant

Category	Consonant	% Omissions	% Substitutions	No. of Errors/ No. of Occurrences
Essentially Equal Distribution Between Error Types	/b/	0	0	1/976
	/ʒ/	0	0	0/1
	/m/	0	0	1/1,273
	/n/	0	0	4/1,997
	/h/	0	0	1/1,327
	/w/	0	0	1/1,043
	/j/	0	0	2/364
Greater Frequency of Omissions	/t/	2	0	58/3,145
	/d/	1	0	13/1,431
	/s/	2	0	35/1,491
	/z/	2	0	27/1,160
	/ʃ/	1	0	2/269
	/tʃ/	3	0	2/61
Greater Frequency of Substitutions	/k/	0	2	21/1,211
	/g/	0	5	41/736
	/p/	0	1	4/764
	/f/	0	3	12/394
	/v/	1	3	12/288
	/θ/	4	48	83/171
	/ð/	1	60	912/1,512
	/dʒ/	0	4	4/95
	/ŋ/	0	4	20/474
	/l/	3	5	89/1,227
	/r/	0	11	172/1,500
Total		1	6	1,522/22,910

Note. The following sound was not entered: /ʔ/.

Correct Production of Distinctive Features

Irwin-Wong Distinctive Feature System

The analysis of phonemes by distinctive features yielded a total of 379,890 feature specifications for the Irwin-Wong (1977) feature system. Percentages of correct use were derived not only for the feature sets of the Irwin-Wong system, but also for each of the individual specifications within each set. Each of the specifications within the feature sets appeared with at least 95 percent accuracy except Closure-3 (82 percent) and Place-3 (42 percent). The percentages of correct usage for each feature set and specification are presented in Table 5.6.

Table 5.7 presents each subject's mean percentage of correct usage for each of the 10 feature sets, as well as the group means. No individual subject varied more than 5 percent from any of the group means for any feature set.

Text continued on p. 98

TABLE 5.6 Correct Usage of Irwin-Wong Feature Sets and Feature Specifications by Percent and Number Based on Total Sample

Feature Set	Feature Specification	% Correct	No. of Correct Occurrences/ No. of Total Occurrences
Oronasal	0	—	0/0
	1	100	34,243/34,244
	2	—	0/0
	3	—	0/0
	4	100	3,743/3,745
	Set Mean	100	37,986/37,989
Motion	0	—	0/0
	1	100	1,167/1,167
	2	100	329/329
	3	100	5,453/5,461
	4	96	21,680/22,613
	5	100	8,417/8,419
	Set Mean	98	37,046/37,989
Fusion	0	—	0/0
	1	100	37,833/37,833
	2	97	152/156
	Set Mean	100	37,985/37,989
Lateral	0	—	0/0
	1	96	1,344/1,402
	2	—	0/0
	3	100	36,584/36,587
	Set Mean	100	37,928/37,989
Labial	0	—	0/0
	1	100	3,317/3,333
	2	99	25,297/25,426
	3	100	6,210/6,217
	4	100	3,011/3,013
	Set Mean	100	37,835/37,989

TABLE 5.6 *Continued*

Feature Set	Feature Specification	% Correct	No. of Correct Occurrences/ No. of Total Occurrences
Tenseness	0	—	0/0
	1	100	29,774/29,780
	2	100	8,206/8,209
	Set Mean	100	37,980/37,989
Vertical	0	100	1,327/1,327
	1	100	3,655/3,655
	2	95	16,349/17,277
	3	100	15,669/15,730
	Set Mean	97	37,000/37,989
Place	0	—	0/0
	1	100	4,054/4,056
	2	98	667/682
	3	42	699/1,683
	4	99	18,654/18,881
	5	100	3,169/3,177
	6	99	8,104/8,183
	7	100	1,327/1,327
	Set Mean	97	36,674/37,989
Laryngeal	0	—	0/0
	1	100	7,490/7,506
	2	100	1,327/1,327
	3	100	29,129/29,156
	4	—	0/0
	Set Mean	100	37,946/37,989
Closure	0	—	0/0
	1	100	8,077/8,078
	2	100	12,451/12,461
	3	82	4,354/5,286
	4	98	12,160/12,164
	Set Mean	98	37,042/37,989
Total for All Sets		99	375,422/379,890

TABLE 5.7 Comparison of Individual Subjects with Group Means
by Percentage of Correct Usage of Irwin-Wong Feature Sets

Subject Number	Oronasal	Motion	Fusion	Lateral	Labial
101	100	96	100	100	100
102	100	99	100	100	100
103	100	99	100	100	100
104	100	99	100	100	99
105	100	97	100	100	100
106	100	100	100	100	100
107	100	99	100	100	100
108	100	97	100	100	100
109	100	100	100	100	100
110	100	96	100	100	100
111	100	97	100	100	99
112	100	95	100	99	99
113	100	98	100	100	100
114	100	97	100	100	99
115	100	96	100	100	100
116	100	97	100	100	99
117	100	96	100	100	100
118	100	96	100	100	99
119	100	96	100	100	100
120	100	98	100	100	100
Range of % for Individual	100	95–100	100	99–100	99–100
Group Mean	100	98	100	100	100

Tenseness	Vertical	Place	Laryngeal	Closure	Overall
100	96	96	100	96	98
100	99	99	100	99	100
100	98	98	100	99	99
100	99	99	99	99	100
100	97	96	100	97	99
100	100	100	100	100	100
100	99	99	100	99	100
100	97	96	100	97	99
100	99	99	100	100	100
100	96	95	100	96	98
100	97	96	100	97	98
100	94	93	100	95	98
100	98	97	100	98	99
100	97	96	100	97	99
100	96	95	100	96	98
100	97	95	100	97	99
100	96	93	100	96	98
100	96	94	100	96	98
100	96	94	100	96	98
100	98	97	100	98	99
100	94–100	93–100	99–100	95–100	98–100
100	97	97	100	98	99

Chomsky-Halle Distinctive Feature System

The analysis of phonemes by distinctive features yielded a total of 490,739 feature specifications for the modified Chomsky-Halle (1968) system. Percentages of correct use were derived not only for feature sets in the Chomsky-Halle system, but for each of the individual specifications within that set as well. All of the specifications within the feature sets appeared with at least 98 percent accuracy except Continuant-2 (91 percent). The percentages of correct usage for each feature set and specification are presented in Table 5.8.

Table 5.9 displays each subject's mean percentage of correct usage for each of the 13 feature sets, as well as the group means. No individual subject varied more than 5 percent from any of the group means for any feature set.

Text continued on p. 102

TABLE 5.8 Correct Usage of Modified Chomsky-Halle Feature Sets and Feature Specifications by Percent and Number Based on Total Sample

Feature Set	Feature Specification	% Correct	No. of Correct Occurrences/ No. of Total Occurrences
Vocalic	0	—	0/0
	1	100	20,180/20,184
	2	99	17,580/17,805
	Set Mean	99	37,760/37,989
Consonantal	0	—	0/0
	1	100	17,635/17,637
	2	99	20,130/20,352
	Set Mean	99	37,765/37,989
High	0	—	0/0
	1	99	28,692/28,922
	2	99	8,985/9,067
	Set Mean	99	37,677/37,989
Back	0	—	0/0
	1	99	28,538/28,763
	2	99	9,148/9,226
	Set Mean	99	37,686/37,989
Low	0	—	0/0
	1	100	33,772/33,773
	2	100	4,216/4,216
	Set Mean	100	37,988/37,989
Anterior	0	—	0/0
	1	100	21,903/21,984
	2	100	15,947/16,005
	Set Mean	100	37,850/37,989
Coronal	0	—	0/0
	1	100	23,111/23,194
	2	98	14,497/14,795
	Set Mean	99	37,608/37,989

TABLE 5.8 *Continued*

Feature Set	Feature Specification	% Correct	No. of Correct Occurrences/ No. of Total Occurrences
Round	0	99	21,457/21,679
	1	100	11,490/11,494
	2	100	4,814/4,816
	Set Mean	99	37,761/37,989
Tense	0	99	21,457/21,679
	1	100	11,017/11,022
	2	100	5,287/5,288
	Set Mean	99	37,761/37,989
Voice	0	—	0/0
	1	100	8,817/8,833
	2	100	29,129/29,156
	Set Mean	100	37,946/37,989
Continuant	0	—	0/0
	1	100	27,064/27,067
	2	91	9,992/10,922
	Set Mean	98	37,056/37,989
Nasal	0	—	0/0
	1	100	34,243/34,244
	2	100	3,743/3,745
	Set Mean	100	37,986/37,989
Strident	0	—	0/0
	1	100	34,156/34,230
	2	99	3,739/3,759
	Set Mean	100	37,895/37,989
Total for All Sets		99	490,739/493,857

TABLE 5.9 Comparison of Individual Subjects with Group Means by Percentage of Correct Usage of Modified Chomsky-Halle Feature Sets

Subject Number	Vocalic	Consonantal	High	Back	Low	Anterior	Coronal
1	100	100	100	100	100	100	100
2	100	100	100	100	100	100	100
3	100	100	100	100	100	100	99
4	100	100	99	99	100	100	99
5	100	100	99	100	100	100	99
6	100	100	100	100	100	100	100
7	100	100	99	100	100	100	99
8	99	99	99	99	100	100	99
9	100	100	100	100	100	100	100
10	99	99	99	99	100	100	99
11	100	100	100	100	100	100	99
12	98	98	98	98	100	99	98
13	99	99	99	99	100	100	99
14	99	99	99	99	100	100	99
15	99	99	99	99	100	100	99
16	99	99	99	99	100	100	98
17	98	99	97	97	100	98	97
18	99	99	98	99	100	99	98
19	99	99	99	99	100	100	99
20	99	99	99	99	100	100	99
Range of % for Individual	98–100	98–100	97–100	97–100	100	98–100	97–100
Group Mean	99	99	99	99	100	100	99

Round	Tense	Voice	Continuant	Nasal	Strident	Overall
100	100	100	96	100	100	100
100	100	99	100	100	100	100
100	100	100	99	100	100	100
100	100	99	100	100	100	100
100	100	100	97	100	100	99
100	100	100	100	100	100	100
100	100	100	99	100	100	100
99	99	100	97	100	100	99
100	100	100	100	100	100	100
99	99	100	96	100	100	100
100	100	100	97	100	99	99
98	98	100	95	100	100	99
99	99	100	98	100	100	99
99	99	100	97	100	100	99
99	99	100	96	100	100	99
99	99	100	97	100	100	99
98	98	100	96	100	100	98
99	99	100	96	100	100	99
99	99	100	96	100	100	99
99	99	100	98	100	100	99
98–100	98–100	99–100	95–100	100	99–100	98–100
99	99	100	98	100	100	99

Replacement Characteristics

Irwin-Wong Distinctive Feature System

For each error made on any vowel or consonant sound, the replacement sound, the frequency of replacement, and the feature/degree difference of the replacement sound were tabulated. Table 5.10 displays these results. In only one case was a vowel replaced by more than one sound; for consonants, on the other hand, the number of replacements ranged up to five.

The mean feature and mean degree differences between target sounds and replacement (error) sounds are presented in Table 5.11. Both mean feature difference and mean degree difference are calculated for each phoneme on the basis of number of errors and of total occurrences. For vowel sounds, the mean feature difference based on error occurrences was highest for /o/ and /ə/ (4.00). For frequently missed consonants, the mean feature difference per error was greatest on /f/ and /l/ (4.92 and 4.09, respectively). The mean number of feature/degree differences between error and target sounds was markedly higher for consonants, indicating that consonant replacements tend to differ more from the target sound than do vowel replacements.

TABLE 5.10 Error Productions by Replacement, Frequency of Replacement, and Feature/Degree Differences of Replacement as Specified in Irwin-Wong System

Phonetic Classification	Phoneme in Error	Replacement 1	Replacement 2	Replacement 3	Replacement 4	Replacement 5
Vowel	/ɪ/	/n/:1–2/5[a]				
	/ɛ/	/ɪ/:3–1/1				
	/æ/	/aɪ/:1–3/6				
	/ɚ/	/ɪ/:2–3/3	/o/:1–2/2			
	/ə/	/i/:1–4/4				
	/ʌ/	/ə/:1–1/1				
	/o/	/ɑ/:1–4/4				
Consonant	/k/	/t/:17–1/2	/d/:1–2/4	/w/:1–6/13		
	/g/	/d/:40–1/2				
	/t/	/k/:2–1/2	/d/:2–1/2	/s/:1–5/5		
	/p/	/d/:2–4/8	/b/:2–1/2			
	/f/	/p/:7–4/6	/l/:3–7/10	/w/:2–5/7		
	/v/	/b/:3–4/6	/f/:6–1/2			
	/θ/	/k/:1–4/6	/t/:20–4/4	/d/:2–5/6	/f/:58–2/2	/w/:1–5/7
	/ð/	/t/:4–5/6	/d/:888–4/4	/f/:10–3/4	/θ/:2–1/2	
	/s/	/t/:1–5/5				
	/dʒ/	/d/:4–3/3				
	/n/	/ʃ/:1–7/10	/m/:2–3/6			
	/ŋ/	/ə/:1–4/8	/n/:18–1/2			
	/l/	/d/:4–3/6	/f/:3–7/10	/w/:51–4/7		
	/r/	/w/:166–1/3				
	/j/	/ʃ/:1–6/7				

[a]That is, the replacement /n/, which occurred once, is removed from /ɪ/ by a feature/degree difference of 2/5.

TABLE 5.11 Mean Feature/Degree Difference Values by Phoneme as Specified in Irwin-Wong System

Phonetic Classification	Phoneme in Error	Number of Errors	Number of Occurrences	$\bar{X}$ Feature Difference Based on Errors	$\bar{X}$ Feature Difference Based on Occurrences	$\bar{X}$ Degree Difference Based on Errors	$\bar{X}$ Degree Difference Based on Occurrences
Vowel	/ɪ/	1	2,779	2.00	.00	5.00	.00
	/ɛ/	3	1,187	1.00	.00	1.00	.00
	/æ/	1	1,079	3.00	.00	6.00	.01
	/ɚ/	3	400	2.67	.02	2.67	.02
	/ə/	1	1,822	4.00	.00	4.00	.00
	/ʌ/	1	975	1.00	.00	1.00	.00
	/o/	1	1,174	4.00	.00	4.00	.00
Consonant	/k/	19	1,211	1.32	.02	2.68	.04
	/g/	40	736	1.00	.05	2.00	.11
	/t/	5	3,145	1.80	.00	2.60	.00
	/p/	4	764	2.50	.01	5.00	.03
	/f/	12	394	4.92	.15	7.17	.22
	/v/	9	288	2.00	.06	3.33	.10
	/θ/	82	171	2.62	1.26	2.70	1.29
	/ð/	904	1,512	3.99	2.38	4.00	2.39
	/s/	2	1,491	3.50	.00	4.00	.01
	/dʒ/	4	95	3.00	.13	3.00	.13
	/n/	3	1,997	4.33	.01	7.33	.01
	/ŋ/	19	474	1.16	.05	2.32	.09
	/l/	58	1,227	4.09	.19	7.09	.33
	/r/	166	1,500	1.00	.11	3.00	.33
	/j/	1	364	6.00	.02	7.00	.02
Total		1,339	24,785	3.34	.18	3.85	.21

Chomsky-Halle Distinctive Feature System

Table 5.12 presents the errors made on vowel and consonant sounds by replacement sound, frequency of replacement, and feature/degree difference of the relevant replacement sound. The mean number of feature differences between target sounds and error sounds for vowels and consonants is presented in Table 5.13.

TABLE 5.12   Error Productions by Replacement, Frequency of Replacement, and Feature Differences of Replacement as Specified in Modified Chomsky-Halle System

Phonetic Classification	Phoneme in Error	Replacement 1	Replacement 2	Replacement 3	Replacement 4	Replacement 5
Vowel	/ɪ/	/n/:1–8[a]				
	/ɛ/	/ɪ/:3–1				
	/æ/	/aɪ/:1–2				
	/ɚ/	/ɪ/:2–2	/o/:1–4			
	/ə/	/i/:1–3				
	/ʌ/	/ə/:1–2				
	/o/	/ɑ/:1–3				
Consonant	/k/	/t/:17–4	/d/:1–5	/w/:1–5		
	/g/	/d/:40–4				
	/t/	/k/:2–4	/d/:2–1	/s/:1–2		
	/p/	/d/:2–2	/b/:2–1			
	/f/	/p/:7–2	/l/:3–4	/w/:2–8		
	/v/	/b/:3–2	/f/:6–1			
	/θ/	/k/:1–5	/t/:20–1	/d/:2–2	/f/:58–2	/w/:1–8
	/ð/	/t/:4–2	/d/:888–1	/f/:10–3	/θ/:2–1	
	/s/	/t/:1–2	/f/:1–1			
	/dʒ/	/d/:4–3				
	/n/	/ʃ/:1–6	/m/:2–1			
	/ŋ/	/ə/:1–7	/n/:18–4			
	/l/	/d/:4–2	/f/:3–4	/w/:51–8		
	/r/	/w/:166–7				
	/j/	/ʃ/:1–6				

[a]That is, the replacement /n/, which occurred once, is removed from /ɪ/ by a feature difference of 8.

DISCUSSION

The results of this study strongly suggest that children may be producing many more sounds, with higher levels of correctness, at much younger ages than previously reported. The level of correct production of vowels was 100 percent, and 22 of 24 consonants were produced with at least 93 percent accuracy. Consonant errors were characterized primarily by substitution. Finally, a high percentage of accuracy was obtained for the distinctive feature sets in both the Irwin-Wong and the modified Chomsky-Halle systems. These high levels of phonological development may simply reflect a biased sample, but present data do not permit an adequate test of this possibility.

TABLE 5.13 Mean Feature Difference Values as Specified in Modified Chomsky-Halle System

Phonetic Classification	Phoneme in Error	Number of Errors	Number of Occurrences	$\bar{X}$ Feature Difference Based on Errors	$\bar{X}$ Feature Difference Based on Occurrences
Vowel	/ɪ/	1	2,779	8.00	.00
	/ɛ/	3	1,187	1.00	.00
	/æ/	1	1,079	2.00	.00
	/ɝ/	3	400	2.67	.02
	/ə/	1	1,822	3.00	.00
	/ʌ/	1	975	2.00	.00
	/o/	1	1,174	3.00	.00
Consonant	/k/	19	1,211	4.11	.06
	/g/	40	736	4.00	.22
	/t/	5	3,145	2.40	.00
	/p/	4	764	1.50	.01
	/f/	12	394	3.50	.11
	/v/	9	288	1.33	.04
	/θ/	82	171	1.87	.89
	/ð/	904	1,512	1.03	.61
	/s/	2	1,491	1.50	.00
	/dʒ/	4	95	3.00	.13
	/n/	3	1,997	2.67	.00
	/ŋ/	19	474	4.16	.17
	/l/	58	1,227	7.38	.35
	/r/	166	1,500	7.00	.77
	/j/	1	364	6.00	.02
Total		1,339	24,785	2.33	.13

6   Development at 4 Years   Cynthia Bassi

METHOD

Subjects

Number

Twenty subjects were selected for the present study. At the time of testing, all subjects resided in the eastern section of Memphis, Tennessee.

Criteria

Ten white females and 10 white males ranging in age from 3 years 10 months to 4 years 2 months were selected as subjects for this study. Subjects were required to satisfy two preliminary criteria: (1) parental statement that there were no known physical anomalies or history of developmental deficits; and (2) no previous history of speech therapy.

The subjects satisfied three test criteria. First, no oral-facial structural anomalies existed. The size, shape, and mobility of the face, lips, teeth, palate, uvula, tonsils, pharynx, and tongue were examined. Only children found to be within gross normal limits were retained.

Second, the children were required to demonstrate hearing of at least 20 dB at 500, 1,000, 2,000, 4,000 and 6,000 Hz in at least one ear to establish the potential for acquiring normal speech and language. Hearing was screened by air conduction in a room free from outside noises on a Beltone Model No. 10 audiometer which was calibrated monthly.

Third, to insure adequate language development and intellectual skills, the cognitive portion of the Revised Lexington Developmental Scales for preschool children was administered to each child immediately prior to the spontaneous sampling. The Revised Lexington Screening Scale, Cognitive

Area, was administered according to the manual. A minimal cognitive age of 3 years 4 months, as measured by the scale, was required for inclusion in the study.

Data Collection

Setting

The subjects were seen in an environment familar to the child, either in the home or school, for one session lasting approximately 40 minutes.

Participants

The parent was present during the various screening procedures, but was asked to leave the room following completion of the screening tasks. The examiner and child were alone during the data collection period.

Equipment

Equipment consisted of a Panasonic casette recorder (Model No. RQ-22AS) with the stationary microphone positioned three to six feet from the child. Memorex MRX_2 Oxide tapes were utilized. Tape speed was 3.75 inches per second. At the initiation of each session, the volume was adjusted to record at zero dB peak volume for each child's speech.

Modes of Stimulation

The child was encouraged to converse with the examiner. If necessary, open-ended questions were utilized to begin a topic. The examiner played the role of a neutral participant by responding with nonjudgmental, paraphrasing remarks, such as "You had a birthday yesterday." The free speech session generally lasted from 20 to 30 minutes.

Corpus

A spontaneous corpus of at least 60 acceptable utterances was obtained from each subject. The first 10 acceptable utterances were excluded; these utterances were treated as a rapport-building period (Dale, 1976). Additional utterances excluded were: (1) False starts—a simple repetition or slightly altered rephrasing, such as "I'm driving [omitted]—I'm driving to town [included]"; (2) Repetitions not functioning as false starts, such as "My sister has one [included]—has one [omitted]"; (3) Starters—stereotypic fillers that carry little meaning, such as "Uh," "Oh," "Let's see" [all omitted]; (4) Unintelligible units not understood by the examiner; and (5) Nonlinguistic sound-making; for example, "My car goes" would be included, but "varooom" would be omitted (Barrie-Blackley, Musselwhite, and Rogister, 1978). Fifty acceptable utterances from each subject were entered for analysis.

Recording

Four steps were taken in preparing data. First, each acceptable utterance was written in adult English. Second, broad IPA transcriptions were made of the adult English. Each IPA phoneme was then coded by number for entry into the computer. (The word "cat," for example, was transcribed phonemically as /kæt/, then numerically as 41, 5, 43.) Third, the differences between the conventional adult English code and the child's production were coded numerically and treated as errors. Lastly, all /s/ and /z/ phonemes were coded for their morphological significance. For example, a child's statement "I saw two cat" would be coded as:

adult English	I	saw	two	cats
numerical code of IPA	21	5112	4314	41054351
error code				90
/s/, /z/ code		09		01

Reliability

Inter- and intrajudge reliability established agreement between the investigator and an independent observer for (1) utterance selection, and (2) phonetic transcription. Criteria for selection of the independent observer included knowledge of and experience with phonetic transcription using IPA. Intrajudge reliability for utterance selection and phonetic transcription was established by listening to each audiotape a second time, two weeks following the initial listening for interjudge reliability purposes.

A representative sample of each child's utterances was used in computing reliability. To insure an understanding of the procedures, an audiotape from a child not in the study was used to familiarize the independent observer with the criteria used for selecting utterances and marking transcripts for analysis.

Utterance Selection

In order to establish interjudge reliability, the independent observer was instructed to select 10 utterances from each subject's audiotape according to the examiner's criteria for admission into the corpus, beginning at a randomly chosen point between the tenth and fortieth utterances. Point by point interjudge agreement was obtained for utterance selection of each subject's audiotape by comparing the examiner's transcript with that of the independent observer. Utterances were selected for admission to the analysis according to the examiner's transcript. Interjudge reliability was 97.3 percent for utterance selection.

In order to establish intrajudge reliability, ten utterances were selected from each audiotape for admission into the corpus by starting at the point chosen during the first listening. A comparison of the first utterances selected with the second utterances yielded a percentage of agreement for each subject's corpus. Intrajudge reliability was 99.7 percent for the examiner and 96.8 percent for the independent observer.

Phonetic Transcription

Interjudge reliability was established through the following procedure. Following utterance selection, the independent observer was instructed to transcribe in broad IPA the first five utterances of each audiotape which both the independent observer and examiner agreed upon for admission into the corpus. Point by point (phoneme by phoneme) percentage of agreement was obtained for each subject's audiotape by comparing the independent observer's transcription with the investigator's original transcription. Interjudge reliability was 94.0 percent for phonetic transcription.

All utterances transcribed during interjudge reliability procedures (five utterances per child) were noted and transcribed a second time in order to establish intrajudge reliability. A comparison of the first and second transcriptions of both the examiner and observer respectively yielded a point by point percentage of agreement for each subject's corpus. Intrajudge reliability was 97.9 percent for the examiner and 92.5 percent for the independent observer.

RESULTS

Phoneme Distribution by Individual Sounds

A total of 16,199 phonemes was entered for phonemic analysis. This represents a mean of 809.95 phonemes per child and a mean length of 16.20 phonemes per utterance.

Based on data obtained from all subjects, the percentage of vowellike sounds (including syllabics and diphthongs) in the phoneme distribution was 39 percent (N = 6,337) and that of consonants was 61 percent (N = 9,862). No child's vowel/consonant distribution differed from the mean by more than ±2 percent.

Based on the total of 16,199 phonemes, the range of frequency distributions for individual vowel sounds was from 0 percent to 6 percent of the total sample. The frequency distribution for individual consonant sounds was from 0 percent to 9 percent of the sample. Vowel sounds that constituted at least 3 percent of the total phoneme count were /i/, /o/, /u/, /aɪ/, /æ/, /ɪ/, and /ʌ/. Consonant sounds that constituted at least three percent of the total phonemes produced were /k/, /t/, /d/, /ð/, /s/, /z/, /m/, /n/, /l/, /r/, /h/, and /w/. A summary of the frequency of occurrence of the individual vowels and consonants is shown in Table 6.1.

TABLE 6.1 Percentage of Occurrence of Individual Vowellike and Consonant Phonemes Based on Total Phoneme Sample (N = 16,199)

Phoneme Category	% of Distribution	Phoneme
Vowellike	0	/ʒ, ʊ, ɔɪ, ɪu, n̩, l̩, m̩/
	1	/ɝ, ɚ, ə, ɔ, aʊ/
	2	/e, ɛ, ə/
	3	/o, u, aɪ/
	4	/i, æ/
	5	/ɪ/
	6	/ʌ/
Consonant	0	/ʒ, tʃ, dʒ, ʔ/
	1	/f, v, θ, ʃ, ŋ, j/
	2	/g, p, b/
	3	/k, ð, m, l, r, h, w, z/
	4	/s/
	5	/d/
	7	/n/
	9	/t/

Percent of Correct Production by Phoneme

Vowellike Sounds

The mean level of correct production of vowellike sounds, based on the total sample obtained from 20 subjects, was 96 percent (6,114 of 6,337). Correct production for individual children ranged from 67 percent to 100 percent.

Based on the total sample, only 4 of the 21 vowellike sounds occurred with less than 92 percent accuracy: /ɚ, ə, u, and ɪu/. Two sounds (/ʊ, ɝ/) occurred with 100 percent accuracy. Of the 7 vowellike sounds that made up 3 percent or more of the total phoneme sample, six phonemes (/æ, ʌ, aɪ, i, o, ɪ/) occurred with at least 96 percent accuracy; one phoneme of the group (/u/) occurred with 87 percent accuracy.

Table 6.2 is a summary of the percentage of accuracy of each vowellike sound based on data obtained from the total group.

TABLE 6.2   Percentage of Correct Production of Individual Vowellike Sounds Based on Total Occurrence of Each Phoneme

Sounds	Phoneme	% Correct Production	No. of Correct Occurrences/ No. of Total Occurrences
Vowels	/ʊ/	100	49/49
	/ɝ/	100	1/1
	/æ/	99	653/660
	/ʌ/	99	926/935
	/ɛ/	98	310/316
	/ɑ/	98	336/344
	/ɔ/	98	160/163
	/i/	97	634/653
	/e/	97	348/357
	/o/	97	482/496
	/ɪ/	96	769/804
	/ɝ/	92	99/108
	/ɚ/	87	127/146
	/u/	87	364/420
	/ə/	84	79/84
Diphthongs	/aɪ/	99	552/560
	/aʊ/	99	154/155
	/ɔɪ/	96	27/28
	/ɪu/	67	2/3
Syllabics	/l̩/	93	42/45
	/m̩/	0	0/0
	/n̩/	0	0/0
Total		96	6,114/6,337

Consonants

The mean percentage of correct production of consonants, based on the total sample obtained from 20 subjects, was 88 percent (8,702 of 9,862). The range of correct production for individual children was from 46 percent to 99 percent. Of the 23 consonant phonemes analyzed, 11 occurred with at least 95 percent accuracy: /k, g, p, b, f, ʃ, m, n, h, w, j/. Nine consonants (/r, l, z, s, θ, dʒ, tʃ, t, v/) ranged from 74 percent to 89 percent accuracy, while the remaining three consonants (/d, ð, ŋ/) were produced with less than 70 percent accuracy. Of the 11 consonant sounds that made up at least 3 percent of the total phoneme sample, 10 phonemes (/k, m, l, h, w, s, r, n, t, z/) were produced with at least 80 percent accuracy. Of this group, /d/ and /ð/ were produced with 68 percent and 64 percent accuracy, respectively.

Table 6.3 is a summary of the percentage of accuracy for each consonant sound based on data obtained from the whole group.

TABLE 6.3   Percentage of Correct Production of Individual Consonants Based on Total Occurrence of Each Phoneme

Phoneme	% Correct Production	No. of Correct Occurrences/ No. of Total Occurrences
/g/	99	350/353
/f/	99	148/150
/m/	99	538/544
/w/	99	501/505
/p/	98	245/249
/n/	98	1,180/1,210
/k/	97	458/471
/h/	97	442/456
/b/	95	325/343
/ʃ/	95	97/103
/j/	95	116/122
/t/	89	1,269/1,423
/z/	89	403/455
/s/	87	571/660
/l/	85	451/530
/θ/	81	79/98
/r/	81	387/478
/v/	76	134/176
/dʒ/	75	50/67
/tʃ/	74	29/39
/d/	68	569/833
/ð/	64	297/462
/ŋ/	46	63/136
Total	88	8,702/9,862

Error Type Distribution

Vowellike Sounds

With the exception of four vowellike sounds (/ɚ, u, ə, ɪu/), all vowellike sounds were produced with at least 96 percent accuracy. Among the less accurately produced vowels, only /u/ constituted at least 3 percent of the total vowel sample. Total vowellike errors were characterized by twice as many substitutions (2 percent, N = 148) as omissions (1 percent, N = 75).

Generally, the errors on individual phonemes were equally distributed between omission and substitution types. The error distributions for the four vowel phonemes which occurred with less than 96 percent accuracy, however, were characterized by an imbalance of substitution and omission errors: /ə/ (13 percent omission, 3 percent substitution); /u/ (1 percent omission, 12 percent substitution); /ɚ/ (1 percent omission, 12 percent substitution); and /ɪu/ (0 percent omission, 33 percent substitution). Table 6.4 summarizes error type distributions for vowellike sounds.

Consonants

The distribution of error type (either substitution or omission) was generally similar for the consonant group. Based on all consonant phonemes, omis-

---

TABLE 6.4   Error Type Distribution (Percent Omissions and Percent Substitutions) for Each Vowellike Sound

Category	Vowellike Sound	% Omissions	% Substitutions	No. of Errors/ No. of Occurrences
Essentially Equal Distribution Between Error Types	/i/	1	2	9/653
	/ɪ/	4	1	35/804
	/e/	1	2	9/357
	/ɛ/	1	1	6/316
	/æ/	0	1	7/660
	/ɝ/	0	8	9/108
	/ʌ/	1	0	9/935
	/ɑ/	0	2	8/344
	/ɔ/	0	2	3/163
	/o/	1	2	14/496
	/aɪ/	0	1	8/560
	/au/	1	0	1/155
	/ɔɪ/	0	4	1/28
	/ʎ/	0	7	3/45
Greater Frequency of Omissions	/ə/	13	3	15/94
Greater Frequency of Substitutions	/ɚ/	1	12	9/146
	/u/	1	12	56/420
	/ɪu/	0	33	1/3
Total		1	2	223/6,337

Note. The following sounds were not entered: /ɜ/, /n̩/, /m̩/.

sions constituted 7 percent of all occurrences while substitutions made up 5 percent of all occurrences. But for the phonemes /ð/, /tʃ/, dʒ/, /ŋ/ and /r/, substitution errors were more common; for /t/, /d/, and /v/, omission errors were more frequent. Table 6.5 summarizes error type distributions for the consonants.

Correct Production of Distinctive Features

Irwin-Wong Distinctive Feature System

The analysis of phonemes by the Irwin and Wong (1977) feature system yielded a total of 161,990 different feature specifications. A mean of 8,099.5 specifications was analyzed for each child. Each of the 10 feature sets included in the articulatory based feature system by Irwin-Wong (1977) was produced with at least 97 percent accuracy, based on the total group. Rank order of percentage of accuracy was: Oronasal, Fusion, Lateral, Laryngeal (100 percent); Tenseness (99 percent); Motion, Labial, Vertical Closure (98 percent); and Place (97 percent).

TABLE 6.5 Error Type Distribution (Percent Omissions and Percent Substitutions) for Each Consonant

Category	Consonant	% Omissions	% Substi-tutions	No. of Errors/ No. of Occurrences
Essentially Equal Distri-bution Between Error Types	/k/	2	1	3/471
	/g/	1	0	3/353
	/p/	1	0	4/249
	/b/	5	1	18/343
	/f/	1	0	2/150
	/θ/	10	9	19/98
	/s/	4	8	89/660
	/z/	5	6	52/455
	/ʃ/	1	4	5/102
	/m/	1	0	6/544
	/n/	2	0	30/1,210
	/l/	6	8	79/530
	/h/	3	0	14/456
	/w/	0	0	4/504
	/j/	0	5	6/122
Greater Frequency of Omissions	/t/	10	0	154/1,423
	/d/	31	1	264/833
	/v/	19	5	42/176
Greater Frequency of Substitutions	/ð/	5	31	165/462
	/tʃ/	0	26	10/39
	/dʒ/	0	25	17/67
	/ŋ/	4	50	73/136
	/r/	4	15	91/478
Total		7	5	1,160/9,862

Percentages of correct use were also obtained for each specification within the 10 Irwin-Wong sets. Only six specifications occurred with less than 95 percent accuracy. They are ranked from high to low as follows:

Place-5	94%
Labial-1	94%
Labial-3	94%
Closure-3	93%
Fusion-2	75%
Place-3	74%

The percentage of accuracy for each of the Irwin-Wong features and specifications, based on group means, is presented in Table 6.6.

Examination of each subject's percentage of correct use for each of the less accurate (less than 95 percent) feature specifications reveals a wide range of individual accuracy. For example, while overall percentage of accuracy for the Irwin-Wong feature Lateral was 92 percent, individual subjects' accuracy ranged from 54 percent to 100 percent on this feature.

No individual subject varied in overall feature set production by more than 6 percent from the group mean in spite of wide variance in the accuracy of the feature specifications. Those feature sets with the greatest deviation from individual means (7 percent) were Labial, Tenseness, and Place. Table 6.7 provides a comparison of individual subject data with the group means for the 10 Irwin-Wong feature sets.

Text continued on p. 120

TABLE 6.6 Correct Usage of Irwin-Wong Feature Sets and Feature Specifications by Percent and Number Based on Total Sample

Feature Set	Feature Specification	% Correct	No. of Correct Occurrences/ No. of Total Occurrences
Oronasal	0	—	0/0
	1	100	14,301/14,309
	2	—	0/0
	3	—	0/0
	4	100	1,888/1,890
	Set Mean	100	16,189/16,199
Motion	0	—	0/0
	1	99	580/588
	2	99	157/158
	3	97	2,030/2,091
	4	98	9,427/9,584
	5	99	3,756/3,778
	Set Mean	98	15,950/16,199
Fusion	0	—	0/0
	1	100	16,085/16,093
	2	75	79/106
	Set Mean	100	16,164/16,199

TABLE 6.6 *Continued*

Feature Set	Feature Specification	% Correct	No. of Correct Occurrences/ No. of Total Occurrences
Lateral	0	—	0/0
	1	92	527/575
	2	—	0/0
	3	100	15,613/15,624
	Set Mean	100	16,140/16,199
Labial	0	—	0/0
	1	94	1,355/1,441
	2	99	10,961/11,018
	3	94	2,459/2,604
	4	100	1,132/1,136
	Set Mean	98	15,907/16,199
Tenseness	0	—	0/0
	1	100	12,175/12,201
	2	96	3,836/3,998
	Set Mean	99	16,011/16,199
Vertical	0	100	456/456
	1	99	1,894/1,910
	2	98	6,509/6,675
	3	98	7,034/7,158
	Set Mean	98	15,893/16,199
Place	0	—	0/0
	1	100	1,636/1,641
	2	98	321/326
	3	74	413/560
	4	97	8,206/8,424
	5	94	641/679
	6	98	4,033/4,113
	7	100	456/456
	Set Mean	97	15,706/16,199
Laryngeal	0	—	0/0
	1	99	3,169/3,192
	2	100	456/456
	3	100	12,514/12,551
	4	—	0/0
	Set Mean	100	16,139/16,199
Closure	0	—	0/0
	1	100	3,436/3,445
	2	97	4,830/4,983
	3	93	1,949/2,103
	4	100	5,648/5,668
	Set Mean	98	15,863/16,199
Total for All Sets		99	159,962/161,990

TABLE 6.7 Comparison of Individual Subjects with Group Means by Percentage of Correct Usage of Irwin-Wong Feature Sets

Subject Number	Oronasal	Motion	Fusion	Lateral	Labial
401	100	100	100	100	100
402	100	99	100	99	99
403	100	99	100	100	99
404	100	99	100	100	99
405	100	100	100	100	99
406	100	96	100	99	96
407	100	99	100	100	100
408	100	99	100	100	99
409	100	99	100	100	99
410	100	97	100	100	99
411	100	98	99	100	99
412	100	99	100	100	99
413	100	98	100	98	97
414	100	96	100	99	95
415	100	99	100	100	93
416	100	96	100	99	98
417	100	97	99	99	99
418	100	100	100	100	99
419	100	98	99	100	98
420	100	100	100	100	99
Range of % for Individual	100	96–100	99–100	98–100	93–100
Group Mean	100	98	100	100	98

[a]Range greater than 7 percent.

Tenseness	Vertical	Place	Laryngeal	Closure	Overall
100	100	99	100	100	100
100	98	98	99	99	99
99	99	99	100	99	99
99	98	98	100	98	99
100	100	99	100	100	100
100	98	95	100	95	98
100	99	98	100	99	99
99	98	98	100	98	99
100	100	99	100	99	100
100	97	96	100	97	99
99	98	97	100	100	99
99	98	98	100	99	99
99	96	95	99	98	98
96	95	92	99	95	97
93	97	92	98	97	97
99	96	94	100	95	98
99	98	98	99	98	99
99	99	99	100	99	99
98	97	96	100	97	98
99	99	99	100	99	100
93–100[a]	95–100	92–99[a]	98–100	95–100	97–100
99	98	97	100	98	99

Chomsky-Halle Distinctive Feature System

The analysis using the Chomsky-Halle (1968) features yielded 210,587 different features for a mean of 10,529 feature specifications per child. Based on group mean data, each of the 13 feature sets was achieved with at least 98 percent accuracy.

Rank order of percentage of accuracy from greatest to least accuracy was Vocalic, Low, Voice, Nasal (100 percent); Tense, Consonantal, Back, Anterior, Coronal, Continuant, Round, Strident (99 percent); and High (98 percent). The lowest percentage of accuracy for a single specification (9 percent) was found in the feature Tense. The percentage of accuracy for each feature and specification, based on group means, is presented in Table 6.8.

Individual means for the Chomsky-Halle features revealed that no subject varied over 5 percent from the group mean for any feature set. The features displaying the greatest variability for individual means were Coronal, Round, Continuant, and Strident. Table 6.9 provides a comparison of individual subject data for the 13 Chomsky-Halle features.

Replacement Characteristics

Irwin-Wong Distinctive Feature System

An analysis of all phonemes and their replacement phonemes and feature/degree differences is summarized in Table 6.10.

While most phonemes have several different replacements, usually one replacement occurred most frequently. For example, /ð/ was replaced by /d/ most frequently, with a feature/degree difference of 4/4. That is, phonemes /ð/ and /d/ differ on four features: Motion, Vertical, Place, and Closure. Each

Text continued on p. 126

TABLE 6.8 Correct Usage of Modified Chomsky-Halle Feature Sets and Feature Specifications by Percent and Number Based on Total Sample

Feature Set	Feature Specification	% Correct	No. of Correct Occurrences/ No. of Total Occurrences
Vocalic	0	—	0/0
	1	100	8,837/8,854
	2	99	7,286/7,345
	Set Mean	100	16,123/16,199
Consonantal	0	—	0/0
	1	100	7,364/7,375
	2	99	8,699/8,824
	Set Mean	99	16,063/16,199
High	0	—	0/0
	1	99	12,394/12,475
	2	96	3,562/3,724
	Set Mean	98	15,956/16,199

TABLE 6.8 *Continued*

Feature Set	Feature Specification	% Correct	No. of Correct Occurrences/ No. of Total Occurrences
Back	0	—	0/0
	1	99	11,478/11,581
	2	98	4,536/4,618
	Set Mean	99	16,014/16,199
Low	0	—	0/0
	1	100	14,141/14,151
	2	99	2,034/2,048
	Set Mean	100	16,175/16,199
Anterior	0	—	0/0
	1	99	8,920/9,021
	2	99	7,114/7,178
	Set Mean	99	16,034/16,199
Coronal	0	—	0/0
	1	99	9,456/9,543
	2	98	6,509/6,656
	Set Mean	99	15,965/16,199
Round	0	99	9,158/9,280
	1	99	5,539/5,580
	2	99	1,322/1,339
	Set Mean	99	16,019/16,199
Tense	0	99	9,158/9,280
	1	100	4,121/4,138
	2	97	2,698/2,781
	Set Mean	99	15,977/16,199
Voice	0	—	0/0
	1	99	3,627/3,648
	2	100	12,514/12,551
	Set Mean	100	16,141/16,199
Continuant	0	—	0/0
	1	100	11,940/11,960
	2	95	4,029/4,239
	Set Mean	99	15,969/16,199
Nasal	0	—	0/0
	1	100	14,301/14,309
	2	100	1,888/1,890
	Set Mean	100	16,189/16,199
Strident	0	—	0/0
	1	100	14,535/14,550
	2	94	1,542/1,649
	Set Mean	99	16,077/16,199
Total for All Sets		99	208,702/210,587

TABLE 6.9 Comparison of Individual Subjects with Group Means by Percentage of Correct Usage of Modified Chomsky-Halle Feature Sets

Subject Number	Vocalic	Consonantal	High	Back	Low	Anterior	Coronal
1	100	100	99	100	100	100	99
2	99	99	98	99	100	99	99
3	100	100	99	99	100	99	99
4	100	100	99	100	100	100	100
5	100	100	99	100	100	99	100
6	99	97	99	98	100	99	95
7	100	100	99	99	100	99	99
8	100	100	99	99	100	100	100
9	100	99	99	99	100	100	99
10	100	100	99	99	100	99	99
11	100	100	99	99	100	99	99
12	100	100	99	99	100	100	100
13	98	97	96	97	100	97	97
14	99	99	97	98	100	98	99
15	100	100	97	98	100	98	99
16	99	97	98	98	100	99	96
17	100	97	100	99	99	99	98
18	100	100	99	99	100	99	99
19	99	99	97	98	100	99	98
20	100	100	99	99	100	100	100
Range of % for Individual	98–100	97–100	96–100	97–100	99–100	97–100	95–100[a]
Group Mean	100	99	98	99	100	99	99

[a]Range greater than 5 percent.

Round	Tense	Voice	Continuant	Nasal	Strident	Overall
100	100	100	100	100	100	100
99	99	99	99	100	100	99
99	100	100	100	99	100	100
100	100	99	99	99	100	100
100	100	100	100	100	100	100
95	97	100	97	100	100	98
100	100	100	99	100	100	100
99	99	99	100	99	100	100
99	99	100	99	100	100	100
100	100	100	97	100	100	99
100	99	100	98	100	99	99
100	99	100	99	100	100	100
97	97	99	98	100	99	98
99	98	99	96	100	97	98
99	98	98	99	100	94	99
96	96	100	95	100	100	98
97	97	99	98	100	99	99
99	99	100	100	100	100	99
99	98	100	99	100	99	99
100	99	100	100	100	100	100
95–100[a]	96–100	98–100	95–100[a]	99–100	94–100	98–100
99	97	100	99	100	99	99

TABLE 6.10 Error Productions by Replacement, Frequency of Replacement, and Feature/Degree Differences of Replacement as Specified in Irwin-Wong System

Phonetic Classification	Phoneme in Error	Replacement 1	Replacement 2	Replacement 3
Vowels	/i/	/ʌ/:7–4/5[a]	/e/:1–1/1	/ɪu/:1–3/5
	/ɪ/	/æ/:2–2/3	/i/:1–1/1	/ɛ/:1–1/1
	/e/	/ʌ/:3–3/4	/ɝ/:2–2/2	/i/:2–1/1
	/ɛ/	/ʌ/:1–2/3	/ə/:1–2/2	/ɪ/:1–2/2
	/æ/	/ʌ/:2–2/3	/ɪ/:2–2/3	/o/:1–5/6
	/ɝ/	/ɜ/:5–2/2	/ʊ/:2–4/4	/ʌ/:1–4/4
	/ɚ/	/ə/:14–2/2	/ʌ/:1–3/3	/ʊ/:1–3/3
	/ə/	/l̩/:1–5/6	/r/:1–4/4	/ɚ/:1–2/2
	/ʌ/	/æ/:1–2/3	/ʊ/:1–2/2	/ə/:1–1/1
	/ɑ/	/ʌ/:3–1/1	/aɪ/:2–2/4	/o/:1–4/4
	/ɔ/	/ə/:2–3/3	/ɑ/:1–1/1	
	/o/	/ʌ/:10–3/3	/ə/:1–4/4	
	/u/	/ʌ/:46–4/4	/ʊ/:2–2/2	/ə/:1–5/5
Diphthongs	/aɪ/	/ɑ/:3–2/4	/ʌ/:2–3/5	/ɪ/:1–5/9
	/ɔɪ/	/ə/:1–5/7		
	/ɪu/	/u/:1–1/2		
Syllabics	/l̩/	/o/:1–5/7	/ʌ/:1–4/6	/ə/:1–4/5
Consonants	/k/	/ʃ/:1–6/6	/ɪ/:1–5/8	/n/:1–4/8
	/t/	/d/:3–1/2	/h/:1–5/12	/ə/:1–5/8
	/d/	/f/:1–6/8	/s/:1–6/7	/ʌ/:1–4/7
	/p/	/w/:1–4/7		
	/b/	/r/:1–4/8	/m/:1–2/4	
	/v/	/b/:5–4/6	/f/:3–1/2	
	/θ/	/t/:3–4/4[a]	/f/:3–2/2	/ʔ/:1–5/12
	/ð/	/d/:130–4/4	/n/:5–4/6	/θ/:3–1/2
	/s/	/θ/:44–3/3	/z/:6–1/2	/ʂ/:5–6/7
	/z/	/θ/:13–5/4	/ð/:13–3/3	/s/:1–1/2
	/ʃ/	/s/:3–2/3	/ð/:1–4/6	
	/tʃ/	/t/:4–3/3	/s/:2–7/8	/d/:2–4/5
	/dʒ/	/d/:13–3/3	/θ/:3–7/9	/ʒ/:1–5/5
	/m/	/n/:2–3/6		
	/n/	/k/:1–4/8		
	/ŋ/	/n/:67–1/2	/dʒ/:1–5/7	
	/l/	/w/:27–4/7	/ʌ/:6–5/7	/ə/:5–5/6
	/r/	/w/:28–1/3	/ə/:23–4/4	/ʌ/:7–4/5
	/w/	/l/:2–4/7		
	/j/	/tʃ/:5–5/8	/d/:1–3/5	

[a]That is, the replacement /ʌ/, which occurred 7 times, is removed from /i/ by a feature/degree difference of 4/5.

Replacement 4	Replacement 5	Replacement 6	Replacement 7	Replacement 8
/r/:1−4/4				
/ʌ/:1−3/4				
/ɑ/:1−1/2				
/w/:1−3/6				
/ɔɪ/:1−3/5				
/ɑ/:1−4/5	/o/:1−1/1			
/e/:1−4/7				
/k/:1−1/2				
/ə/:1−4/6	/l/:1−3/6	/tʃ/:1−1/2		
/d/:1−5/6	/i/:1−5/6			
/h/:1−5/10	/l/:1−5/6	/f/:1−3/4		
/ʃ/:3−2/3	/ð/:2−4/5	/ɪ/:1−5/6		
/θ/:1−6/7	/s/:1−5/5			
/r/:3−3/4	/o/:1−6/8	/n/:1−5/10	/u/:1−5/7	/j/:1−2/3
/ɜ/:6−3/3	/ʊ/:2−4/5	/ɚ/:2−2/2	/tʃ/:1−6/9	/ɪu/:1−4/5

specification is one degree from the correct specification (e.g., Motion-5 is one degree from Motion-4, but two degrees from Motion-3). Thus, there is a one-degree difference for each of the features, or a total of four degree differences.

Each feature set found to be produced with less accuracy also showed one feature specification which occurred most often. These least accurate specifications are often characteristic of those phonemes produced with less accuracy.

Place-5 (linguapalatal), produced with 94 percent accuracy, is characteristic of the /ʃ/, /ʒ/, /tʃ/, dʒ/, /j/, /ɝ/, /ɚ/, and /ə/ phonemes. Seventy-one percent of the replacement specifications were accounted for by Place-4 (lingua-alveolar). The remaining 29 percent of the errors were as follows: 13 percent Place-3 (linguadental); 13 percent Place-6 (linguavelar); and 3 percent Place-1 (bilabial).

Closure-3 (obstructed airflow) was produced with 93 percent accuracy. Phonemes such as /f/, /v/, /θ/, /ð/, /s/, /z/, /ʃ/, and /ʒ/ display this specification. Ninety-four percent of all errors produced were replaced by Closure-4 (occlusion). The remaining 6 percent of errors was replaced by Closure-1 (1 percent) or Closure-2 (5 percent).

Labial-1 (characterized by lip spread) was 94 percent accurate. Consonants characterized by Labial-1 are /f/, /v/, /s/, and /z/. Ninety-one percent of the errors were accounted for by Labial-2 (lips in neutral position); the remaining were replaced by Labial-3 (lips rounded) 3 percent of the time and Labial-4 (lips closed) 6 percent of the time.

Labial-3 (lips rounded) also occurred with 94 percent accuracy, and is characteristic of the phonemes /ɚ/, /ɔ/, /o/, /u/, /ʊ/, /ɪ/, /ɔɪ/, /ɪu/, /tʃ/, /dʒ/, /r/, /ʃ/, /ʒ/, and /w/. This specification was replaced by Labial-2 (neutral lip position) 97 percent of the time and by Labial-1 (lips rounded) the remaining 3 percent.

Using the graded Irwin and Wong feature system, feature/degree differences for errors produced in vowel and consonant groups were obtained. Two types of mean errors were computed. First, the mean number of both feature and degree differences based on *only* error productions in each phonemic category was computed (number of feature differences/number of errors, and the number of degree differences/number of errors). The second computation was the two means, feature and degree, based on *all* phoneme occurrences (correct and incorrect) which were contained in each phonemic category. These computations are summarized in Table 6.11.

A comparison of the vowel errors revealed that the mean number of feature/degree differences was highest for syllabic errors, followed by vowel and diphthong errors, regardless of how the means were computed. Comparison of vowel errors and consonant errors revealed that the mean number of feature/degree differences (based on error productions) was higher for vowel errors (3.68/4.37) than for consonant errors (3.18/4.06). The number of mean feature/degree differences between errors and target sounds, when based on all phoneme occurrences and weighted by frequency of occurrence, was higher for consonants (.63/.77) than for vowels (.23/.24). The weighted means

TABLE 6.11 Mean Feature/Degree Difference Values by Phoneme as Specified in Irwin-Wong System

Phonetic Classification	Phoneme in Error	Number of Errors	Number of Occurrences	$\bar{X}$ Feature Difference Based on Errors	$\bar{X}$ Feature Difference Based on Occurrences	$\bar{X}$ Degree Difference Based on Errors	$\bar{X}$ Degree Difference Based on Occurrences
Vowels	/i/	10	653	3.60	.06	.07	4.50
	/ɪ/	6	804	1.50	.01	.01	2.00
	/e/	7	357	2.14	.04	.05	2.57
	/ɛ/	3	316	2.00	.02	.02	2.33
	/æ/	6	660	2.33	.02	.03	3.33
	/ɝ/	9	108	2.78	.23	.26	3.11
	/ɚ/	17	146	2.00	.23	.23	2.00
	/ə/	3	94	3.67	.12	.13	4.00
	/ʌ/	3	935	1.67	.01	.01	2.00
	/ɑ/	7	344	2.00	.04	.06	2.86
	/ɔ/	3	163	2.33	.04	.04	2.33
	/o/	11	496	3.09	.07	−.07	3.09
	/u/	51	420	3.88	.47	.47	3.09
Diphthongs	/aɪ/	7	560	3.00	.04	.07	5.43
	/ɔɪ/	1	28	5.00	.18	.25	7.00
	/ɪu/	1	3	1.00	.33	.67	2.00
Syllabics	/l̩/	3	45	4.33	.29	.40	6.00
Consonants	/k/	3	471	5.00	.03	.05	7.33
	/t/	7	1,423	2.00	.01	.02	4.00
	/d/	6	833	4.00	.03	.04	6.00
	/p/	1	249	4.00	.02	.03	7.00
	/b/	2	343	3.00	.02	.03	6.00
	/v/	8	176	2.88	.13	.20	4.50
	/θ/	9	98	3.67	.34	.43	4.67
	/ð/	141	462	3.94	1.20	1.25	4.09
	/s/	61	660	3.07	.28	.31	3.34
	/z/	27	455	3.41	.20	.23	3.93
	/ʃ/	4	102	2.50	.10	.15	3.75
	/tʃ/	10	39	4.50	1.15	1.28	5.00
	/dʒ/	17	67	3.82	.97	1.06	4.18
	/m/	2	544	3.00	.01	.02	6.00
	/n/	1	1,210	4.00	.00	.01	8.00
	/ŋ/	68	136	1.06	.53	1.04	2.07
	/l/	45	530	4.22	.36	.57	6.69
	/r/	70	478	2.69	.39	.54	3.67
	/w/	2	505	4.00	.02	.03	7.00
	/j/	6	122	4.67	.23	.37	7.50
Total		638	15,035	3.16	.13	.17	3.90

reflect the greater frequency of occurrence and higher proportion of errors on consonant phonemes.

Fusion-2, which indicates blending of a stop and continuant, is applicable to the phonemes /tʃ/ and /dʒ/, and appeared only with 75 percent accuracy. All Fusion-2 errors were substituted by Fusion-1 (the absence of blending of a stop and continuant).

Lateral-1, indicating a bilateral airflow around the tongue blade, is produced with /l/ and /ḽ/ phonemes, and was substituted entirely by Lateral-3 (no movement of air around the tongue blade).

Place-3 (linguadental) was achieved with the lowest accuracy, at 74 percent. It is characteristic of the /ð/ and /θ/ phonemes. Its most frequent feature specification replacement was Place-4 (lingua-alveolar), which was substituted 96 percent of the time. Two infrequent replacements were Place-2 (labiodental) and Place-7 (glottal), which accounted for 3 percent and 1 percent of the remaining substitutions, respectively.

Analysis of the data indicates a lack of consistent pattern for phoneme substitutions in terms of feature/degree differences. That is, a more similar sound, indicated by a lower feature/degree difference, is not always the most frequent replacement.

Chomsky-Halle Distinctive Feature System

An analysis of all phonemes and their replacement phonemes and feature differences is summarized in Table 6.12. Since the Chomsky-Halle feature system is binary, no degree differences can be calculated between the target and replacement phonemes. While most phonemes have several replacements, usually one occurred most frequently. Those features found to be less accurate are often those features found in less accurate phonemes. For example, the Chomsky-Halle feature continuancy, in which the presence of the feature indicates a constricted air passage, was always replaced by the absence of continuancy. The consonants /f/, /v/, /θ/, /ð/, /s/, /z/, /ʃ/, /ʒ/, /l/, /r/, /h/, /w/, /j/, and /ʔ/ are characterized by the presence of the continuancy feature. Stridency (marked acoustically by greater noisiness as a result of air turbulence) is characteristic of the consonants /f/, /v/, /s/, /z/, /ʃ/, /ʒ/, /tʃ/, and /dʒ/.

The feature differences between target phonemes and replacement phonemes indicate that the most frequent subsitutions are not necessarily characterized by a lesser feature difference than infrequent phoneme substitutions.

A comparison of vowel errors revealed that the mean number of feature differences was higher for syllabic errors, followed by vowel and diphthong errors. A comparison of the vowel and consonant errors revealed a higher feature error for consonants (3.15) than vowels (2.25) based on the number of error occurrences. When feature differences were weighted for total phoneme occurrences, consonant errors reflected a much larger feature difference (.63) than vowels (.20). Mean feature differences are summarized in Table 6.13.

DISCUSSION

This study has analyzed the spontaneous speech of children 46 to 50 months of age in terms of phonemes and distinctive features.

The data support the contention by Sander (1972) that most sounds are "customarily produced" (with greater than 50 percent accuracy) by age 4. Sander felt that altered sampling methods and differing criteria for mastery yielded results varying from previous studies (Wellman et al., 1931; Poole, 1934; Templin, 1947). The present data show consistently higher percentages of accuracy for the phonemes /ʃ/, /tʃ/, /ð/, /ʒ/, /dʒ/, /θ/, /v/, and /z/ than does Sander's application of the 50 percent criterion to the work of Wellman et al. (1931) and Templin (1947).

The frequency of consonant occurrence in the present data parallels that of Denes (1963). In addition, the sequence of mastery, as judged by the percentages of accuracy, parallels that of Wellman et al. (1931), Poole (1934), and Templin (1957).

Three types of errors were defined—omission, substitution, and distortion. Children of 46 to 50 months of age appear to show preference for omitting or substituting particular phonemes. Group means seem to indicate that children are just as likely to omit a sound as to replace it with another. Inspection of individual phoneme errors, however, reveals that some phonemes are consistently replaced while others are more often omitted.

The spontaneous speech of 4-year-old children is remarkably similar to adult speech in the distribution of vowels and consonants, as well as in the frequency of occurrence of individual sounds. Accuracy scores of each sound may indicate, as Sander (1972) postulated, that deviant articulatory patterns may be established prior to the accepted age of consonant mastery at 6 or 8. From these data, children who articulate any sound except /ŋ/ with less than 50 percent accuracy could be considered as having delayed articulation development. If further investigation reveals that /ŋ/ is dialectally bound, then these data suggest that all phonemes should be "customarily produced" (with greater than 50 percent accuracy) by 50 months. Additional evaluation of word types and error position may reveal the exact nature of the misarticulations, particularly for the phonemes /ð/ and /ŋ/, which are susceptible to regional variations.

Data revealed that regardless of the feature system used (Irwin-Wong or Chomsky-Halle), all feature sets were produced with a high degree of accuracy by children of 46 to 50 months. Thus, all features are considered "available" at this age. Phoneme errors analyzed for the number of feature/degree and feature differences between the target and error phonemes revealed that the more frequent replacements are not characterized by a lower feature/degree difference. However, when weighted for frequency of occurrence, consonants show higher feature/degree differences, reflecting the more complex articulatory postures necessary for consonant production.

In summary, according to the preceding data, all phonemes should be "customarily produced" by 4 years of age, and all distinctive features—by either the Irwin-Wong or Chomsky-Halle system—should be available. Fur-

Text continued on p. 132

TABLE 6.12 Error Productions by Replacement, Frequency of Replacement, and Feature Differences of Replacement as Specified in Modified Chomsky-Halle System

Phonetic Classification	Phoneme in Error	Replacement 1	Replacement 2	Replacement 3
Vowels	/i/	/ʌ/:7–3ᵃ	/e/:1–1	/ɪu/:1–2
	/ɪ/	/æ/:2–2	/i/:1–1	/ɛ/:1–1
	/e/	/ʌ/:3–2	/ɝ/:2–1	/i/:2–1
	/ɛ/	/ʌ/:1–1	/ə/:1–1	/i/:1–2
	/æ/	/ʌ/:2–2	/ɪ/:2–2	/o/:1–4
	/ɝ/	/ɜ/:5–2	/ʊ/:2–5	/ʌ/:1–3
	/ɚ/	/ə/:14–2	/ʌ/:1–2	/ʊ/:1–4
	/ə/	/l̩/:1–6	/r/:1–5	/ɚ/:1–2
	/ʌ/	/æ/:1–2	/ʊ/:1–2	/ə/:1–2
	/ɑ/	/ʌ/:3–1	/aɪ/:2–1	/o/:1–3
	/ɔ/	/ə/:2–1	/ɑ/:1–2	
	/o/	/ʌ/:10–2	/ə/:1–2	
	/u/	/ʌ/:46–2	/ʊ/:2–2	/ə/:1–4
Diphthongs	/aɪ/	/ɑ/:3–1	/ʌ/:2–2	/ɪ/:1–4
	/ɔɪ/	/ə/:1–3		
	/ɪu/	/u/:1–1		
Syllabics	/l̩/	/o/:1–7	/ʌ/:1–7	/ə/:1–6
Consonants	/k/	/ʃ/:1–4	/ɪ/:1–6	/n/:1–6
	/g/	—	—	—
	/t/	/d/:3–1	/h/:1–5	/ə/:1–7
	/d/	/f/:1–4	/s/:1–3	/ʌ/:1–7
	/p/	/w/:1–8		
	/b/	/r/:1–4	/m/:1–1	
	/v/	/b/:5–2	/f/:3–1	
	/θ/	/t/:3–1	/f/:3–2	/ʔ/:1–6
	/ð/	/d/:130–1	/n/:5–2	/θ/:3–1
	/s/	/θ/:44–1	/z/:6–1	/ṣ/:5–2
	/z/	/θ/:13–2	/ð/:13–1	/s/:1–1
	/ʃ/	/s/:3–2	/ð/:1–4	
	/tʃ/	/t/:4–3	/s/:2–3	/d/:2–4
	/dʒ/	/d/:13–3	/θ/:3–5	/ʒ/:1–1
	/m/	/n/:2–1		
	/n/	/k/:1–6		
	/ŋ/	/n/:67–4	/dʒ/:1–4	
	/l/	/w/:27–8	/ʌ/:6–7	/ə/:5–6
	/r/	/w/:28–7	/ə/:23–5	/ʌ/:7–6
	/w/	/l/:2–8		
	/j/	/tʃ/:5–7	/d/:1–7	

ᵃThat is, the replacement /ʌ/, which occurred 7 times, is removed from /i/ by a feature difference of 3.

Replacement 4	Replacement 5	Replacement 6	Replacement 7	Replacement 8
/r/:1–6				
/ʌ/:1–2				
/ɑ/:1–1				
/w/:1–7				
/ɔɪ/:1–2				
/ɑ/:1–3	/o/:1–2			
/e/:1–2				
/k/:1–4				
/ə/:1–6	/l/:1–2	/tʃ/:1–1		
/d/:1–2	/i/:1–9			
/h/:1–5	/l/:1–1	/f/:1–3		
/ʃ/:3–2	/ð/:2–2	/ɪ/:1–10		
/θ/:1–4	/ʃ/:1–1			
/r/:3–1	/o/:1–7	/n/:1–6	/u/:1–8	/j/:1–7
/ɜ/:6–4	/ʊ/:2–7	/ɚ/:2–4	/tʃ/:1–5	/ɪu/:1–7

ther sampling in terms of race, socioeconomic status, and regional dialect, as well as analysis of word errors, may lead to a greater understanding of phoneme and feature usage.

TABLE 6.13   Mean Feature Difference Values as Specified in Modified Chomsky-Halle System

Phonetic Classification	Phoneme in Error	Number of Errors	Number of Occurrences	$\bar{X}$ Feature Difference Based on Errors	$\bar{X}$ Feature Difference Based on Occurrences
Vowels	/i/	10	653	3.00	.05
	/ɪ/	5	804	1.60	.01
	/e/	7	357	1.43	.03
	/ɛ/	3	316	1.33	.01
	/æ/	6	660	2.17	.02
	/ɝ/	9	108	3.33	.28
	/ɚ/	17	146	2.12	.25
	/ə/	3	94	4.33	.14
	/ʌ/	3	935	2.00	.01
	/ɑ/	7	344	1.43	.03
	/ɔ/	3	163	1.33	.02
	/o/	11	496	2.00	.04
	/u/	51	420	2.06	.25
Diphthongs	/aɪ/	7	560	1.86	.02
	/ɔɪ/	1	28	3.00	.11
	/ɪu/	1	3	1.00	.33
Syllabics	/l̩/	3	45	6.67	.44
Consonants	/k/	3	471	5.33	.03
	/t/	6	1,423	3.17	.01
	/d/	6	833	3.83	.03
	/p/	1	249	8.00	.03
	/b/	2	343	2.50	.01
	/v/	8	176	1.63	.07
	/θ/	9	98	2.89	.27
	/ð/	141	462	1.08	.27
	/s/	61	660	1.31	.22
	/z/	27	455	1.48	.09
	/ʃ/	4	102	2.50	.10
	/tʃ/	10	39	3.10	.79
	/dʒ/	17	67	3.24	.79
	/m/	2	544	1.00	.00
	/n/	1	1,210	6.00	.00
	/ŋ/	68	136	4.00	2.00
	/l/	45	530	7.09	.60
	/r/	70	478	5.87	.86
	/w/	2	505	8.00	.03
	/j/	6	122	7.00	.34
Total		636	9,862	2.95	.12

7   Development at 6 Years   Electa Harmon and Stephen Harmon

METHOD

Subjects

Twenty Caucasian children, 10 male and 10 female, served as subjects. These children had no known gross intellectual, neurological, or physiological deviations, and were from middle- to upper-middle-class homes. All the subjects were enrolled in a public school kindergarten and ranged in age at the time of testing from 5 years 10 months to 6 years 2 months.

Data Collection

Each child was seen in a classroom at his/her school, and was presented with a uniform variety of play objects. The child was encouraged to verbalize about his/her activities. If the child did not converse readily, the examiner asked questions designed to elicit connected speech. Each child's verbalizations were recorded on a portable Panasonic cassette recorder equipped with a condenser microphone.

A 250-phoneme sample (to the nearest complete utterance) was extracted from each child's recording. The first 15 phonemes that the child said were excluded in obtaining the 250-phoneme count. Broad phonetic transcriptions of the sample, using the International Phonetic Alphabet, were made from the audiotape recordings.

Reliability

Interjudge reliability was established by having an objective listener phonetically transcribe 20 consecutive phonemes in each child's sample. The transcribed portion began after the first 20 phonemes in each child's sample.

The overall percentage of agreement between the investigator and the independent observer for phonetic transcription was 88 percent. Intrajudge reliability was not established.

RESULTS

Phoneme Distribution by Individual Sounds

Analyses were made for each individual child as well as for the total group of 20 subjects. A grand total of 4,906 phonemes distributed in 294 utterances was entered for analysis. The mean number of phonemes per subject was 245.

Based on data from all subjects, vowellike and consonant sounds accounted for 42 percent and 58 percent of the phoneme distribution, respectively.

Table 7.1 presents the range of frequency distribution for both the vowellike and consonant sounds. The range of frequency distribution for individual vowel sounds was from 0 percent to 8 percent; the range of frequency distribution for individual consonant sounds was from 0 percent to 9 percent. So, while some phonemes constituted essentially 0 percent of the children's speech, no phoneme constituted more than 9 percent. The vowel /ɪ/ and the consonant /t/ were the most frequently used vowel and consonant.

TABLE 7.1 Percentage of Occurrence of Individual Vowellike and Consonant Sounds Based on Total Phoneme Sample (N = 4,906)

Phoneme Category	% of Distribution	Phoneme
Vowellike	0	/ʒ, ɔɪ, ɪu, n̩, m̩, l̩/
	1	/ɝ, ɚ, ɔ, ʊ, aʊ/
	2	/e, ɛ, ɑ, o, u/
	3	/i, ʌ, aɪ/
	4	/æ, ə/
	8	/ɪ/
Consonant	0	/ʒ, tʃ, dʒ, ʔ/
	1	/f, v, θ, ʃ, ŋ, h, j/
	2	/g, p, b/
	3	/z, m, r, w/
	4	/k, d, ð, l/
	5	/s/
	6	/n/
	9	/t/

Percentage of Correct Production by Phoneme

Vowellike Sounds

As shown in Table 7.2, the majority of the vowels were produced correctly essentially 100 percent of the time. The /ɚ/ and /ɝ/ phonemes were consistently misarticulated with the highest percentage of error among the vowels. Percentages ranged from 4 to 8 percent incorrect for the phonemes in the individual samples.

TABLE 7.2   Percentage of Correct Production of Individual Vowellike Sounds Based on Total Occurrence of Each Phoneme

Sounds	Phoneme	% Correct Production	No. of Correct Occurrences/ No. of Total Occurrences
Vowels	/i/	100	136/136
	/e/	100	118/118
	/ɛ/	100	91/91
	/ɑ/	100	92/92
	/ɔ/	100	37/37
	/ʊ/	100	42/42
	/æ/	99	189/191
	/ə/	99	225/227
	/ʌ/	99	146/148
	/o/	99	109/110
	/u/	99	83/84
	/ɪ/	98	389/398
	/ɝ/	95	38/40
	/ɚ/	94	46/49
Diphthongs[a]	/aɪ/	100	174/174
	/aʊ/	100	46/46
	/ɔɪ/	100	3/3
Syllabics	/n̩/	100	14/14
	/l̩/	100	17/17
	/m̩/	100	1/1
Total		99	1,996/2,018

[a]The following diphthong was not entered: /ɪu/.

Consonants

Of the 24 different consonants that appeared, as shown in Table 7.3, 15 were used correctly by the total group of subjects more than 90 percent of the time. For the remaining consonants (/ʃ, v, dʒ, r, θ, ð, ʒ/), the majority of misarticulations may be interpreted as being developmentally based.

Error Type Distribution

Vowellike Sounds

Table 7.4 presents vowel sounds by error type distribution. All but two vowels appeared with at least 98 percent total accuracy: /ɜ/ was produced 95 percent correct, and /ɚ/ was produced 94 percent correct. Because of the relatively few errors, the classification by percentage of error type is not particularly meaningful.

TABLE 7.3 Percentage of Correct Production of Individual Consonants Based on Total Occurrence of Each Phoneme

Phoneme	% Correct Production	No. of Correct Occurrences/ No. of Total Occurrences
/k/	100	183/183
/f/	100	47/47
/tʃ/	100	13/13
/m/	100	165/165
/t/	99	482/483
/p/	99	109/110
/b/	99	116/117
/n/	99	329/330
/w/	99	141/142
/j/	98	49/50
/g/	97	90/93
/l/	95	178/188
/z/	94	131/140
/s/	93	227/243
/h/	91	67/74
/ʃ/	87	33/38
/v/	83	49/59
/dʒ/	83	15/18
/r/	82	143/175
/θ/	78	25/32
/d/	77	164/212
/ð/	65	128/196
/ŋ/	57	34/60
/ʒ/	0	0/1
Total	92	2,918/3,169

Note. The following phoneme did not occur in sample: /ʔ/.

TABLE 7.4 Error Type Distribution (Percent Omissions and Percent Substitutions) for Each Vowellike Sound

Category	Vowellike Sound	% Omissions	% Substitutions	No. of Errors/ No. of Occurrences
Essentially Equal Distribution Between Error Types	/i/	0	0	0/136
	/e/	0	0	0/118
	/ɛ/	0	0	0/91
	/æ/	1	1	2/191
	/ɑ/	0	0	0/92
	/ɔ/	0	0	0/37
	/ʊ/	0	0	0/42
	/aɪ/	0	0	0/174
	/aʊ/	0	0	0/46
	/ɔɪ/	0	0	0/3
	/n̩/	0	0	0/14
	/l̩/	0	0	0/17
	/m̩/	0	0	0/1
Greater Frequency of Omissions	/ə/	1	0	2/227
	/o/	1	0	1/110
	/u/	1	0	1/84
Greater Frequency of Substitutions	/ɪ/	1	2	9/398
	/ɝ/	0	5	2/40
	/ɚ/	0	6	3/49
	/ʌ/	0	1	2/148
Total		0	1	22/2,018

Consonants

Total consonant errors were generally equally distributed between omissions (37 percent) and substitutions (39 percent). A small percentage of errors (6 percent) was characterized by distortion. Table 7.5 presents the consonant sounds by error type distribution.

Correct Production of Distinctive Features

Irwin-Wong Distinctive Feature System

The analysis of phonemes by distinctive features yielded a total of 51,870 feature specifications for the Irwin-Wong (1977) feature system. Percentages of correct use were derived not only for the feature sets of the Irwin-Wong system, but also for each of the individual specifications within each set. Each of the specifications within the feature sets appeared with at least 95 percent accuracy except Fusion-2 (90 percent), Place-3 (78 percent), and Closure-3 (91 percent). The percentages of correct usage for each of the feature sets are presented in Table 7.6.

Table 7.7 provides a comparison of the mean percent of correct usage of each of the 10 feature sets by each subject with the group mean. Only one individual subject, Subject Seven, varied more than 5 percent from the group means for any feature set. Subject Seven varied from eight to eleven percentage points from the group mean in the following features: Motion, Lateral, Labial, Tenseness, Vertical, and Closure. For this child, the overall mean varied six percentage points from the group's overall mean. Phonological analysis of his sample revealed the following:

Phoneme	Percent Correct Production
/ð/	8
/s/	0
/z/	14
/ʃ/	0
/ŋ/	50 (1 out of 2 occurrences)
/r/	78

All other consonants were produced correctly by this child.

Text continued on p. 144

Phonological Development in Children

TABLE 7.5 Error Type Distribution (Percent Omissions and Percent Substitutions) for Each Consonant

Category	Consonant	% Omissions	% Substitutions	% Distortions	No. of Errors/ No. of Occurrences
Essentially Equal	/k/	0	0	0	0/183
Distribution Between	/f/	0	0	0	0/47
Error Types	/tʃ/	0	0	0	0/13
	/m/	0	0	0	1/483
	/w/	1	1	0	2/142
Greater Frequency	/t/	1	0	0	6/483
of Omissions	/b/	1	0	0	1/117
	/n/	1	0	0	3/330
	/g/	3	0	0	3/93
	/h/	9	0	0	7/74
	/v/	17	0	0	10/59
	/dʒ/	17	0	0	3/18
	/d/	23	0	0	48/212
Greater Frequency	/p/	0	1	0	1/110
of Substitutions	/j/	0	2	0	1/50
	/l/	1	5	0	10/188
	/r/	5	14	0	32/175
	/ɚ/	12	22	0	68/196
	/ŋ/	0	43	0	26/60
	/ʒ/	0	1	0	1/100
Greater Frequency	/s/	0	0	6	16/24
of Distortions	/ʃ/	0	5	8	5/38
Total		37	39	6	244/3,195

Note. The following phoneme was not entered: /ʔ/.

TABLE 7.6 Correct Usage of Irwin-Wong Feature Sets and Feature Specifications by Percent and Number Based on Total Sample

Feature Set	Feature Specification	% Correct	No. of Correct Occurrences/ No. of Total Occurrences
Oronasal	0	—	0/0
	1	100	4,167/4,617
	2	—	0/0
	3	—	0/0
	4	100	569/570
	Set Mean	100	5,186/5,187
Motion	0	—	0/0
	1	100	177/177
	2	100	46/46
	3	99	622/629
	4	98	3,038/3,106
	5	100	1,229/1,229
	Set Mean	99	5,112/5,187
Fusion	0	—	0/0
	1	100	5,155/5,156
	2	90	28/31
	Set Mean	100	5,183/5,187
Lateral	0	—	0/0
	1	96	197/205
	2	—	0/0
	3	100	4,958/4,982
	Set Mean	99	5,155/5,187
Labial	0	—	0/0
	1	96	468/489
	2	100	3,536/3,553
	3	97	733/752
	4	100	392/393
	Set Mean	99	5,129/5,187
Tenseness	0	—	0/0
	1	100	4,052/4,054
	2	98	1,107/1,133
	Set Mean	99	5,159/5,187

TABLE 7.6 *Continued*

Feature Set	Feature Specification	% Correct	No. of Correct Occurrences/ No. of Total Occurrences
Vertical	0	100	74/74
	1	100	542/543
	2	97	2,180/2,249
	3	99	2,307/2,321
	Set Mean	98	5,103/5,187
Place	0	—	0/0
	1	100	533/535
	2	100	106/106
	3	78	178/228
	4	99	2,703/2,736
	5	97	425/436
	6	97	1,044/1,072
	7	100	74/74
	Set Mean	100	5,063/5,187
Laryngeal	0	—	0/0
	1	100	1,148/1,149
	2	100	74/74
	3	100	3,956/3,964
	4	100	1,799/1,799
	Set Mean	100	5,178/5,187
Closure	0	—	0/0
	1	100	1,032/1,034
	2	99	1,582/1,598
	3	91	689/756
	4	100	1,799/1,799
	Set Mean	98	5,102/5,187
Total for All Sets		99	51,370/51,870

TABLE 7.7 Comparison of Individual Subjects with Group Means by Percentage of Correct Usage of Irwin-Wong Feature Sets

Subject Number	Oronasal	Motion	Fusion	Lateral	Labial
1	100	99	100	100	100
2	100	99	100	100	100
3	100	96	100	100	97
4	100	100	100	100	100
5	100	100	100	100	99
6	100	100	100	100	100
7	100	88	100	91	90
8	100	100	100	100	100
9	100	100	100	100	100
10	100	100	100	100	99
11	100	100	100	100	100
12	100	99	100	100	100
13	100	98	100	100	100
14	100	100	100	100	100
15	100	99	100	100	100
16	100	97	100	97	97
17	100	100	100	100	99
18	100	100	100	100	100
19	100	99	100	100	100
20	100	100	100	100	98
Range of % for Individual	100	88–100	100	91–100	90–100
Group Mean	100	99	100	99	99

Tenseness	Vertical	Place	Laryngeal	Closure	Overall
100	99	98	100	99	99
100	99	98	100	99	99
100	97	94	100	96	98
100	100	100	100	100	100
100	100	98	100	99	100
99	100	100	96	99	99
91	91	88	94	88	93
100	100	100	100	100	100
100	100	100	99	100	100
100	99	98	100	100	100
100	99	99	100	99	100
100	99	99	100	99	100
99	98	96	100	97	99
100	100	100	100	100	100
100	99	98	100	99	99
100	94	93	100	97	97
100	100	99	100	100	100
100	100	99	100	100	100
100	99	98	100	99	100
100	100	96	100	99	99
91–100	88–100	93–100	98–100	88–100	93–100
100	99	93	100	98	99

Chomsky-Halle Distinctive Feature System

The analysis of phonemes by distinctive features yielded a total of 66,920 feature specifications for the Chomsky-Halle (1968) system as modified for this analysis. Percentages of correct use were derived not only for feature sets in the Chomsky-Halle system but for each of the individual specifications within that set as well. All of the specifications within the feature sets appeared with at least 98 percent accuracy except High-2 (97 percent), Continuant-2 (97 percent), and Strident-2 (95 percent). The percentages of correct usage are presented in Table 7.8.

Table 7.9 provides a comparison of the mean percent of correct usage of each of the 13 feature sets by each subject with the group mean. There were two instances in which a subject varied more than 5 percent from the group mean. Subject Seven was eight percentage points (91 percent) from the group mean (99 percent) for correct usage of the feature Vocalic, and nine percentage points (91 percent) from the group mean (100 percent) for correct usage of the feature Strident.

Text continued on p. 148

TABLE 7.8 Correct Usage of Modified Chomsky-Halle Feature Sets and Feature Specifications by Percent and Number Based on Total Sample

Feature Set	Feature Specification	% Correct	No. of Correct Occurrences/ No. of Total Occurrences
Vocalic	0	—	0/0
	1	99	2,796/2,821
	2	99	2,339/2,366
	Set Mean	99	5,135/5,187
Consonantal	0	—	0/0
	1	100	2,252/2,252
	2	99	2,001/2,935
	Set Mean	99	5,153/5,187
High	0	—	0/0
	1	99	3,901/3,929
	2	97	1,217/1,258
	Set Mean	99	5,118/5,187
Back	0	—	0/0
	1	99	3,944/3,973
	2	98	1,185/1,214
	Set Mean	99	5,129/5,187
Low	0	—	0/0
	1	100	4,645/4,653
	2	100	533/534
	Set Mean	100	5,178/5,187
Anterior	0	—	0/0
	1	99	2,799/2,833
	2	100	234/2,354
	Set Mean	99	5,143/5,187

Phonological Development in Children

TABLE 7.8 *Continued*

Feature Set	Feature Specification	% Correct	No. of Correct Occurrences/ No. of Total Occurrences
Coronal	0	—	0/0
	1	99	2,971/2,998
	2	98	2,142/2,189
	Set Mean	99	5,113/5,187
Round	0	99	2,975/3,009
	1	100	1,611/1,617
	2	100	560/561
	Set Mean	99	5,146/5,187
Tense	0	99	2,975/3,009
	1	100	1,465/1,467
	2	100	710/711
	Set Mean	99	5,150/5,187
Voice	0	—	0/0
	1	100	1,223/1,223
	2	100	3,956/3,964
	Set Mean	100	5,179/5,187
Continuant	0	—	0/0
	1	100	3,785/3,785
	2	97	1,355/1,402
	Set Mean	99	5,140/5,187
Nasal	0	—	0/0
	1	100	4,617/4,617
	2	100	569/570
	Set Mean	100	5,186/5,187
Strident	0	—	0/0
	1	100	4,619/4,628
	2	95	531/559
	Set Mean	99	5,150/5,187
Total for All Sets		99	66,920/67,431

TABLE 7.9 Comparison of Individual Subjects with Group Means by Percentage of Correct Usage of Modified Chomsky-Halle Feature Sets

Subject Number	Vocalic	Consonantal	High	Back	Low	Anterior	Coronal
1	100	100	100	100	100	100	100
2	100	100	99	99	100	100	99
3	99	98	98	99	100	99	98
4	100	100	100	100	100	100	100
5	100	100	98	98	100	98	98
6	98	97	97	98	100	100	96
7	91	99	98	99	100	99	98
8	100	100	100	100	100	100	100
9	100	100	99	100	100	99	100
10	100	100	98	98	100	99	98
11	100	100	98	99	99	99	99
12	100	100	99	99	100	99	99
13	100	100	99	98	100	99	98
14	100	100	100	100	100	100	100
15	100	100	100	100	100	100	100
16	97	96	95	96	100	96	95
17	100	100	99	100	100	100	100
18	100	100	100	100	100	99	99
19	100	100	98	98	100	98	98
20	97	97	97	97	100	100	96
Range of % for Individual	91–100	96–100	95–100	96–100	99–100	96–100	95–100
Group Mean	99	99	99	99	99	99	99

Round	Tense	Voice	Continuant	Nasal	Strident	Overall
100	100	100	99	100	100	100
100	100	100	99	100	100	100
98	98	100	96	100	100	99
100	100	100	100	100	100	100
100	100	100	100	100	100	99
97	97	100	100	100	100	98
99	99	98	97	100	91	97
100	100	100	100	100	100	100
100	100	100	100	100	100	99
100	100	100	100	100	100	99
100	100	100	100	100	100	100
100	100	100	100	100	100	100
100	99	100	98	100	100	99
100	100	100	100	100	100	100
100	100	100	99	100	100	100
96	96	100	97	100	100	97
100	100	100	100	100	100	100
100	100	100	100	100	100	100
100	100	100	99	100	100	99
96	97	100	100	100	100	98
96–100	96–100	98–100	96–100	100	91–100	97–100
99	99	100	99	100	100	99

Replacement Characteristics

Irwin-Wong Distinctive Feature System

Each error (excluding omissions) made on any vowel or consonant sound was analyzed by nature of replacement, frequency of replacement, and feature/degree difference of the replacement. In this analysis, degree differences refer to within-feature variations. Table 7.10 displays these results. The consonant sounds most frequently replaced were /ð/, /s/, /ŋ/, and /r/.

The mean feature and mean degree differences between target sounds and replacement (error) sounds are presented in Table 7.11. Both mean feature difference and mean degree difference are calculated for each phoneme on the basis of number of occurrences and of total occurrences. In comparing errors made on vowel sounds, the greatest feature differences occurred on /æ/ and /ɝ/ (3 and 3). For frequently missed consonants, the mean feature difference per error was greatest on /s/ and /z/, with values of 6 and 7 respectively. The phoneme /ʒ/ has been excluded from this comparison because it was not represented frequently in the sample. The higher feature differences for consonants (mean = 3.78) as compared to vowels (mean = 2.26) indicated that consonant replacements tended to differ more from the target sound than did vowel replacements.

TABLE 7.10 Error Productions by Replacement, Frequency of Replacement, and Feature/Degree Differences of Replacement as Specified in Irwin-Wong System

Phonetic Classification	Phoneme in Error	Replacement 1	Replacement 2	Replacement 3
Vowel	/ɪ/	/i/:1–1/1[a]	/æ/:1–2/3	—
	/æ/	/e/:1–3/3		
	/ɝ/	/ʌ/:1–4/4		
	/ɚ/	/ə/:2–2/2		
	/ʌ/	/ɛ/:1–2/3	/ə/:1–1/1	
Consonant	/d/	/dʒ/:1–3/3		
	/p/	/t/:1–3/6		
	/θ/	/f/:3–2/2		
	/ð/	/t/:1–5/6	/d/:35–4/4	/v/:3–2/2
	/s/	/l/:15–6/7		
	/z/	/l/:6–7/9		
	/ʃ/	/s/:2–7/8	/l/:3–7/8	
	/ʒ/	/ʔ/:1–7/10		
	/dʒ/	/d/:1–3/3		
	/n/	/d/:1–2/4		
	/ŋ/	/n/:1–1/2	/n/:14–1/2	
	/l/	/ə/:1–5/6	/l/:1–1/1	/w/:7–4/7
	/r/	/ə/:3–4/4	/w/:12–1/3	

Note. Omissions not included.

[a]That is, the replacement /i/, which occurred once, is removed from /ɪ/ by a feature/degree difference of 1/1.

Phonological Development in Children

TABLE 7.11 Mean Feature/Degree Difference Values by Phoneme as Specified in Irwin-Wong System

Phonetic Classification	Phoneme in Error	Number of Errors	Number of Occurrences	$\bar{X}$ Feature Difference Based on Errors	$\bar{X}$ Feature Difference Based on Occurrences	$\bar{X}$ Degree Difference Based on Errors	$\bar{X}$ Degree Difference Based on Occurrences
Vowel	/ɪ/	6	398	1.83	.03	.04	2.67
	/æ/	1	191	3.00	.02	.02	3.00
	/ɝ/	2	40	3.00	.15	.15	3.00
	/ɚ/	3	49	2.00	.12	.12	2.00
	/ʌ/	2	148	1.50	.02	.03	2.00
Consonant	/d/	1	212	3.00	.01	.01	3.00
	/p/	1	110	3.00	.03	.05	6.00
	/θ/	6	32	2.50	.47	.69	3.67
	/ð/	44	196	3.89	.87	.88	3.91
	/s/	15	243	6.00	.37	.43	7.00
	/z/	6	140	7.00	.30	.39	9.00
	/ʃ/	5	38	5.00	.66	.79	6.00
	/ʒ/	1	1	7.00	7.00	10.00	10.00
	/dʒ/	3	18	3.00	.50	.50	3.00
	/n/	1	330	2.00	.01	.01	4.00
	/ŋ/	26	60	1.00	.43	.87	2.00
	/l/	9	188	3,78	.18	.30	6.22
	/r/	24	175	1.50	.21	.43	3.17
	/w/	1	142	5.00	.04	.05	7.00
	/j/	1	50	3.00	.06	.12	6.00
Total		158	2,761	3.16	.18	.23	4.09

Table 7.12 analyzes the errors made on vowel and consonant sounds by replacement, frequency of replacement, and feature/degree difference of the relevant replacement.

The mean number of feature differences between target sounds and error sounds for vowels and consonants is presented in Table 7.13.

DISCUSSION

In analyzing the total sample, the /ɜ, ɪu, ʔ/ phonemes were not used at all, except as substitution errors. If a 95 percent correct criterion is established, all vowels and vowellike phonemes were correct except for the unstressed /ɚ/ (94 percent).

TABLE 7.12   Error Productions by Replacement, Frequency of Replacement, and Feature Differences of Replacement as Specified in Modified Chomsky-Halle System

Phonetic Classification	Phoneme in Error	Replacement 1	Replacement 2	Replacement 3
Vowel	/ɪ/	/i/:1–1[a]	/æ/:5–2	
	/æ/	/e/:1–2		
	/ɝ/	/ɜ/:1–2	/ʌ/:1–3	
	/ɚ/	/æ/:3–2		
	/ʌ/	/ɛ/:1–1	/ə/:1–2	
Consonant	/d/	/dʒ/:1–3		
	/p/	/t/:1–1		
	/θ/	/f/:5–2	/ʔ/:1–6	
	/ð/	/t/:1–2	/d/:50–1	/v/:3–2
	/s/	/l/:15–2		
	/z/	/l/:6–3		
	/ʃ/	/s/:2–2	/l/:3–4	
	/ʒ/	/ʔ/:1–8		
	/dʒ/	/d/:3–3		
	/n/	/d/:1–1		
	/ŋ/	/ɲ/:1–4	/n/:25–4	
	/l/	/ə/:1–6	/l̩/:1–0	/w/:7–8
	/r/	/ə/:4–5	/w/:20–7	
	/w/	/æ/:1–6		
	/j/	/w/:1–2		

[a]That is, the replacement /i/, which occurred once, is removed from /ɪ/ by a feature difference of 1.

In evaluating consonant production, all phonemes met a 95 percent correct criterion with the exception of the following: /z, s, h, ʃ, v, dʒ, r, θ, d, ð, ŋ, ʒ/. Of these /d, v, h/ showed only omission errors, and these errors were considered to be consistent with normal, conversational coarticulation (e.g., "gimme one" for *"give* me one"). Also, substitution of /n/ for /ŋ/ was interpreted as a dialectal variation rather than a true error (e.g., "comin'" for *"coming"*). When these errors were eliminated, the outstanding errors were in the fricative class. The majority of /s, z, ʃ/ errors were made by Subject Seven, who, though selected at random and not enrolled in speech therapy at the time of the study, would be considered by the present authors to display a mild-to-moderate articulatory disorder.

TABLE 7.13   Mean Feature Difference Values as Specified in Modified Chomsky-Halle System

Phonetic Classification	Phoneme in Error	Number of Errors	Number of Occurrences	$\bar{X}$ Feature Difference Based on Errors	$\bar{X}$ Feature Difference Based on Occurrences
Vowel	/ɪ/	6	398	1.83	.03
	/æ/	1	191	2.00	.01
	/ɝ/	2	40	2.50	.13
	/ɚ/	3	49	2.00	.12
	/ʌ/	2	148	1.50	.02
Consonant	/d/	1	212	3.00	.01
	/p/	1	110	1.00	.01
	/θ/	6	32	2.67	.50
	/ð/	44	196	1.09	.24
	/s/	15	243	2.00	.12
	/z/	6	140	3.00	.13
	/ʃ/	5	38	3.20	.42
	/ʒ/	1	1	8.00	8.00
	/dʒ/	3	18	3.00	.50
	/n/	1	330	1.00	.00
	/ŋ/	26	60	4.00	1.73
	/l/	9	188	6.89	.33
	/r/	24	175	6.67	.91
	/w/	1	142	6.00	.04
	/j/	1	50	2.00	.04
Total		158	2,761	3.23	.19

8 Summary John V. Irwin and Seok P. Wong

DESCRIPTIVE STATISTICS

Phonemes

Distribution of Phonemes

The distribution of phonemes entered for analysis is shown by basic phonetic classification and age group in Table 8.1. A total of 86,861 phonemes was entered in the IPA transcription of the presumed adult model. Distribution by individual phonemes will be presented later in this chapter.

Stability of Vowel-Consonant Ratio. Figure 8.1 presents the vowel/consonant distribution graphically by relative percentage of occurrence. At each age group, more consonants than vowels have been entered. In addition, data from the adult studies of Dewey (1923) and Denes (1963) have been plotted in Figure 8.1. Dewey based his data on dictionary transcriptions of written samples; Denes, on adult spoken speech (samples). For each of the

TABLE 8.1 Phoneme Frequency by Basic
Phonetic Classification and Age Group

| Age | *Phonetic Classification* | | |
	Vowels	*Consonants*	*Total*
1.5	5,448	7,327	12,775
2	5,914	8,797	14,711
3	15,079	22,910	37,989
4	6,337	9,862	16,199
6	2,018	3,169	5,187
Total	34,796	52,065	86,861

five ages, the ratios bear a striking similarity to the adult ratios, although at age 1.5 the vowel/consonant ratio is approximately 43/57 as opposed to the 39/61 of the two adult studies.

It should be noted that the values referred to represent the phonemes entered in the adult model and not the phonemes actually attempted. This fact is particularly important at ages 1.5 and 2, where the ratio of consonant to

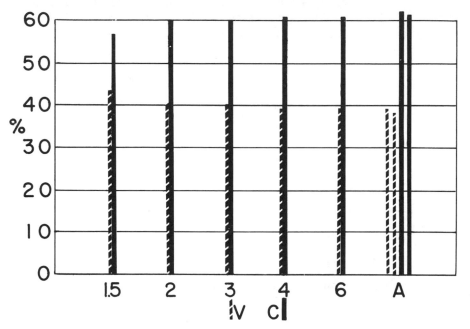

FIGURE 8.1   Distribution of vowels and consonants by percentage of occurrence for five age groups and two adult studies

TABLE 8.2   Percent of Vowellike and Consonant Sounds from Children in Project and from Two Adult Studies

Source	Vowels		Consonants	
	Produced[a]	Entered[b]	Produced[a]	Entered[b]
Children				
1.5	49	43	51	57
2	46	40	54	60
3	40	40	60	60
4	39	39	61	61
6	40	39	60	61
Adult				
Dewey	—	39	—	61
Denes	—	39	—	61

[a]Produced: includes sounds scored as correct, substitution, or distortion but not as omission.
[b]Entered: includes all phonemes recorded in IPA transcription of assumed adult form, irrespective of success in production.

Phonological Development in Children

vowel omissions is greater than at ages 3, 4, and 6. Thus, as shown in Table 8.2, for the 18-month-old group the vowel-consonant *production* ratio is 49/51; for the 2-year-old group, 46/54. Except for these two younger groups, the production ratios are essentially the same as the ratios graphed in Figure 8.1.

Variation in Occurrence of Individual Phonemes. Table 8.3 summarizes the frequency of occurrence of the individual vowellike sounds by age group. Each of the vowels except /ɜ/ occurs regularly at all ages. The diphthong /ɪu/ occurred primarily at age 1.5. The syllabic /m̩/ occurred only once.

Table 8.4 presents the frequency distribution of the individual consonants by age group. Note that /ʒ/ occurs only twice. These consonant data will be examined more closely in the section on inferential analyses.

TABLE 8.3   Frequency Distribution of Vowellike Sounds by Age Groups

| Phonemes | Age Group | | | | | Total |
	1.5	2	3	4	6	
/i/	797	889	997	653	136	3,392
/ɪ/	479	452	2,779	804	398	4,912
/e/	337	522	712	357	118	2,056
/ɛ/	162	204	1,187	316	91	1,980
/æ/	484	459	1,079	660	191	2,873
/ɝ/	97	109	159	108	40	513
/ʒ/	0	0	6	1	0	7
/ɚ/	131	93	400	146	49	819
/ɔ/	244	258	1,822	94	227	2,642
/ʌ/	292	314	975	935	148	2,664
/ɑ/	452	707	643	344	92	2,238
/ɔ/	436	154	437	163	37	1,227
/o/	462	539	1,174	496	110	2,781
/u/	147	386	744	420	84	1,711
/ʊ/	164	161	293	49	42	709
Subtotal	4,684	5,247	13,407	5,546	1,763	30,647
/aɪ/	361	345	1,126	560	174	2,566
/aʊ/	130	172	329	155	46	832
/ɔɪ/	30	86	41	28	3	188
/ɪu/	141	1	0	3	0	145
Subtotal	662	604	1,496	746	223	3,731
/n̩/	6	15	1	0	14	36
/l̩/	96	48	175	45	17	381
/m̩/	0	0	0	0	1	1
Subtotal	102	63	176	45	32	418
Total	5,448	5,914	15,079	6,337	2,018	34,796

Three Most Frequent Vowellike Sounds. Table 8.5 presents the three most frequently appearing vowels by age group from this study and also from Dewey's adult norms. The phonemes are ranked from left to right in decreasing percentage of occurrence. Except at age 4, high front vowels /i, ɪ/ appear most frequently. The percentages show rough correspondence to the values of Dewey.

Three Most Frequent Consonant Sounds. Table 8.6 presents the three most frequent consonants by age group from this study and again from Dewey's adult norms. It is interesting to see that at the two lowest ages, the labial /b/ is the most frequent consonant, but that beginning with age 3 and continuing on through age 6, the lingua-alveolars predominate. Again, percentages are roughly consistent with those of Dewey.

Phonemes Not Entered in the Adult Form. As shown in Table 8.7, in all of the age groups, all but 3 of the 46 eligible phonemes were used. It should also be pointed out that the glottal stop did not appear in any adult form, but as this sound has not been classified in this study as a standard phoneme of English, it is not listed in these tables.

TABLE 8.4   Frequency Distribution of Consonants by Age Group

| Phonemes | Age Group | | | | | Total |
	1.5	2	3	4	6	
/k/	865	772	1,211	471	183	3,502
/g/	289	381	736	353	93	1,852
/t/	609	879	3,145	1,423	483	6,539
/d/	567	648	1,431	833	212	3,691
/p/	409	464	764	249	110	1,996
/b/	1,370	1,067	976	343	117	3,873
/f/	142	208	394	150	47	941
/v/	40	15	288	176	59	578
/θ/	113	49	171	98	32	463
/ð/	75	233	1,512	462	196	2,478
/s/	333	493	1,491	660	243	3,220
/z/	138	171	1,160	455	140	2,064
/ʃ/	106	143	269	102	38	658
/ʒ/	0	0	1	0	1	2
/tʃ/	96	184	61	39	13	393
/dʒ/	58	57	95	67	18	295
/m/	524	739	1,273	544	165	3,245
/n/	375	691	1,997	1,210	330	4,603
/ŋ/	94	53	474	136	60	817
/l/	452	437	1,227	530	188	2,834
/r/	329	645	1,500	478	175	3,127
/h/	247	263	1,327	456	74	2,367
/w/	79	152	1,043	505	142	1,921
/j/	17	53	364	122	50	606
Total	7,327	8,797	22,910	9,862	3,169	52,065

Phonological Development in Children

Phonemes Appearing as Additions. Table 8.8 lists the phonemes appearing as additions. In interpreting the data from this table, it should be noted that the computer program is able to process only additions coded at the end of a word. Perhaps because of this restriction in the coding, additions were entered by only three of the five investigators. To the extent that it is safe to indicate a trend, the number of additions seems to increase in the middle age ranges and then decrease completely. No particular pattern of phonemes emerges.

TABLE 8.5 Three Most Frequent Vowellike Sounds by Age and Percentage of Distribution

Age	Phonemes					
1.5	/i/	6	/æ/	4	/ɪ/	4
2	/i/	6	/ɑ/	5	/o/	4
3	/ɪ/	7	/ə/	5	/ɛ/	4
4	/ʌ/	6	/ɪ/	5	/æ/	4
6	/ɪ/	8	/ə/	4	/æ/	4
Adult[a]	/ɪ/	8	/ə/	5	/ɛ/	4

[a]Dewey.

TABLE 8.6 Three Most Frequent Consonants by Age and Percentage of Distribution

Age	Phonemes					
1.5	/b/	11	/k/	7	/t/	5
2	/b/	7	/t/	6	/k/	5
3	/t/	8	/n/	5	/ð/	4
4	/t/	9	/n/	7	/d/	5
6	/t/	9	/n/	6	/s/	5
Adult[a]	/n/	7	/t/	7	/r/	7

[a]Dewey.

TABLE 8.7 Phonemes Not Entered in Adult Form

Age	Phonemes
1.5	/ɜ, m̩, ʒ/
2	/ɜ, m̩, ʒ/
3	/ɪu, m̩/
4	/n̩, m̩, ʒ/
6	/ɪu, ʒ/

TABLE 8.8 Phonemes Appearing as Additions

Age	Phonemes
1.5	/i, ə, ɑ/
2	/e, ə, t, d, s, dʒ, j/
3	
4	/ɪ, ə, ʌ, t, d, s, z/
6	

Percentage of Correct Production

Individual Phonemes by Age. The percentage of correct production by individual vowellike sound is shown in Table 8.9 and by consonant in Table 8.10. These tables are intended primarily for basic reference; detailed comments will be made in later sections concerning specific sounds and groups of sounds.

Phonemes 100 Percent Correct. Phonemes produced with 100 percent correctness are shown in Table 8.11. The number of phonemes judged to have been produced with 100 percent correctness ranged from none at age 1.5 to 16 at age 6. The generally accelerated development of the 3-year-old group manifests itself clearly in this table.

TABLE 8.9   Percentage of Correct Usage of Vowellike Sounds by Age

		Age in Years				
Sounds	Phonemes	1.5	2	3	4	6
Vowels	/i/	76	96	100	97	100
	/ɪ/	73	84	99	96	98
	/e/	46	89	100	97	100
	/ɛ/	35	89	100	98	100
	/æ/	50	96	100	99	99
	/ɝ/	2	45	100	92	95
	/ɜ/	—	—	100	100	—
	/ɚ/	3	27	99	87	94
	/ə/	60	86	100	84	99
	/ʌ/	73	99	100	99	99
	/ɑ/	81	97	100	98	100
	/ɔ/	53	97	100	98	100
	/o/	58	91	100	97	99
	/u/	59	99	100	87	99
	/ʊ/	77	93	100	100	100
Subtotal		61	91	100	96	99
Diphthongs	/aɪ/	47	98	100	99	100
	/aʊ/	62	99	100	99	100
	/ɔɪ/	60	97	100	96	100
	/ɪu/	40	100	—	67	—
Subtotal		49	98	100	99	100
Syllabics	/n̩/	0	73	100	—	100
	/l̩/	27	50	100	93	100
	/m̩/	0	—	—	—	100
Subtotal		25	56	100	93	100
Total		59	91	100	96	99

TABLE 8.10 Percentage of Correct Usage of Consonants by Age

Phonemes	Age in Years				
	1.5	2	3	4	6
/k/	47	71	98	97	100
/g/	49	71	94	99	97
/t/	36	55	98	89	99
/d/	63	64	99	68	77
/p/	56	66	99	98	99
/b/	90	97	100	95	99
/f/	67	65	97	99	100
/v/	13	7	96	76	83
/θ/	0	2	49	81	78
/ð/	5	1	40	64	65
/s/	8	54	98	87	93
/z/	1	33	98	89	94
/ʃ/	2	43	99	95	87
/ʒ/	—	—	100	—	—
/tʃ/	22	35	97	74	100
/dʒ/	9	53	96	75	83
/m/	84	97	100	99	100
/n/	63	75	100	98	99
/ŋ/	3	74	96	46	57
/l/	4	27	93	85	95
/r/	2	20	89	81	82
/h/	68	78	100	97	91
/w/	63	94	100	99	99
/j/	71	55	99	95	98
/ʔ/	—	—	—	—	—
Total	50	63	93	88	92

TABLE 8.11 Phonemes 100 Percent Correct by Age

Age	Phonemes
1.5	None
2	/ɪu/
3	/e, ɚ, ɜ, ɑ, ɔ, u, ʊ, aɪ, aʊ, ɔɪ, n̩, l̩, ʒ/
4	/ɜ, ʊ/
6	/i, e, ɛ, ɑ, ɔ, ʊ, aɪ, aʊ, ɔɪ, n̩, l̩, m̩, k, f, tʃ, m/

Phonemes Most Frequently in Error. Phonemes appearing most frequently in error are shown in Table 8.12. At each age, the linguadental consonants /θ/ and /ð/ are most frequently in error. Note that at age 1.5 the voiced member of this pair, /ð/, was in error 95 percent of the time. Note also the consistent improvement across age. This trend holds even for the 3-year-old group, which, in general, was considerably accelerated. A possible conclusion is that the linguadentals are true developmental measures in the sense that the ability to make this light contact is tied more closely to chronological age than is the production of any other English phoneme set.

Replacements for Phonemes

The replacement of error phonemes has been summarized in detail in Chapters 3, 4, 5, 6, and 7 for each of the five age groups. At each age there tends to be some consistency in the pattern of replacement. It should also be noted that the tendency is for more than one replacement to be used for error phonemes. For example, at age 4, /tʃ/ is replaced by /t, d, θ, s, ʃ/.

This section will deal only with the most consistent of the replacement patterns, that is, the replacements for the phonemes /θ/ and /ð/. As has been previously noted in this chapter, the improvement in percent correct of /θ/ and /ð/ was the most uniform change among all of the consonants. The replacement patterns for these phonemes are also the most consistent in the study. Tables 8.13 and 8.14 summarize the replacement pattern for the two phonemes by age group. For the unvoiced cognate /θ/, the most frequent replacement at each age is /f/. On the other hand, for the voiced cognate /ð/, the most frequent replacement is consistently /d/ at each age. Of course, in terms of absolute frequency of the replacements, /d/ is used much more frequently because as shown in Table 8.4, /ð/ occurs 2,478 times in the entire distribution whereas /θ/ occurs only 463 times.

It is difficult to suggest an explanation as to why the unvoiced cognate goes forward to /f/ and the voiced cognate shifts backward to /d/. Both /f/ and /d/, as shown in Table 8.4, occur frequently and, as shown in Table 8.10, with a relatively high degree of accuracy. Obviously, this pattern of replacement maintains the voicing feature, but one may speculate why not /v/ for /ð/ or /t/

TABLE 8.12   Phonemes Most Frequently in Error by Age and Percent

Age	Phonemes	% Error
1.5	/θ/	100[a]
2	/ð/	90
3	/ð/	60
4	/ð/	36
6	/ð/	35

[a]/ð/ = 95% in error.

for /θ/, which would maintain a uniform place characteristic as well as the voicing characteristic. Finally, note also that the forward shift to /f/ for /θ/ retains the fricative characteristic, whereas the backward shift to /d/ for /ð/ changes the manner characteristic to plosive.

Distinctive Features

Correlation Between the Two Systems

A total of 47 phonemes was entered in both the Irwin-Wong and the Chomsky-Halle systems. The total of 47 includes the glottal stop /ʔ/, which was not entered in any of the data analyzed in this work. Because of the

TABLE 8.13 /θ/ Replacements
by Phoneme and Frequency
of Replacement

Age	Replacement	Frequency of Replacement
1.5	/d/	35
	/f/	5
	/t/	5
	/k/	3
	/r/	3
	/ə/	3
	/h/	2
	/g/	1
	/v/	1
	/n/	1
	/w/	1
2	/f/	13
	/s/	7
	/d/	2
	/t/	1
	/v/	1
	/n/	1
	/ʔ/	1
3	/f/	58
	/t/	20
	/d/	2
	/k/	1
	/w/	1
4	/f/	3
	/t/	3
	/i/	1
	/d/	1
	/ʔ/	1
6	/f/	5
	/ʔ/	1

TABLE 8.14 /ð/ Replacements
by Phoneme and Frequency
of Replacement

Age	Replacement	Frequency of Replacement
1.5	/d/	53
	/t/	2
	/b/	2
	/g/	1
	/dʒ/	1
2	/d/	194
	/t/	7
	/s/	3
	/n/	2
3	/d/	888
	/f/	10
	/t/	4
	/θ/	2
4	/d/	130
	/n/	5
	/θ/	3
	/f/	1
	/l/	1
	/h/	1
6	/d/	40
	/v/	3
	/t/	1

potential importance of the off-target hypothesis, the feature/degree or feature difference value was computed for each possible substitution for each phoneme in both systems. The number of possible pairs of comparisons was 1,081 ($47 \times 46/2$). For example, in the Irwin-Wong system, the substitution of /d/ for /g/ represents a feature difference of one. In the Chomsky-Halle system, the substitution is a four-feature difference.

The correlations between the difference values for all possible substitutions in the two systems are shown in Table 8.15. The Pearson r is significant ($r = .45$; $df = 1,080$; $p < .001$). The r^2 value—the coefficient of determination—is .20, suggesting that the correlation between the two systems accounts for only some 20 percent of the variance.

In the Irwin-Wong system, a degree difference is also calculated. As used here, the term *degree* refers to the differences within a feature. For example, the substitution of a Place-4 plosive for a Place-1 plosive is a place feature difference of one but a degree difference of three ($4 - 1 = 3$). Obviously, the degree difference can never be less than the feature difference, but can be greater. The Pearson r between Irwin-Wong degree differences and Chomsky-Halle feature differences is significant ($r = .47$; $df = 1,080$; $p < .001$), with an r^2 value of .22.

The values of the respective coefficients of determination (.20 for feature-to-feature correlation and .22 for degree-to-feature correlation between the two systems) suggest that the off-target hypothesis is unlikely to hold for all substitutions in both systems. For example, the substitution of /d/ for /ð/ gives in the Irwin-Wong system a feature/degree difference of 4/4 and in the Chomsky-Halle system a feature difference of one. The substitution of /f/ for /θ/ gives an Irwin-Wong feature/degree difference of 2/2 and a Chomsky-Halle feature difference of 2. Degree and feature differences, then, become not so much a test of the off-target hypothesis as an expression of how narrowly or how broadly the system defines a particular difference. This observation raises the interesting speculation that one way to develop a meaningful system

TABLE 8.15 Correlation Matrix for Two Feature Systems by Differences Between All Possible Pairs (1,081) of 47 Phonemes

Variable	Irwin-Wong Feature		Irwin-Wong Degree		Chomsky-Halle Feature	
	r	r^2	r	r^2	r	r^2
Irwin-Wong Feature	1.00	1.00	.79	.62	.45	.20
Irwin-Wong Degree	.79	.62	1.00	1.00	.47	.22
Chomsky-Halle Feature	.45	.20	.47	.22	1.00	1.00

1. 47 phonemes.

2. Number of comparisons $= \dfrac{(N)(N - 1)}{2} = \dfrac{(47)(46)}{2} = \dfrac{2,162}{2} = 1,081$

3. a. Irwin-Wong. Mean Feature Difference for 1,081 pairs = 4.5541.
   b. Irwin-Wong. Mean Degree Difference for 1,081 pairs = 7.5375.
   c. Chomsky-Halle. Mean Feature Difference for 1,081 pairs = 5.5338.

would be to design it—if possible—so that the frequent replacements would have small differences. A possible first step in this direction is the Irwin-Wong Five-Feature System for Consonants. This simplified system, which is not described in the current publication, handles differences in replacements with small differences—but the correlation with frequency is not always one to one.

Incidentally, for the 25 consonants, the mean difference for all possible combinations in the Irwin-Wong system is 4.59; in the Chomsky-Halle system, 4.34. The range of mean differences is also similar. In the Irwin-Wong, the range is from 3.79 for /w/ to 5.50 for /ʔ/; in the Chomsky/Halle, 3.32 for /ð/ and 6.68 for /ʔ/. The mean feature/degree differences for both the Irwin-Wong and Chomsky-Halle systems for all possible pairs of consonants appear as footnotes to Table 8.15.

Acquisition of Distinctive Features

Irwin-Wong. As shown in Figure 8.2, only two of the Irwin-Wong specifications were produced with less than 50 percent correctness at ages 1.5 and 2, and only one at age 3. Fifteen specifications were produced with less than 90 percent correctness at 1.5 years; this number decreased until only one was produced with less than 90 percent correctness at 6 years.

TABLE 8.16 Place-3 (Linguadental) Percent Correct and Replacement Percent by Age

Age	% Correct	Replacement Code	Description	% Used
1.5	3	Place-4	(Alveolar)	82
2	18	Place-4	(Alveolar)	94
3	42	Place-4	(Alveolar)	93
4	74	Place-4	(Alveolar)	96
6	78	Place-4	(Alveolar)	82

TABLE 8.17 Mean Percent Correct for /s/ and /z/ by Age and Inflection

	/s/			/z/			/s/ and /z/
Age	Inflected	Uninflected	Total	Inflected	Uninflected	Total	Total
1.5	38.10	6.09	8.11	1.35	1.56	1.45	6.16
2	92.00	52.14	54.16	33.33	31.25	32.75	48.64
3	94.16	98.83	97.65	97.43	98.93	97.67	97.66
4	75.38	89.25	86.52	88.27	89.47	88.57	87.35
6	92.42	93.79	93.42	93.33	94.29	93.57	93.47

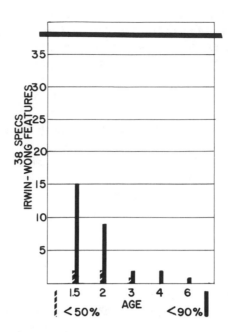

FIGURE 8.2   Number of Irwin-Wong features occurring with less than 50 percent or less than 90 percent correctness by subject age in years

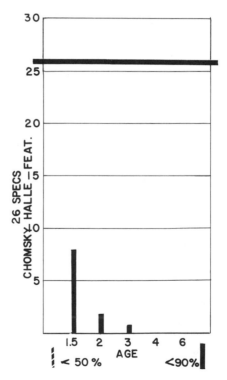

FIGURE 8.3   Number of Chomsky-Halle features occurring with less than 50 percent or less than 90 percent correctness by subject age in years

Place-3 (linguadental constriction) was the Irwin-Wong specification most frequently in error. Table 8.16 shows the percent correct for Place-4 (lingua-alveolar). These figures reflect the phoneme replacement for /θ/ and /ð/ as shown previously in Tables 8.13 and 8.14.

Chomsky-Halle. As shown in Figure 8.3, even at age 1.5, only 8 of the 26 Chomsky-Halle specifications were less than 90 percent correct. The Chomsky-Halle feature specification most frequently in error was + strident.

Discussion. Except for Place-3 (linguadental) in the Irwin-Wong system, all specifications in both systems are generally acquired by age 2. These findings are consistent with those of Hodson and Paden (1978), who found development relatively established at age 4 and did not look at ages 1.5, 2, and 3. These data, then, suggest that phonological development is not controlled primarily by the physiological availability of distinctive features.

Morphological Functions of /s/ and /z/

All occurrences of /s/ and /z/ were coded as inflected (plural, possessive, third person singular, contraction, or superlative) or root. Table 8.17 presents the mean percent correct for both phonemes by the five age groups. At age 1.5, the percent correct of inflected /s/ was some six times greater than root /s/, and at age 2, the percent correct of inflected /s/ was approximately 1.8 times greater than root /s/. Otherwise, the percents correct were roughly the same for both the inflected and root forms of both phonemes at each age.

INFERENTIAL STATISTICS

Vowel-Consonant, Sex, and Age

The basic data for these analyses are shown in Table 8.18. A three-factor analysis of variance with five levels of Age, two levels of Sex, and two levels of Phoneme Type, with repeated measures for Phoneme Type, was completed. The three-way interaction was not significant (F = 0.42; df = 4,90; p = .787). The interaction between Vowel-Consonant and Sex was not sig-

TABLE 8.18   Percent of Correct Production by Phoneme Type, Age, and Sex

| | | Age in Months | | | | | | | | | | |
| | | 18 | | 24 | | 36 | | 48 | | 72 | | |
Phoneme Type	Statistic	F	M	F	M	F	M	F	M	F	M	Total
Vowel	Mean	56.3	53.6	92.2	90.9	99.8	99.9	96.6	96.3	99.1	98.7	88.3
	SD	9.3	14.9	3.1	5.7	0.4	0.3	1.5	2.2	1.7	1.6	
Consonant	Mean	49.4	50.0	74.9	71.7	95.8	95.9	93.0	90.2	96.1	93.0	81.0
	SD	6.8	12.9	4.8	12.6	2.4	2.3	1.6	3.5	1.5	4.0	
Total	Mean	52.9	51.8	83.5	81.3	97.8	97.9	94.8	93.3	97.6	95.8	84.7

nificant (F = 0.20; df = 1,90; p = .658). The Age-Sex interaction was not significant (F = 0.18; df = 4,90; p = .947). But the interaction between Vowel-Consonant and Age was significant (F = 73.66; df = 4,90; p ⩽ .000). The F-Ratio for sex was not significant (F = 1.94; df = 1,90; p = .167).

Because of the significant interaction between Vowel-Consonant and Age, a t-test was run for the difference in Vowel-Consonant percent correct at each of the five age levels. Table 8.19 displays the means for Vowels and Consonants, the difference scores (Vowel minus Consonant), the respective standard deviations, and the t-tests for each of the five age levels.

An F-test comparing the vowel percent correct of the five age groups was significant (F = 205.68; df = 4,95; p ⩽ .000). Bonferroni multiple comparisons showed that at the 1 percent level, the vowel percent correct for the 18-month-old group was significantly less than that for the other four age groups, and that for 2-year-olds was significantly less than for the 3- and 6-year-old groups. An F-test comparing the consonant percent correct of the five age groups was significant (F = 101.22; df = 4,95; p ⩽ .000). The results of the Bonferroni multiple comparisons for consonants were similar to those for the vowels.

These data suggest that the articulation of the children did differ by age. As shown in Table 8.18, the direction of change for both vowels and consonants is to improve at 24 months over 18 months and at 36 months over 24. After the peak of 36 months, there is a slight decline at 48 months for both vowels and consonants, followed by an improved percentage correct again at 72 months. Developmental data previously cited in Chapter 2 would suggest that the peak at age 3 may be in part an artifact of subject selection, but the present data do not permit a test of this hypothesis.

These analyses suggest that the accuracy of production of vowels and consonants differs by age. As shown in Table 8.19, the difference in accuracy of vowel and consonant production is not statistically significant at 18 months but is significant at each of the four older ages.

TABLE 8.19   t Tests of Difference in Percent Correct Production of Vowels and Consonants by Age

| Statistic | Age in Months | | | | |
	18	24	36	48	72
Vowel Mean	54.95	91.55	99.85	96.45	98.90
Vowel SD	12.15	4.54	.37	1.85	1.62
Consonant Mean	49.70	73.30	95.85	91.60	94.55
Consonant SD	10.04	9.40	2.28	3.00	3.35
Vowel $\overline{X}$ − Consonant $\overline{X}$	5.25	18.25	4.00	4.85	4.35
Difference SD	17.01	6.62	2.29	2.13	3.31
t	1.38	12.34	7.80	10.16	5.87
p	<.183	<.000	<.000	<.000	<.000

Phonological Development in Children

Mean Percents Correct by Cognate Pairs

The criterion variable was the percent correct for each of 100 subjects by six pairs of cognates. The six pairs of cognates selected for analysis are: /p – b, t – d, k – g, f – v, θ – ð, s – z/. The phonetic classification and frequency of occurrence of the 12 phonemes making up these six pairs of cognates appear in Table 8.20. Findings for these cognate pairs are summarized in Tables 8.21 through 8.26. Means and standard deviations by age group and phoneme are shown in Table 8.21.

TABLE 8.20 Traditional Classification of 18 Selected Consonants by Manner, Voicing, and Place of Constriction

| | Manner | | | | | | | | |
| | Fricatives | | Plosives | | Nasals | | Liquids/Glides | | |
	u	v	u	v	u	v	u	v	Totals
Bilabial			/p/ (1,996)	/b/ (3,873)	—	/m/ (3,245)	—	/w/ (1,921)	11,035
Labiodental	/f/ (941)	/v/ (578)							1,519
Linguadental	/θ/ (463)	/ð/ (2,478)							2,941
Alveolar	/s/ (3,220)	/z/ (2,064)	/t/ (6,539)	/d/ (3,691)	—	/n/ (4,603)	—	/l, r/ (2,834/3,127)	26,178
Velar			/k/ (3,502)	/g/ (1,852)	—	/ŋ/ (817)			6,171
Subtotals	4,624	5,120	12,037	9,416					
Totals	9,744		21,453		8,665		7,882		47,744

TABLE 8.21 Means and Standard Deviations by Age Group and Phoneme

| Age Group | Statistic | Plosives | | | | | | Fricatives | | | | | |
		/p/	/b/	/t/	/d/	/k/	/g/	/f/	/v/	/θ/	/ð/	/s/	/z/
1.5 years	X̄	37.0	91.1	27.4	56.9	26.0	33.8	23.1	01.8	00.0	02.0	03.8	02.6
	SD	34.6	06.7	29.1	30.2	30.2	36.5	34.8	06.0	00.0	05.8	09.1	11.2
2 years	X̄	59.4	96.6	54.8	62.5	68.2	68.0	51.6	01.2	02.5	00.7	51.2	21.8
	SD	33.9	04.1	29.0	18.4	28.8	25.9	42.4	05.6	11.2	02.2	30.1	26.5
3 years	X̄	99.4	100.0	98.0	99.2	98.2	95.2	97.0	96.0	38.9	37.0	97.6	97.2
	SD	01.7	00.2	02.0	01.8	02.6	08.7	04.1	06.4	34.3	34.7	03.1	03.9
4 years	X̄	97.6	95.0	88.8	70.4	97.4	99.2	99.0	74.8	82.2	65.4	87.5	88.2
	SD	06.1	04.9	05.5	11.2	04.8	02.5	03.1	19.4	28.7	26.0	17.5	17.8
6 years	X̄	94.5	99.4	98.6	76.2	100.0	97.6	85.0	83.1	51.6	70.8	94.6	93.6
	SD	22.4	02.7	02.1	22.9	00.0	06.1	36.6	28.3	49.2	27.1	22.3	19.5

The first hypothesis tested was whether the five age groups have the same profiles with respect to the means of the six pairs of phonemes. As shown in Table 8.22, the null hypothesis can be rejected ($p < .02$) for all pairs except /k – g/ ($p > .05$), permitting the conclusion that, disregarding /k – g/, the relative mean percents correct for each cognate pair do differ by age.

The next hypothesis tested was whether the age groups differed for the six pairs, each considered as a whole. As shown in Table 8.23, hypotheses of no difference across age can be rejected, suggesting that age is a major variable in the accuracy of production. With the possible exception of /b/, /θ/, and /ð/, acceptability of production tends to peak at age 3 and to remain constant at ages 4 and 6. The consonant /b/ is produced with a high percentage of accuracy at all five ages. /θ/ and /ð/ tend to increase slowly in accuracy until age 4 and then fall back slightly at 5 and 6.

Univariate analyses of variance were completed for the five age groups on each of the cognate pairs. As shown in Table 8.24, hypotheses of no difference can be rejected for each pair. This suggests that performance by age will vary within each pair.

TABLE 8.22   Profile Analysis for Six Pairs of Cognates

Hypothesis	Statistic ($df = 4,95$)	Cognates					
		/p – b/	/t – d/	/k – g/	/f – v/	/θ – ð/	/s – z/
H_{01}	F	20.97	11.90	0.8452	7.27	3.02	12.38
	p	<.001	<.001	<.5	<.001	<.02	<.001

TABLE 8.23   Multivariate Analyses of Variance for Five Age Groups on Six Pairs of Cognates

Criterion Variables	Cognates					
	/p – b/	/t – d/	/k – g/	/f – v/	/θ – ð/	/s – z/
F (8,188)	22.89	26.82	18.08	50.87	21.50	49.96
p	<.001	<.001	<.001	<.001	<.001	<.001

TABLE 8.24   Univariate Analyses of Variance for Five Age Groups on Six Pairs of Cognates

Statistic	Criterion Variables											
	/p	–	b/	/t	–	d/	/k	–	g/	/f	–	v/
F (4,95)	57.59	37.53	57.05	14.11	27.29	13.77	24.73	165.58	26.38	42.21	88.28	130.97
p	<.001	<.001	<.001	<.001	<.001	<.001	<.001	<.001	<.001	<.001	<.001	<.001

Bonferroni comparisons of the five age groups are shown in Table 8.25. In general, the seven possible comparisons involving ages 1.5 and/or 2 are significant for /p, b, t, k, f, v, θ, ð, s, z/. The same comparisons are nonsignificant for /d/ and /g/. No age reversals appear in these seven comparisons. Comparisons of age 3 vs. 4, 3 vs. 6, and 4 vs. 6 tend to be nonsignificant and to show a relatively high degree of age reversal.

Finally, as is shown in Table 8.26, the two members of the six cognate pairs were compared at each age level. Nineteen of the 30 possible comparisons are nonsignificant, suggesting that the mean percents correct for each member of a cognate pair tend to be somewhat similar at any given age.

TABLE 8.25 Bonferroni Multiple Comparison of Five Age Groups

Age Groups Compared		/p – b/		/t – d/		/k – g/		/f – v/		/θ – ð/		/s – z/	
1.5	2	1	1	1	N	5	1	5	N	N	N	1	1
1.5	3	1	1	1	1	1	1	1	1	1	1	1	1
1.5	4	1	1	1	N	1	N	1	1	1	1	1	1
1.5	6	1	1	1	5	1	1	1	1	1	1	1	1
2	3	1	1	1	1	1	N	1	1	1	1	1	1
2	4	1	1	1	N	1	N	1	1	1	1	1	1
2	6	1	1	1	N	1	N	1	1	1	1	1	1
3	4	N	N	N	1[a]	N	1[a]	N	1[a]	1	1	N	N
3	6	N	N	N	1[a]	N	N	N	N	N	1	N	N
4	6	N	N	N	N	N	5	N	N	5[a]	N	N	N

[a]Mean of percents correct is higher for younger group.
1: p < .01
5: p < .05
N: p > .05

TABLE 8.26 Comparisons of Six Cognate Pairs by Age Group

Age Group	Cognate Pairs					
	/p vs. b/	/t vs. d/	/k vs. g/	/f vs. v/	/θ vs. ð/	/s vs. z/
1.5	N	5	1	5[a]	N	N
2	N	N	1[a]	1[a]	N	1[a]
3	N	N	N	N	N	N
4	N	1[a]	N	1[a]	5[a]	N
6	N	1[a]	N[a]	N	N	N

[a]Mean of percents correct is higher for unvoiced.
1: p < .01
5: p < .05
N: p > .05

Mean Percents Correct by Unvoiced and Voiced Plosives and Fricatives

The criterion variable was the percent correct for each of 100 subjects by four groups of consonants: (1) unvoiced plosives, (2) voiced plosives, (3) unvoiced fricatives, (4) voiced fricatives. The constitutency of each of these four groups is specified in Table 8.20. Means and standard deviations by age and phoneme group are shown in Table 8.27.

The first hypothesis tested was whether the five age groups have the same profiles with respect to the mean of the unvoiced and voiced members of the plosives and of the fricatives. As shown in Table 8.28, the null hypothesis can be rejected, permitting the conclusion that the relative mean percents correct for unvoiced versus voiced members of the plosive and fricative groups do differ by age.

The next hypothesis tested was whether the age groups differed for the phonetic groups each considered as a whole. As shown in Table 8.29, hypotheses of no difference across age can be rejected for both plosives and fricatives, suggesting that age is a major variable in the accuracy of the respective voiced and unvoiced members of these groups. As is shown in Table 8.27, the unvoiced plosives seemed to be produced less accurately until age 3 and more accurately after age 3. On the other hand, the unvoiced fricatives seemed to be produced more accurately at all ages.

Univariate analyses of variance were completed for the five age groups on the voiced and unvoiced comparisons of plosives and fricatives. As shown in Table 8.30, the hypotheses of no difference can be rejected for each of the four subgroups. This suggests that performance by age will vary within each of the four consonant groups.

TABLE 8.27   Mean Percentages Correct and Standard Deviations by Age and Two Phoneme Groups

| Age Group | Statistic | Phonetic Classification | | | | | |
| | | Plosives | | | Fricatives | | |
		Unvoiced	Voiced	Unvoiced Minus Voiced	Unvoiced	Voiced	Unvoiced Minus Voiced
1.5	$\overline{X}$	36.0	76.0	−40.0	8.8	5.0	3.8
	SD	22.9	16.4		14.9	12.1	
2	$\overline{X}$	61.2	81.2	−20.0	51.2	10.5	40.7
	SD	28.1	9.0		30.3	13.3	
3	$\overline{X}$	98.3	98.3	0.0	93.3	67.8	25.4
	SD	1.7	2.6		4.2	19.4	
4	$\overline{X}$	92.0	82.2	9.8	88.6	75.3	13.3
	SD	3.2	6.6		12.6	18.8	
6	$\overline{X}$	99.2	88.0	11.2	93.6	80.2	13.5
	SD	1.2	10.3		15.8	19.2	

Bonferroni comparisons of the five age groups are shown in Table 8.31. For the seven comparisons involving at least one of the age groups 1.5 and 2, both the unvoiced plosives and the unvoiced fricatives are produced with significantly greater accuracy at each age. With the exception of the 1.5 vs. 2 comparison, the same statement holds for the voiced fricatives. Voiced plosives, on the other hand, were not significant in four of the seven comparisons.

In comparisons of 3 vs. 4, 3 vs. 6, and 4 vs. 6, no significant differences were noted except between ages 3 vs. 4 and 3 vs. 6, at which ages the younger children produced the voiced plosives with greater accuracy. These two reversals reflect the previously noted high rate of development of age group 3.

TABLE 8.28   Profile Analyses for Five Age Groups on Voiced and Unvoiced Plosives and Fricatives

Statistic	Unvoiced Plosives versus Voiced Plosives	Unvoiced Fricatives versus Voiced Fricatives
F	23.69	10.85
df	4,95	4,95
p	<.001	<.001

TABLE 8.29   Multivariate Analyses of Variance for Five Age Groups on Voiced and Unvoiced Plosives and Fricatives

| | Criterion Variable | |
Statistic	Unvoiced Plosives and Voiced Plosives	Unvoiced Fricatives and Voiced Fricatives
F	28.70	48.23
df	8,188	8,188
p	<.001	<.001

TABLE 8.30   Univariate Analyses of Variance for Five Age Groups on Voiced and Unvoiced Plosives and Fricatives

| | Criterion Variable | | | | | |
Statistic	Unvoiced Plosives	and	Voiced Plosives	Unvoiced Fricatives	and	Voiced Fricatives
F (4,95)	58.43		14.29	87.93		95.35
p	<.001		<.001	<.001		<.001

Finally, in Table 8.32, both the unvoiced and voiced plosives and fricatives are compared at each of the five age levels. These comparisons show that for the plosives, the unvoiced members are significantly better than the voiced members at ages 1.5 and 2, that no difference obtains at age 3, and that at ages 4 and 6 the voiced plosives are superior. On the other hand, no significant difference exists at age 1.5 for the fricatives, but for the four older ages, the voiced fricatives are produced with a higher percentage of accuracy than the unvoiced.

Mean Percents Correct by Manner

The criterion variable was the percent correct for each of 100 subjects by four groups of consonants classified by manner of production. The four groups as defined are: (1) plosives, (2) fricatives, (3) nasals, and (4) liquids/glides. The constituency of each group for the 47,744 phonemes entered is specified in Table 8.20 by phoneme and by frequency. The six plosives (N = 21,453) constitute the largest manner group; the liquids and glides (N = 7,882), the smallest. Means and standard deviations by age and phoneme group are presented in Table 8.33.

The first hypothesis tested was whether the five age groups have the same profiles with respect to the means of each of the four groups of phonemes. As shown in Table 8.34, the null hypothesis can be rejected, permitting the conclusion that the relative mean percents for each phonetic group do differ by age.

The next hypothesis tested was whether the age groups differed for the manner groups considered as a whole. As shown in Table 8.35, hypotheses of no difference across age can be rejected, suggesting that age is a major vari-

TABLE 8.31   Bonferroni Multiple Comparisons for Five Age Groups

Age Groups Compared		Criterion Variable			
		Unvoiced Plosives	Voiced Plosives	Unvoiced Fricatives	Voiced Fricatives
1.5	2	1	N	1	N
1.5	3	1	1	1	1
1.5	4	1	N	1	1
1.5	6	1	1	1	1
2	3	1	1	1	1
2	4	1	N	1	1
2	6	1	N	1	1
3	4	N	1[a]	N	N
3	6	N	5[a]	N	N
4	6	N	N	N	N

[a]Mean of percents correct is higher for younger group.
1: p < .01
5: p < .05
N: p > .05

TABLE 8.32 Bonferroni Multiple Comparisons of Unvoiced Plosives vs. Voiced Plosives and Unvoiced Fricatives vs. Voiced Fricatives

Age Group	Voicing Groups	
	Unvoiced Plosives versus Voiced Plosives	Unvoiced Fricatives versus Voiced Fricatives
1.5	1[a]	N
2	1[a]	1
3	N	1
4	1	1
6	1	1

[a]Mean of percents correct is lower for first named group.
1: p < .01
5: p < .05
N: p > .05

TABLE 8.33 Means and Standard Deviations by Age Group and Four Groups of Phonemes Classified by Manner

Age Group	Statistic	Phonetic Classification			
		Plosives	Fricatives	Nasals	Liquids and Glides
1.5	$\overline{X}$	61.9	21.0	61.8	8.2
	SD	12.5	18.7	24.1	9.0
2	$\overline{X}$	73.0	45.8	83.1	31.2
	SD	13.3	19.4	11.6	13.3
3	$\overline{X}$	98.4	82.6	99.3	92.6
	SD	1.8	9.7	.9	5.5
4	$\overline{X}$	87.8	84.2	93.9	88.9
	SD	3.0	11.5	3.1	14.0
6	$\overline{X}$	95.1	86.0	94.7	91.2
	SD	3.5	15.1	5.7	15.6

TABLE 8.34 Profile Analysis for Five Age Groups on Four Phonetic Classifications by Manner

Statistic	
F	16.18
df	12,246
p	<.001

TABLE 8.35 Multivariate Analysis of Variance for Five Age Groups Using Plosives, Fricatives, Nasals, and Liquids and Glides as Criterion Variables

Statistic	
F	27.39
df	16,282
p	<.001

able in the accuracy of production of these phoneme groups. As is shown in Table 8.33, mean percents correct increase with age through 3 and then remain relatively constant. As has been noted, the relatively high degree of accuracy at age 3 is considered to be, in part, at least, an artifact of the sample.

Univariate analyses of variance were completed for the five age groups on each of the consonant groups. As shown in Table 8.36, the hypotheses of no difference can be rejected for each group. This suggests that performance by age will vary within each consonant type.

Bonferroni multiple comparisons of the five age groups are shown in Table 8.37. In general, the pairs 1.5 vs. 2 and either 1.5 or 2 vs. 3, 4, and 6 are statistically significant for each phoneme group. But comparisons of possible pairs within ages 3, 4, and 6 tend to be nonsignificant. In only one instance, age 3 vs. age 4 for plosives, is the younger age superior. These comparisons suggest a steady improvement in mean percents correct by age until age 3, after which the change, as measured by consonant group, becomes reduced.

TABLE 8.36 Univariate Analyses of Variance for Five Age Groups on Four Groups of Phonemes Classified by Manner

	Criterion Variables			
Statistic	Plosives	Fricatives	Nasals	Liquids and Glides
F (4,95)	66.82	72.47	29.82	217.94
p	<.001	<.001	<.001	<.001

TABLE 8.37 Bonferroni Multiple Comparison of Five Age Groups

	Criterion Variables			
Age Groups Compared	Plosives	Fricatives	Nasals	Liquids and Glides
1.5 2	1	1	1	1
1.5 3	1	1	1	1
1.5 4	1	1	1	1
1.5 6	1	1	1	1
2 3	1	1	1	1
2 4	1	1	N	1
2 6	1	1	5	1
3 4	1[a]	N	N	N
3 6	N	N	N	N
4 6	N	N	N	N

[a]Mean of percents correct is higher for younger group.
1: p < .01
5: p < .05
N: p > .05

Phonological Development in Children

These figures may be interpreted as suggesting an essentially complete phonological development by age 3.

Finally, as shown in Table 8.38, the six possible pairs of consonant groups were compared at each age level. These data suggest that plosives and nasals are mastered earlier than are fricatives and liquids/glides. But the differences between nasals and plosives, on the one hand, and fricatives and liquids/glides, on the other hand, tend to be neither consistent nor significant.

Mean Percents Correct by Place

The criterion variable was the percent correct for each of 100 subjects by five groups of consonants classified by place of constriction. The five places selected for analysis are: (1) bilabial, (2) labiodental, (3) linguadental, (4) alveolar, and (5) velar. The constituency of each place group for the 47,744 phonemes entered is specified in Table 8.20. The seven phonemes classified as alveolar make up the largest group (N = 26,178); the labiodentals, the smallest (N = 1,519). Means and standard deviations by age and phoneme group are shown in Table 8.39.

The first hypothesis tested was whether the five age groups have the same profiles with respect to the means of each of the five groups of phonemes classified by place. As shown in Table 8.40, the null hypothesis can be rejected, permitting the conclusion that the relative mean percents correct for each place group do differ by age.

The next hypothesis tested was whether the age groups differed for the place groups considered as a whole. As shown in Table 8.41, hypotheses of no difference across age can be rejected, suggesting that age is a major variable in the accuracy of production. Of the five phoneme groups, as shown in Table 8.33, mean percents correct tended to peak at age 3 for all groups except linguadental, which continues to show a steady improvement on

TABLE 8.38 Bonferroni Multiple Comparison of Four Manner Groups by Age Group

Age Group	Manner Groups					
	Plosives vs. Fricatives	Plosives vs. Nasals	Plosives vs. Liquids and Glides	Fricatives vs. Nasals	Fricatives vs. Liquids and Glides	Nasals vs. Liquids and Glides
1.5	1	N	1	1[a]	N	1
2	1	5[a]	1	1[a]	N	1
3	1	N	1	1[a]	1[a]	1
4	N	1[a]	N	1[a]	N	N
6	N	N	N	N	N	N

[a]Mean of percents correct is lower for first named group.
1: p < .01
5: p < .05
N: p > .05

through ages 4 and 6. The bilabials and velars remain relatively constant after age 3, but the labiodentals and alveolars show some fallback, particularly at age 4.

Univariate analyses of variance were completed for the five age groups on each of the consonant groups. As shown in Table 8.42, the hypothesis of no difference can be rejected for each group. This suggests that the performance by age will vary within each consonant type.

TABLE 8.39   Means and Standard Deviations by Age Group and Phonetic Classification by Place

Age Group	Statistic	Bilabials	Labiodentals	Linguadentals	Alveolars	Velars
1.5	$\overline{X}$	78.8	21.4	1.7	32.8	28.4
	SD	10.4	33.0	5.7	17.3	27.6
2	$\overline{X}$	90.6	49.1	.8	49.1	70.5
	SD	5.5	39.9	2.0	14.8	24.4
3	$\overline{X}$	99.8	96.4	36.9	96.4	96.6
	SD	.4	3.1	33.6	2.6	5.1
4	$\overline{X}$	98.0	86.4	68.3	86.8	90.6
	SD	3.1	10.7	24.7	4.7	4.1
6	$\overline{X}$	99.2	91.0	70.4	93.0	92.0
	SD	1.6	15.7	25.4	6.0	7.8

TABLE 8.40   Profile Analyses for Five Age Groups on Five Phonetic Classifications by Place

	Statistic
F	20.83
df	16,282
p	<.001

TABLE 8.41   Multivariate Analysis of Variance for Five Age Groups Using Five Places as Criterion Variables

	Statistic
F	22.16
df	20,303
p	<.001

TABLE 8.42   Univariate Analyses of Variance for Five Age Groups on Five Groups of Phonemes Classified by Place

Statistic	Criterion Variables				
	Labials	Labiodentals	Linguadentals	Alveolars	Velars
F (4,95)	52.47	34.44	47.92	141.93	54.53
p	<.001	<.001	<.001	<.001	<.001

Bonferroni comparisons of the five age groups are shown in Table 8.43. Each of the seven possible pairs involving age groups 1.5 or 2 is statistically significant for all places, with the exception of the linguadental comparison at age 1.5 vs. 2. But comparisons of 3 vs. 4, 3 vs. 6, and 4 vs. 6 are non-significant, except for linguadentals. The linguadental comparisons were significant for all ages except 4 vs. 6. In no instance was the younger age superior in mean percents correct. These comparisons suggest that for all phonetic groups, performance improves with age until age 4, and that for linguadentals this improvement continues through age 4.

TABLE 8.43 Bonferroni Multiple Comparisons of Five Age Groups

Age Groups Compared		Criterion Variables				
		Labials	Labiodentals	Linguadentals	Alveolars	Velars
1.5	2	1	1	N	1	1
1.5	3	1	1	1	1	1
1.5	4	1	1	1	1	1
1.5	6	1	1	1	1	1
2	3	1	1	1	1	1
2	4	1	1	1	1	1
2	6	1	1	1	1	1
3	4	N	N	1	N	N
3	6	N	N	1	N	N
4	6	N	N	N	N	N

Note. Mean of percents correct is higher for younger group.
1: p < .01
5: p < .05
N: p > .05

TABLE 8.44 Bonferroni Multiple Comparisons of Five Place Groups by Age Groups

Age Group	Place Groups									
	Labials vs. Labio-dentals	Labials vs. Lingua-dentals	Labials vs. Alve-olars	Labials vs. Velars	Labio-dentals vs. Lingua-dentals	Labio-dentals vs. Alve-olars	Labio-dentals vs. Velars	Lingua-dentals vs. Alve-olars	Lingua-dentals vs. Velars	Alve-olars vs. Velars
1.5	1	1	1	1	N	N	N	1[a]	1[a]	N
2	1	1	1	1	1	N	N	1[a]	1[a]	1[a]
3	1	1	1	N	1	N	N	1[a]	1[a]	N
4	1	1	1	1	5	N	N	5[a]	1[a]	5[a]
6	N	1	1	1	N	N	N	1[a]	5[a]	N

[a]Mean of percents correct is lower for first named group.
1: p < .01
5: p < .05
N: p > .05

Finally, as is shown in Table 8.44, the 10 possible pairs were compared at each age level. These comparisons indicate that the labials are produced with the highest percents correct at all ages except for single exceptions at age 3 and age 6. At age 3, the comparison with the velars is not significant; at age 6, the comparison with the labiodentals is not significant. It is interesting to note further that the labiodentals do not differ significantly from the alveolars or velars at any age, nor from the linguadentals at ages 1.5 and 6. The linguadentals consistently show the lowest mean percents correct. They are significantly lower in all comparisons at all ages except when compared with the labiodentals at ages 1.5 and 6.

References

References

Baltaxe, C. *Foundations of distinctive feature theory*. Baltimore: University Park Press, 1978.

Barrie-Blackley, S., Musselwhite, C., & Rogister, S. *Clinical language sampling*. Danville, Ill.: Interstate Printers and Publishers, 1978.

Bassi, C. Phonemic and distinctive feature acquisition in children 46–50 months of age. Unpublished master's thesis, Memphis State University, 1979.

Blache, S. *The acquisition of distinctive features*. Baltimore: University Park Press, 1978.

Brown, R. *A first language*. Cambridge: Harvard University Press, 1973.

Cairns, H., & Williams, F. An analysis of the substitution errors of a group of Standard English speaking children. *Journal of Speech and Hearing Research,* 15, 1972, 811–20.

Chomsky, N., & Halle, M. *The sound pattern of English*. New York: Harper and Row, 1968.

Compton, A. Generative studies of children's phonological disorders. *Journal of Speech and Hearing Disorders,* 35, 1970, 91–94.

Costello, J. Articulation instruction based on distinctive feature theory. *Language, Speech and Hearing Services in Schools,* 6, 1975, 61–71.

Costello, J., & Onstine, J. The modification of multiple articulation errors based on distinctive feature theory. *Journal of Speech and Hearing Disorders,* 41, 1976, 199–215.

Crystal, D. The case of linguistics: A prognosis. *British Journal of Disorders in Communication,* 7, 1972, 3–16.

Dale, P. *Language development*. 2nd ed. New York: Holt, Rinehart and Winston, 1976.

Daniloff, R., Schuckers, G., & Feth, L. *The physiology of speech and hearing: an introduction*. Englewood Cliffs, N.J.: Prentice-Hall, 1980.

Denes, P. On the statistics of spoken English. *Journal of the Acoustical Society of America,* 35, 1963, 892–904.

Dewey, G. *Relativ frequency of English speech sounds*. Cambridge: Harvard University Press, 1923.

Dyson, A. The suppression of five phonological simplification processes by two-year-olds. Unpublished doctoral dissertation. University of Illinois, 1979.

Fairchild, L., & Beasley, D. A case study of three siblings with deviant speech patterns. Unpublished manuscript, Michigan State University, East Lansing, 1974.

Faircloth, M., & Faircloth, S. An analysis of the articulatory speech defective child in connected speech and in isolated word responses. *Journal of Speech and Hearing Disorders,* 35, 1970, 51–61.

Ferguson, C., & Farwell, C. Words and sounds in early language acquisition. *Language,* 51, 1975, 419–39.

Gleason, H. *An introduction to descriptive linguistics.* New York: Henry Holt and Co., 1962.

Gooze, S. A clinical application of distinctive feature theory to articulation management. Paper presented at the American Speech and Hearing Association Convention, Las Vegas, 1974.

Hare, G. Sound acquisition by phonemes and distinctive features in children aged 21–24 months. Unpublished master's thesis, Memphis State University, 1977.

Hodson, B., & Paden, E. Phonological feature competencies of normal four-year olds. *Acta Symbolica,* 9, 1978, 37–49.

Ingram, D. *Phonological disability in children.* New York: Elsevier, 1976.

Irwin, J., Huskey, R., Knight, N., & Oltman, S. A longitudinal study of the spontaneous remission of articulatory defects of 1665 school children in grades 1, 2, and 3. Part III: The study group. *Acta Symbolica,* 5, 1974, 9–17.

Irwin, J., & Wong, S. Distinctive feature analysis in conversational samples. Paper presented at Mid-South Conference on Communicative Disorders, Memphis, 1977.

Jakobson, R., Fant, C., & Halle, M. *Preliminaries to speech analysis.* Cambridge, Mass.: MIT Press, 1952.

Ladefoged, P. *Preliminaries to linguistic phonetics.* Chicago: University of Chicago Press, 1971.

Leonard, L. The nature of deviant articulation. *Journal of Speech and Hearing Research,* 38, 1973, 156–61.

Leonard, L., Prutting, C., Perozzi, J., & Berkley, R. Nonstandardized approaches to the assessment of language behaviors. *ASHA,* 20, 1978, 371–79.

Leopold, W. *Speech development of a bilingual child.* Evanston: Northwestern University Press, 1947.

McReynolds, L., & Bennett, S. Distinctive feature generalization in articulation training. *Journal of Speech and Hearing Disorders,* 37, 1972, 462–70.

McReynolds, L., & Engman, E. *Distinctive feature analysis of misarticulations.* Baltimore: University Park Press, 1975.

McReynolds, L., & Huston, K. A distinctive feature analysis of children's misarticulations. *Journal of Speech and Hearing Disorders,* 36, 1971, 155–56.

Menyuk, P. The role of distinctive features in children's acquisition of phonology. *Journal of Speech and Hearing Research,* 11, 1968, 138–46.

Northern, J., & Downs, M. *Hearing in children.* Baltimore: Waverly Press, 1974.

Olmsted, D. *Out of the mouth of babes.* The Hague: Mouton, 1971.

Pollack, E., & Rees, N. Disorders of articulation: Some clinical applications of distinctive feature theory. *Journal of Speech and Hearing Disorders,* 37, 1972, 451–61.

Poole, I. Genetic development of articulation of consonant sounds in speech. *Elementary English Review,* 11, 1934, 159–64.

Prather, E., Hedrick, D., & Kern, C. Articulation development in children aged two to four years. *Journal of Speech and Hearing Disorders,* 40, 1975, 179–91.

Sander, E. When are speech sounds learned? *Journal of Speech and Hearing Disorders*, 37, 1972, 55–63.

Schane, S. *Generative phonology*. Englewood Cliffs, N.J.: Prentice-Hall, 1973.

Shriberg, L., & Kwiatkowski, J. *Natural process analysis (NPA): a procedure for phonological analysis of continuous speech samples*. New York: John Wiley & Sons, 1980.

Siegel, G. Prototypes of criteria for counting words. In T. Longhurst (Ed.), *Linguistic analysis of children's speech: readings*. New York: MSS Information, 1974.

Singh, S. Use of a distinctive model in speech pathology. *Acta Symbolica*, 3, 1972, 17–25.

———. *Distinctive features, theory and validation*. Baltimore: University Park Press, 1976.

Singh, S., Woods, D., & Becker, G. Perceptual structures of 22 prevocalic English consonants. *Journal of the Acoustical Society of America*, 52, 1972, 1698–1713.

Smith, N. *The acquisition of phonology*. Cambridge: Cambridge University Press, 1973.

Soli, S. Some effects of acoustic attributes of speech on the processing of phonetic feature information. *Journal of Experimental Psychology: Human Perception and Performance*, 6, 1980, 622–38.

Templin, M. Spontaneous versus imitated verbalization in testing articulation in preschool children. *Journal of Speech and Hearing Disorders*, 12, 1947, 293–300.

———. *Certain language skills in children. University of Minnesota Institute of Child Welfare Monograph, Series No. 26*. Minneapolis: University of Minnesota Press, 1957.

Thomas, C. *An introduction to the phonetics of American English*. 2nd ed. New York: Ronald, 1958.

Trubetzkoy, N. S. *Principles of phonology*. Trans. C. Baltaxe. Berkeley: University of California Press, 1969.

Van Riper, C., & Irwin, J. *Voice and Articulation*. Englewood Cliffs, N.J.: Prentice-Hall, 1958.

Walsh, H. On certain practical inadequacies of distinctive feature systems. *Journal of Speech and Hearing Disorders*, 39, 1974, 32–43.

Wellman, B., Case, E., Mengert, I., & Bradbury, D. Speech sounds of young children. *University of Iowa Studies in Child Welfare, 5:2*. Iowa City: State University of Iowa, 1931.

Wickelgren, W. Distinctive features and errors in short-term memory for English vowels. *Journal of the Acoustical Society of America*, 38, 1965, 583–88.

———. Distinctive features and errors in short-term memory for English consonants. *Journal of the Acoustical Society of America*, 39, 1966, 388–98.

Winitz, H. *Articulatory acquisition and behavior*. New York: Appleton-Century-Crofts, 1969.

Winitz, H. *From syllable to conversation*. Baltimore: University Park Press, 1975.

Wise, C. *Introduction to phonetics*. Englewood Cliffs, N.J.: Prentice-Hall, 1958.

References